More Acclaim for *Cen*

C000003138

"Now, about this magnificent boc
important capacity to put the reader right in the center of the action,
whether it's stories about the Nazis' bombing in London or the
newsroom of the *Winston-Salem Journal* when the Pulitzer Prize
announcement was made. I do hope this book finds its way into the
marketplace where people who care about American journalism can
see what [McNeil has] produced—it's a real gift!"
—Garrett Mitchell, *The Mitchell Report*

"Mary Llewellyn McNeil's warm telling of [Carroll's] extraordinary
life is the best roadmap I know of if we aim to restore journalism's
power to inform and persuade. Virtually every page has something
important to say about integrity in journalism. And on top of all that,
vivid first-hand accounts of some of the most consequential events
and people of the 20th Century, from the London Blitz, Pearl Harbor,
and Vietnam to Churchill, Stalin, Kennedy, and Lyndon Johnson—and,
in the story of his life with Peggy, one of the best love stories you
could ever hope to read."
—Jon Sawyer, Executive Director, the Pulitzer Center

"Wallace Carroll was one of the great journalists of the 20th
century. He covered Europe and the Soviet Union as they braced for
World War II; ran the *New York Times* Washington bureau for Scotty
Reston; was editor and publisher of the *Winston-Salem Journal*, where his
editorial on getting out of Vietnam helped persuade President Johnson
not to seek reelection. This extraordinary life of an exceptionally wise
man is captured in Mary McNeil's compelling and vivid biography,
Century's Witness. Every working journalist today should read it."
—Al Hunt, former Washington bureau chief, *Wall
Street Journal* and columnist, Bloomberg News

"Carroll's story is the kind of romance that persuades many of us to be drawn to journalism as a profession. As a globe-trotting, unflappable observer and interpreter, he had a nose for what was important, and he somehow managed to be on the scene of some of history's major turning points."

—Mark Nelson, former head, Center
for International Media Assistance

"Wallace Carroll was a man of great charm and intelligence as well as a great twentieth-century journalist reporting on some of the most critical moments in American history—McNeil, one of Carroll's students at Wake Forest University, has done her homework well: she shows us what mattered in his life, and what should matter in ours."

—Edwin G. Wilson, former Provost, Wake Forest University

"In my first two newspaper jobs, I worked for Wally Carroll, once at the Washington bureau of the *New York Times* and again at the *Winston-Salem Journal.* He was universally revered in both places, though reverence is in short supply in newsrooms. How I wish I had asked him about reporting from London on the Blitz, or about being one of the first American reporters with the Russian army in World War II. He could be wrong, and McNeil is frank about the two big mistakes of his career. But at his best—and he was mostly at his best—he stood for the greatest values of daily newspapers, as reporter, editor, and publisher."

—Donald Graham, former publisher, *Washington Post*

"To today's journalists, Wallace is less well known than his son, John, who became the editor of the *Los Angeles Times,* but he is no less worthy of recognition. McNeil's thoughtful and well executed study should go a long way toward giving this exemplary journalist his due."

—Margaret Sullivan, Media Columnist, *Washington Post*

Century's
Witness

Century's Witness

The Extraordinary Life of Journalist Wallace Carroll

Mary Llewellyn McNeil

WHALER
BOOKS

Buena Vista, VA

1 3 5 7 9 10 8 6 4 2

Library of Congress Control Number: 2022902904

Century's Witness
By Mary Llewellyn McNeil
p. cm.

1. Biography & Autobiography/Editors, Journalists and Publishers
2. History/Wars & Conflicts/WWII, General
3. History/Modern/20th Century/Cold War

I. McNeil, Mary Llewellyn 1956– II. Title.
ISBN 13: 978-1-7378864-4-0 (softcover : alk. paper)

Whaler Books
An imprint of
Mariner Media, Inc.
131 West 21st Street
Buena Vista, VA 24416
Tel: 540-264-0021
www.marinermedia.com

Printed in the United States of America
This book is printed on acid-free paper meeting the requirements of the American Standard for Permanence of Paper for Printed Library Materials.

Cover Photo: Wallace Carroll inspecting a Hawker Hurricane fighter plane on a visit to Biggin Field during the Battle of Britain, June 1940. Credit: Carroll family.

For my Mother and Father

"I became a journalist to come as close as possible to the heart of the world."

—Henry Luce, American magazine magnate

CONTENTS

Author's Note   xiii
Prologue   xix

Section I: To Go Abroad   1
Chapter 1: A Son of the Midwest   3
Chapter 2: Foreign Correspondent   11
Chapter 3: Love, War, and the League of Nations   23

Section II: Cataclysm   43
Chapter 4: London 1939: On the Brink   45
Chapter 5: Anticipation   57
Chapter 6: Staying Alive   69
Chapter 7: The Road to Moscow—And Back   83

Section III: The Art of Persuasion   113
Chapter 8: What Next?   115
Chapter 9: To Win Hearts and Minds   129
Chapter 10: Up Against Goebbels   147
Chapter 11: "Persuade or Perish"   167

Section IV: Back to the Newsroom   177
Chapter 12: Song of the South   179
Chapter 13: A Call to Washington   201

Section V: To Go Home Again   **231**
Chapter 14: Our Collective Conscience at Work   233
Chapter 15: A World of Influence   253
Chapter 16: To Leave Something Behind   273

Epilogue   287
Timeline   291
Acknowledgments   293
Endnotes   297
Bibliography   313
Index   321
Reader's Guide   345

AUTHOR'S NOTE

When I set about writing a book on Wallace Carroll, a journalist and editor whose career spanned most of the twentieth century, I had little idea of either the scope of the project or where, frankly, it would take me.

Carroll is not well-known today, but he was among the best of what many see as a dying breed. Fiercely independent of business interests and convinced he could influence the public good through the written word, he saw journalism as a commitment to improving his nation and his community. And he lived in an age in which this was possible—before the internet, cable news, and social media—when journalists were recognized, not as opinionated celebrities hired to ensure corporate profits, but more as trusted filters through which the news could be delivered. In this, he was in the tradition of such iconic foreign correspondents as A.J. Liebling, Edward R. Murrow, and Dorothy Thompson, who chronicled a turbulent Europe for their readers and came home to use their experience and skills to strengthen our democracy.

Carroll's death coincided with a massive generational shift in the role and practice of journalism, during which the business model, delivery mechanisms, and the very identity of the journalism profession were changing, becoming something else and declining in the eyes of Americans. Many local newspapers are now in a death spiral, foreign correspondents are being brought home, and Americans receive their news from a wide range of unfiltered sources, ensuring the spreading of both good and bad information. Newspaper staffs are being cut drastically, and in some places in the country there is literally no news coverage at all. Carroll left the international and national scene at the height of his career to strengthen a regional paper in the South, where he felt he could effect change. He was able to do so because the owner of the paper gave him almost total independence and saw the paper not as a profit-making venture but to ensure the public good. For this reason and others, Carroll's life is important to know about; he represents the best qualities of his time, and stands as a virtual mentor today.

As a student I had known Wallace Carroll, having taken his course on the First Amendment at Wake Forest University. I only knew then that he had served as the editor of the city paper, and that he was a man you didn't want to let down. Stern yet approachable, he seemed to emit a kind of quiet charisma that made you want to do your best for him. We all tried.

Years later, reading Lynne Olson's account of influential Americans in London during the Blitz, *Citizens of London,* I came upon the name Wallace Carroll. Apparently, he had been manager of the United Press (UP) office in London at the beginning of World War II, and subsequently directed European operations for the United States' newly created Office of War Information (OWI). He seemed to have had access to every person of importance at the time, from Winston Churchill to Franklin Roosevelt to Dwight Eisenhower. This intrigued me as a former journalist, and my journey into the life of this man began.

Wallace Carroll was a war correspondent, diplomatic reporter, UP bureau chief, government official, adviser to presidents and statesmen, editor and publisher, environmental leader, teacher, poet, and—not least—husband and father. In an almost uncanny way, he was present at most of the significant events of the twentieth century, from his first assignment in 1929 covering the St. Valentine's Day Massacre in Chicago to his 1968 commentary on the Vietnam War, which influenced Lyndon Johnson to begin drawing back from the conflict. Not only did he report on the Blitz, the Battle of Britain, and the Nazi assault on Moscow in 1941, but on his return through Asia, he landed in Pearl Harbor on December 14, 1941, his ship, scheduled to arrive December 7, unexpectedly delayed by a few days. Carroll was among the first to file dispatches on the attack's devastation. This knack for what some would call his "peripheral vision"—his way of seeing where the important story would be or sometimes just landing in the middle of the story at the crucial moment—led Carroll to chart a remarkable course through life.

After his pre- and early war work in the capitals of Europe, he assumed the role of chief propagandist for the Allied cause as the first director of the London office of the U.S. Office of War Information, established in 1942 to consolidate and disseminate information to civilians about the war. He was an adviser to General Eisenhower on the role of information, or what he called "persuasion by words," in advancing the war effort. Later, as director of European Operations for OWI in Washington, D.C., he orchestrated the dropping of millions of leaflets across occupied Europe and coordinated official government news reports of the Allied advance across the continent. As important as military efforts, Carroll believed, were the Allies' efforts to win the proverbial hearts and minds of Europeans trapped under the Nazi boot.

Following the war, and drawing on his knowledge of the Soviet Union, he would consult for the State Department on "psychological warfare," then be recruited as news editor for the Washington bureau of the *New York Times* in the mid-1950s to early 1960s. When he was poised to leave the *Times* in 1963, he was offered "any bureau in the world," but decided instead to take the helm of the *Winston-Salem Journal* and *Sentinel,* a mid-size newspaper in North Carolina, where he would use his influence to transform the community. His position put him at the center of the nation's struggle for civil rights, the fight against the tobacco industry, and the nascent environmental movement.

An acquaintance once remarked that while Carroll was going from A to B, the rest of us were drifting through life. He had a keen strategic mind, honed by a lifetime of reporting the international and national news. His editorial calling for the end of the Vietnam War demonstrated a knowledge far greater than most policy analysts, and its publication was perfectly timed to bring about a significant change in the course of the war. When his managers at the *New York Times* changed the wording of a quote in one of his stories about President John F. Kennedy, he resigned his position in protest. And when others questioned if Great Britain would go to war against Hitler on September 3, 1939, Carroll was standing outside the Cabinet offices at 10 Downing Street, knowing from his contacts that a decision was to be made that morning. So it was that Americans got the first dispatch that war had been declared.

In Winston-Salem he commanded the same respect as he had 300 miles away in his office at the *New York Times*. To those who worked for him he was extraordinarily private and unforthcoming, reticent, and dignified. Yet he was kind, thoughtful, and witty, avuncular in his treatment of others, particularly young journalists. And although there was seldom a person on the global scene that he did not know, he maintained a low-key presence, working through his editorials to advance causes rather than to garner the spotlight. In this he was a "persuader" who saw the value of information gathered by journalists as not just informing the public but helping to guide public action and policy. "It wasn't a matter of where he was," wrote Jonathan Yardley, one of the young journalists he mentored, "but who he was—a man of integrity, quiet but with passionate conviction and decency. A gentleman."

Wallace Carroll's story is a history of the twentieth century and the importance of what it meant to be a journalist during this most violent of times. Carroll was part of this country's "greatest generation," who not only won the war but worked to ensure a peaceful postwar world. Working to win a war, structure the peace, advance desegregation in the South, influence the pullout from the Vietnam War, ensure conservation of our most beautiful lands—these were the accomplishments of his life.

This is his story.

Mary Llewellyn McNeil
Washington, D.C.

PROLOGUE

In the early afternoon of Saturday, September 7, 1940, Hermann Goering, commander in chief of the German Luftwaffe, climbed the cliffs of Cap Gris-Nez in northern France to watch more than 800 German bombers and fighters set off for the English coast. Flying in perfect formation, they formed a block 20 miles wide, their silver wings glistening in the blue skies of a warm day. British spotters on the coast marked their arrival, assuming they would disperse to attack the airfields and sector stations they usually targeted.

That same day journalist Wallace Carroll, eager to take advantage of the beautiful weather, was sunning himself on the upper tower of the United Press (UP) offices on Bouverie Street, off Fleet Street in London. Despite his initial hurry to set up a telephone line to the desk below to call in any action, the tower had sat empty for almost a year. Occasionally one of his reporters would venture up to get a glance at the city or, as Carroll did that day, to sun himself in the late summer air.

But for several days now Carroll had posted himself on a small chair near the tower's edge. He had a distinct feeling that something might be afoot. His numerous sources in British intelligence had told him that landing barges in the estuaries of the Netherlands and France were on the move to the coast, and he knew—after visiting the Royal Air Force (RAF), seeing German pilots in action, and haunting the halls of RAF Command—that both countries' pilots were at a breaking point.

About 3:30 in the afternoon, as he returned from grabbing a sandwich from his offices below, he spotted in the distance, clear as day, a squadron of German bombers—Junkers, the Ju-87—coming down the Thames River in perfect formation at about 4,000 feet, flying over the barrage balloons that were hung with netting to impede aircraft and defend London from the south side of the Thames. The planes flew east to west, past the Houses of Parliament and Big Ben, and drew up just abreast of the UP tower on Bouverie Street. They passed the Tower Bridge and, according to Carroll's account, suddenly peeled off one by one and dived, aiming at the big oil tanks of the East End docks. They released their bombs one by one, followed by tremendous explosions.

Carroll, sensing that this was more than a stray raid, grabbed the telephone line and began dictating blow by blow to one of his staff, Ferdie Kuhn, in the office below. Carroll had experienced high-altitude bombing in Spain, but this was different. Adolf Hitler had dispatched his Stuka bombers, which as they peeled off and headed toward their targets, sounded very close, whistling as they came down. Carroll, ducking with each explosion, stayed up on the tower as another squadron came through, and then another, undeterred by anti-aircraft fire. For four hours he watched the conflagration, as bombs exploded around him and planes flew so close as to almost nick the gray stones of the tower. His only protection was a battered tin helmet he had pilfered from a member of the Old Guard who lived in his apartment building.

By the end of the day, German planes had dropped more than 300 tons of bombs on London. Even though civilian populations were not the target, the poorest of London slum areas—the East End—felt the fallout the most, from direct hits of errant bombs or fires that broke out and spread throughout the vicinity. Eric Sevareid, reporting for CBS Radio that evening, told how "flames swept through dockyards, oil tanks, factories, flats, sending towering pillars of black, oily smoke into the sky." The fires guided German bombers who continued to blast the city throughout the night. The attack killed more than 400 people that afternoon and evening, injured hundreds, and drove thousands from their homes. One bomb, in what was described as a million-to-one chance, made a direct hit on a ventilation shaft in a crowded East London district where a thousand people had sheltered. Fourteen were killed and 40 injured, including children.

Fortunately for Carroll, the British censors had decided to take that Saturday off, or they had been told to let the American reports go through, so Carroll's dictated stories went on the wire directly to New York. Newspapers across the United States published them the next morning. Carroll had been among the first to file an eyewitness report of the attack, and because of him Americans received newspaper accounts even before the British. One of the reporters on the receiving end in the United States was 20-year-old Walter Cronkite, who was working for UP in Kansas City, Missouri. He later recalled Carroll's bravery. "Being a war correspondent was dangerous business," wrote Cronkite. "When German bombers were swooping right past Parliament at only four thousand feet in altitude, Carroll was on duty."

Around 6:30 p.m., an exhausted Carroll descended from his tower, covered in soot and red-eyed from smoke. With nothing more to be done for the moment at the office, he started for home, a five-mile walk to Kensington High Street. With the blackout in full force, it was pitch dark outside. "I could hear the night bombing had started," he recalled. "The bombers were circling around. They couldn't fly in formation in the dark, so bombs were being dropped randomly."

Carroll heard the planes droning above, and "then there was a long series of whistles and off in the distance the sound of bombs being dropped, and then a strange thud sound not far away." He dropped to his belly and covered his head. Rising unhurt he slowly made his way through the moonlight to the gates of Buckingham Palace, where all seemed quiet. Finally reaching home several hours later he fell into bed, too tired to eat the dinner that his wife, Peggy, had laid out for him.

Several days later, in a meeting at the British Ministry of Information, he learned that the dull thuds that September night were bombs falling in the courtyard of Buckingham Palace. Fortunately, they were duds. The Ministry had not released the information for fear that the Luftwaffe would realize how close they had come to the King and Queen, then in residence, and would try the same attack again.

▪ ▪ ▪

That early fall night was the first of 57 consecutive day and night bombing raids on the city. Life in London became both intolerable and strangely exhilarating. "The Blitz affected all the senses, the taste of dirt, the smell of burnt timber, the artificial smell of homes sealed and closed windows, the blackness of blackout, the glare of flares and the blazing orange and red skies after a raid," the BBC reported. The bombs created appalling wreckage, especially in the East End near the docks. One street of tenements would be leveled, while in the next, houses were sliced in two with furniture hanging out of windows or shattered on the streets. Bulldozers each morning pushed the rubble into vast piles.

For most reporters, it was a harrowing experience. Carroll's friend James Reston, who had recently joined the London bureau of the *New York Times*, minced no words about the precarious nature of life in London. "I wasn't scared," he later wrote. "I was terrified. I came even to fear the moonlight, for then the bombers could follow the shine of the Thames." Ultimately he developed an ulcer and then a case of undulant fever, contracted from drinking unpasteurized milk. He left for home shortly after the Blitz began in September. Other journalists lost their lives during the Blitz. Webb Miller, one of UP's most respected reporters, missed his step on a train in the London blackout and was killed. Shortly after, Walter Leysmith, an Australian on the *New York Times'* London staff, died when a stray German plane, lost in the fog, ditched its bombs and one blew up his house. The *New York Times* moved its staff to the Savoy Hotel to spare them the hazards of walking to and from their homes.

But the Blitz also offered an opportunity for many young journalists, drawn to London by the excitement of covering a war. And it was the perfect event for a new breed of radio journalists. "It had immediacy, human drama, and *sound*—sirens, bombs falling and exploding, anti-aircraft guns firing," Edward R. Murrow later wrote.

Such immediacy captured the American public's attention. Before the bombing began, a June 1940 Gallup Poll showed that only 35 percent of Americans favored helping England win the war. Five months later, after Carroll, Murrow, and their colleagues had reported the bombs falling on London, 60 percent thought more aid should go to Britain.

Such efforts did not go unnoticed by the British hierarchy, despite the Ministry of Information's efforts to censor much of what came out in the written media. Murrow was given unprecedented license by the British government to report on the bombings and became the toast of the town. He "dined with the Churchills, was courted by society hostesses, was invited to country house parties by aristocrats." Though less well-known, Carroll, too, would be privy to the inner circles of British power. As the wire services and the radio reporters competed and shared their coverage, U.S. ambassador to Great Britain John "Gil" Winant wrote that his country's journalists "accepted the dangers and risked life cheerfully in their determined effort to keep the American people informed."

Years later, Wallace Carroll would say it was the most exciting time of his life.

TO GO ABROAD

CHAPTER 1

A SON OF THE MIDWEST

"I realized if I didn't just go, I'd never go. Going was the key...."
—a character in a novel by Jayden Hunter

In the early twentieth century, Milwaukee, Wisconsin, was a working-class town at the heart of a changing America. For most of its history the city had been associated with Germany and its chief export, beer. But by the late nineteenth century, what had been called the most German town in America was a melting pot of ethnic workers, led by Polish and Irish immigrants, who had flocked to the city to fill its burgeoning manufacturing jobs.

As Milwaukee grew and thrived, its one-time immigrant workers had created a new and diverse middle class of factory and office employees who relocated to the northern suburbs and built Sears bungalows along paved sidewalks and parks. The city's "sewer socialist" government cleaned up neighborhoods with sanitation, water, and power systems and pumped resources into public education. Milwaukee's economy boomed, and a new consumer class arose.

This was the world into which John Wallace Carroll was born in mid-December 1906. Carroll's father, John Francis, was a beneficiary of this new economy. After losing his Irish immigrant parents at a young age, he had been raised by an aunt and uncle in Zenia, Ohio, and somehow educated as an accountant. For 25 years he worked for the city government, earning a sufficient wage so that his wife, Josephine Meyer Carroll, could remain a homemaker. Fiercely intelligent with a classic Irish wit, he was a passionate lover of classical music and an expert piano player.

Josephine was second-generation German, fluent in the language but increasingly distanced from her German heritage. She was known for her love of baseball and excellent baked stollen, and although John Francis was often critical of the Germans in Milwaukee, his love match with Josephine was to last their whole lives. Together they embodied the new Milwaukee, more tied to the possibilities of America than to their countries of origin, and determined to reach a solid middle-class existence.

When Carroll came into the world, his family lived in a house with no electric light, telephone, or radio. In a note to his grandchildren, Carroll recalled that "When it became dark my father would turn on the gas globe hanging from the ceiling in the kitchen or living room and light it with a match so the family could read." The Carrolls didn't own a car ("Only rich people owned cars," Carroll remembered), but they did own a horse—named Colonel. Carroll recalled going on rides with the family in a wagon pulled by Colonel, perched on a small box behind the single leather seat in front where his mother and sister would sit, and during which he would lean over to pull Colonel's tail.

Later, like many middle-class workers in Milwaukee, the family moved up in the world—to a bungalow on North 28th Street that was three blocks down from the A.O. Smith Corporation, a huge car factory that churned out more than 10,000 steel car frames a day and employed thousands of workers. The bungalow was surprisingly spacious and boasted a broad front porch, stained glass windows, hardwood floors, and an attic easily converted to living space. Like most along its block, it had recently been electrified and included a garage in the back, a much-needed commodity in Milwaukee even though the Carrolls still could not afford to own a car.

As the children of Irish and German Catholic immigrants, the Carrolls made sure their children attended Mass on Sunday morning. Sunday afternoons were spent listening to the sounds of opera wafting from the living room, where John Francis would be listening to his favorite artists on an old beat-up Victrola. The family's prized possession was their player piano, purchased with scarce funds, and the one family outing each year was to attend the Chicago Symphony when it came to town. Other entertainment included visits to Borchert Field to see the local minor league team play—a particular favorite pastime of Josephine—and listening to radio. All in all, it was a happy, loving, and rather cultured existence, even if money was scare and luxuries few.

The Carrolls raised three children in the bungalow on 28th Street. The eldest, a girl, Marian; then John Wallace, or "Bud" as he was called; and the youngest, Emmet. Of the three children, Bud alone would leave Milwaukee for a life on the global stage. He emerged early as the star of the family, and was the first in his family to attend college. To save money, he lived at home throughout the entire four years and worked a variety of part-time jobs to finance the cost. Compact and trim with notoriously bad eyesight, he was known for his prodigious memory and droll wit. A favorite family pastime was to listen to him recite verbatim passages from books and conversations he had heard, a skill that earned him a part-time job reading children's stories over the radio to earn extra money. As a young man—as was true of many Wisconsin natives—he prided himself on his ice skating and skiing abilities. Summer weekends were spent crabbing on the Menominee River and in the winter joining pick-up games of ice hockey.

Bud remained close to his siblings his whole life. Marian was "whip smart," according to those who knew her; like her mother, fluent in German, and always reading. Like her mother, too, she would become a homemaker in Milwaukee. Emmet, handsome and charming, worked as an engineer, among other small jobs, but never left the neighborhood in which he grew up. While abroad, Carroll wrote his parents religiously, and he dedicated his second book, *Persuade or Perish,* to them. In a testament to the family's enduring closeness, family legend has it that when his father died in 1951, shortly after Josephine had passed away, it was from a broken heart from missing her.

It was a secure upbringing, grounded in the solid virtues of a second-generation Midwestern American family. But it was certainly not an environment that portended advancement to the global stage. Nonetheless, it gave Carroll a strong sense of values that were never to leave him. These included an unfailing modesty and unwillingness to talk about himself or inflate the truth, stoicism and politeness, and authenticity. Even into his nineties he would retain his clipped Wisconsin accent.

Bud was quiet but fiercely ambitious, educated and openly curious, and most of all filled with a spirit and confidence that he could do anything if he worked hard enough at it. These were the same values that would help his generation overcome the Depression and win a world war. And like many young men and women of his time, he was seeking adventure, a world different from the one he had grown up in. While he loved his family, he simply wanted more out of life than what Milwaukee offered.

▪ ▪ ▪

There are times when opportunity and destiny intersect, and this was the case when Wallace Carroll entered Marquette University in the fall of 1924. The university had just hired Jeremiah L. O'Sullivan as professor of journalism and manager of the university press. O'Sullivan, a Marquette alumnus, had worked for United Press as bureau chief in Wisconsin and Indianapolis and later as division chief in New York City and Chicago, with responsibility for covering the entire southern and western divisions of the nationwide news service. While in Chicago and New York he had hired and trained beginning journalists, a job that cemented his desire to teach and fit well with his supportive nature. Finding the pressure of daily journalism too much, in 1924 he resigned from UP, writing tersely to his higher ups, "Hours too long. Wages too low. Life too short." He would remain with the school of journalism for the next four decades, and on becoming dean of the college in 1928 he set about elevating the university's school of journalism to national stature.

If Carroll had not considered journalism as a career before entering college, he certainly gained a reason to under the tutelage of O'Sullivan. Marquette University also provided him an opportunity to demonstrate his intellectual skills and to broaden his horizons. One of the leading Catholic universities in the United States, it was then the only one to have a separate college of journalism. It was also the premiere university in Milwaukee, occupying prime space along the town's main thoroughfare. Several years earlier it had begun a building boom, erecting a new law building, a grand structure to house science classrooms and laboratories, a dental school building, and a long-desired gymnasium. Marquette finally had the physical facilities to house its rapidly expanding curriculum. And while most students still hailed from Wisconsin, the school was garnering a national reputation.

The university's president, Father Albert C. Fox, was at the time considered the most informed Jesuit in the United States on education trends, and he strongly supported the premise that the press, next to the pulpit, was the most powerful influence for good in society. Marquette had a reputation as a character-building institution, built on the principle that education dealt with both the mind and the heart. The school, in the Jesuit tradition, strove to instill in its students the will to serve others. Although Carroll had already begun to pull away from Catholic dogma and the formal trappings of the church, the Jesuit teachings had pervaded his thinking; public service and compassion for those less fortunate would be a guiding principle throughout his life.

He was also fortunate to come under the tutelage of a seasoned reporter like O'Sullivan, who was not only toughened by his own experience but loved teaching. With his booming voice and abundant good nature, he set about instilling in his students his three main journalistic dictates: "Truth, Competence, Compassion," and even introduced an entire course on the latter topic. His students adored him. Many who would later rise to prominence would remember how he had helped them through difficulties in their undergraduate years with an encouraging word and a few dollars in book fees from his own pocket. When he became dean, he would maintain a firm belief in the importance of journalism education to democratic society. "If we don't have a good press," he would often say, "then society as we know it will end."

These influences propelled Carroll into what turned out to be a successful academic career and gave him the opportunity to do what he had always wanted to do—write. He promptly joined the staff of the university's newspaper, the *Marquette Tribune,* as well as its yearbook and literary magazine staffs. His early stories in the *Tribune* revealed a tongue-in-cheek approach and fondness for puns. An expose on the school's cafeteria, for instance, spoke of how "it would certainly take a lot of crust to criticize the pies, and the fellow who would pan the bread or roast the meat is only half-baked."

While he moved on to more weighty topics, becoming an editorial writer and associate editor of the paper, his writing continued to tend toward the rather overblown and dramatic. A later piece, entitled "Barber of Seville Has Nothing on the Barber of Union House," encouraged students that "If you wish to see somebody get a good trimming, step over to the Union House barber shop some day and watch the hair fly."

But by the time he graduated, he was vice president of the school's Press Club and Journalism Honorary Society, editor of the literary magazine, and secretary of Marquette's Honor Society. He was one of two journalism students to receive the Sigma Delta Chi key, awarded by the Society of Professional Journalists to a graduating senior.

O'Sullivan had emphasized the importance of combining practical experience with academic studies, and no doubt he called on his contacts at the United Press to hire his quiet yet aggressive young student. Several days before graduation, Carroll received a note from UP Chicago offering him a position in the bureau. He jumped at the chance, packing his belongings and leaving the bungalow on 28th Street. Less than three months later, by July 3, 1928, he had been given his first byline as a United Press staff correspondent.

CHAPTER 2

FOREIGN CORRESPONDENT

"Journalism will kill you, but it will keep you alive while you're at it."
—Horace Greeley,
founder and editor of the *New York Tribune*

arroll had scarcely been outside his home state of Wisconsin
when Earl Johnson, the head of the UP Chicago office and
of its nascent international bureau, hired him. Johnson oversaw
a vast network of correspondents for what was then the largest
wire service in the world and the first to give reporters bylines.
Johnson drilled UP's reporting style into his reporters: short,
bright sentences, active verbs, specific nouns, few adjectives.
"News stories on a press wire," Johnson wrote, "are like fire-
crackers. The tighter you roll them, the more noise they make
when they go off." In a slight paradox, Johnson, known for his
unflappable demeanor and slow, loping walk, stressed speed in
posting to the wires as of the utmost importance, along with
brevity.

The wire services, notably UP and the Associated Press(AP),
were the internet of the 1920s and 1930s, virtually the only
sources of immediate mass information to the public. They sent
material to thousands of newspapers, magazines, and later radio
and television stations across the country for yearly subscription
fees. Reporters would enter their stories on a keyboard attached
to a machine that would transmit their characters via electronic

communication—telephone cables or wireless radiotelegraph—to a receiving teletype machine, which would spew forth printed material. The "clattering keys, ringing bells and scrolling paper" that churned from the often squat, black machines were omnipresent in the newsrooms of every newspaper and radio—and later TV—station in the country. They made the news almost instantaneous, and seasoned newspeople kept their ears open for the bell that signaled breaking news. UP's operations relied almost totally on the teletype machine, and papers everywhere relied on their services.

The feisty UP had been created in 1907 by Midwest newspaper publisher E.W. Scripps, who united three small news syndicates he owned and expanded the wire service across the country. From the beginning, it was considered radical. Scripps opposed the concentration of corporate power, championed labor unions, and inveighed against political corruption. He wanted a wire service whose goal was to sell news to anybody, anywhere, and at any time. Copy had to focus on the human element and be colorfully written; its reporters scrupulously independent. Its reporters, known as "Unipressors," were given little formal training; new hires often thrust into a sink-or-swim situation. But the most talented journalists in the country worked for UP, and the low pay was offset by the excitement and challenge often provided by the dashing service.

UP was considered a scrappy alternative to the better-funded and well-heeled Associated Press, and the competition between the two services was legendary. "In bureau after bureau, country after country, the men and women of the United Press turned out stories around the clock," wrote Gregory Gordon and Ronald Cohen in their book, *Down to the Wire: UPI's Fight for Survival*, "their financially fragile network held together with Scotch tape and baling wire." But while many considered AP more polished and prestigious, UP was seen by many cub reporters as a sacred calling. And it was not for the faint of heart. "Only an instinctive counterpuncher could prevail, one with a tough hide," wrote one observer, "and a knack for making correct split-second judgments to scoop people."

The serious, young Carroll took UP's culture to heart, worked extremely hard, and wasted no time in churning out pithy reports on such arcane topics as the price of grain futures. But he increasingly sought out the big news as well. His first major story in Chicago was a rewrite of the infamous St. Valentine's Day Massacre, executed by gangster Al Capone's men on February 14, 1929, and called in by reporters on the scene who could barely string two words together. Carroll waxed poetic about the bloodletting, writing of "men propped against the brick wall of a warehouse like animals and shot down in their tracks, moaning, screaming and cursing as the internal whine and roar of leaden slugs mowed them down."

In short order, his boss, Earl Johnson, would develop a fond attachment to his young reporter from Wisconsin, perhaps because of Carroll's unflappable nature, which mirrored Johnson's own laconic style. "I never saw him [Johnson] rattled, never heard him raise his voice," recalled one colleague. Johnson also had a talent for going immediately to the crux of a story, and what was drawing his attention in the fall of 1928 was the growing political and economic discontent on the European continent. In a remarkable demonstration of confidence in the young Carroll, he agreed to send him to London after only six months on the job. He wanted someone with chutzpah in whom he could trust. Carroll, undaunted, jumped at the chance, setting sail for the British capital in the summer of 1929. It would be up to his own wits and hard work to make a go of it—and he knew Johnson would be watching.

When an inexperienced Carroll arrived in London in 1929, the term "foreign correspondent" was not what we know it to be today. For the most part, correspondents wrote up their stories based on rehashed government documents or called in reports already prepared by bureaucratic government agencies. Most would simply re-run wire reports from home, many of which were unlikely to contain any new or factual information. Seldom did reporters venture out of their offices to witness events. With some exceptions, it was not until the late 1930s and early 1940s—in part fueled by the growing international wire services—that the term earned its connotation of glamour, excitement, and intrigue—of death-defying adventurers willing to risk their lives to get a good story.

Carroll was at the forefront of a new breed of wire reporters who knew that to make a name for themselves, they had to get out and witness events firsthand. He wasted no time in hitting the London streets, unchained from the office by his reluctant manager, Clarence Day, who was "great at keeping the books but had no idea what an eyewitness report was." He began by covering sporting events, but in the nearly two years Carroll spent covering news in and around London, he wrote about everything from "Big Bill" Tilden's win at Wimbledon in 1930 to the invention of the fax machine to the presentation of young American women to the Court of St. James's.

Perhaps his most colorful story was a 1930 account of the Lord Mayor's parade gone haywire, when four elephants, panicked by an effigy of a lion, broke loose and injured more than fifty spectators. Carroll's account reflected his flair for the dramatic as well as his sense of humor:

> ...The lead elephant, apparently convinced that the lion [effigy] was authentic and a natural enemy, raised its trunk, trumpeted angrily and lumbered toward the students. Others in the herd stepped out of the line and followed after.

That was enough for the students. They dropped the effigy in haste and scattered. Their fear was communicated to the vast crowd and soon there was a stampede. Police, doing their utmost to maintain order, kept shouting: "Don't get panic-stricken!" These cries, however, together with strident whistling for police reinforcements, merely seemed to add to the confusion.

At this point the elephants, their objective lost in the surging mass of humanity, appeared as frightened as the rapidly dispersing throng. The terror spread to police mounts and it was with difficulty that the horses were controlled. An Indian boy, seated on one of the elephants, managed to keep his precarious perch despite the animal's excited maneuvers.

Elephant attendants, armed with hooks, prods and the correct vocabulary for dealing with the beasts when fractious, finally got them back in line and the procession continued peacefully to the end.

■ ■ ■

Stampeding elephants notwithstanding, Carroll understood that he had to move on to more serious topics. The growing unrest in England offered him plenty of opportunity.

By 1929 the country was beginning to suffer the effects of what would be known worldwide as the Great Depression, at a time when the country was still far from having recovered from the First World War. Between 1929 and 1933, Britain's world trade would fall by half, the output of heavy industry by a third, and profits plunge in nearly all sectors. At the depth of the Depression in the summer of 1932, the British registered 3.5 million unemployed, and many more had only part-time jobs. Despite this, the Conservative Party in 1931, accepting the necessity of budget tightening, cut unemployment benefits and public sector wages. The result was Britain's largest and most profound economic depression of the twentieth century.

Particularly hard hit were the industrial and mining areas in the north of England, Scotland, Northern Ireland, and Wales. Unemployment in some areas reached 70 percent. Many families depended entirely on payments from local governments, known as the dole. Others were left destitute, with queuing at soup kitchens a way of life.

This impoverishment led to civil unrest, with violent clashes between police and demonstrators erupting throughout the country. The National Unemployed Workers Union (NUWM) had begun as early as 1922 to pressure the government for assistance. It organized a series of hunger strikes, in which thousands of workers, primarily from the South Wales Valley, Scotland, and the North of England, would walk to London to demonstrate against the government. One such march reached the capital soon after Carroll had arrived in the country in the summer of 1929. Hurrying to join the marchers as they headed toward Tower Hill, he was struck by "the terrible shape they were in," and how the police called out in force and on horseback "beat them unmercifully." Narrowly missing a beating himself, he later that day filed a piece that gave the lie to the British press's official reports that no violence had occurred. Carroll had been able to report the truth because he had seen it; he was the only reporter there.

Carroll would file dozens of pieces and slowly inch his way toward reporting more on international and diplomatic affairs, filing stories about the British policy in Palestine, an international meeting of faith leaders in Canterbury, and Britain's rather half-hearted leanings toward home rule in India, among others. In September 1931, he would report on Mahatma Gandhi's decision to postpone a trip to America, "I fear the Americans might misunderstand my mannerisms, my clothes, my rustic speech," he would quote Gandhi as saying, "They would probably lionize me, which I do not desire. It is better that I remain far away, where I am only a legend to the American people."

His more substantive reporting did not escape the attention of Earl Johnson back in Chicago. In October 1931, he rewarded Carroll with a transfer to Paris. Johnson, remembering Carroll's persistence in getting a story and his ability to garner trust among contacts, wanted a reporter with scope to cover the growing political violence in France. Johnson saw it as a prelude to future trouble in Germany. He set about strengthening UP's European bureaus, and two years later would go himself to Berlin to assemble a staff, which included William L. Shirer and Howard K. Smith, that would run rings around AP and other news agencies. For a still very young Carroll, the transfer meant a chance to strengthen his diplomatic credentials and to be more at the heart of what was going on in Europe.

▪ ▪ ▪

There is little we know about Carroll's initial two years in London outside of his work. No doubt he felt relieved to have a job—even at UP's barely subsistence-level wages—given that unemployment was rampant, people regularly lined up at soup kitchens, and the government seemed to turn a blind eye to the people's distress. But London must have been a cultural and literary feast for a young man like Carroll. It was the home of H.G. Wells, George Orwell, Agatha Christie, and Carroll's favorite—Ford Madox Ford. Theatre was hugely affordable, and the city was awash with sophistication. But it was also a city of extremes—the elite who held flamboyant dress parties and drunken treasure hunts throughout the streets at night and the poor who peddled goods on the steps of St. Paul's Church in Covent Garden. Carroll would not forget the contrasts, while at the same time making the most of his adventure. And he had worked almost nonstop to build his reputation and establish contacts.

Paris would be different. More accustomed to life in Europe, Carroll eased into life there. He quickly picked up French and managed to establish himself as a regular at Le Lapin Agile where he would join the crowd in drinking songs and show off his piano-playing skills. Paris, too, was rich with culture, filled with salons, galleries, and cafes. Jazz filtered through the clubs, surrealism flourished, and haute couture, with the help of CoCo Chanel, was reinventing itself.

But by the time Carroll arrived in Paris, France too was suffering the effects of the Great Depression. Pierre Laval, a former socialist, had recently been elected prime minister, yet his tenure would be brief as the country zigzagged back and forth between the left and the right, groping for a solution to the deepening economic crisis. One result was a frightening rise of right-wing movements, including the National Socialist movement next door in Germany. The French continued to be bitterly divided between pacifism and rearmament, with the popular mood soured amid recurrent corruption scandals.

Carroll's bureau chief was Ralph Heinzen, a decided step up from Clarence Day, and someone willing to take risks to cover a story. (Heinzen later would be captured and held a prisoner of war; following his release he would write numerous insider stories on the Nazi regime.) Carroll began to file stories immediately, focusing on the growing drama of economic and political affairs. Topics included France's infamous tariff policies, the deflation of the American dollar, and most important, the ongoing disagreements about war reparations and French rearmament of its naval fleet. Hovering over all of these events was rising tension with Germany. In January 1933, Adolf Hitler would ascend to the German chancellorship, giving him expanded power and causing further consternation among those in France worried about Germany's intentions. And in 1934, France would be rocked by the Stavisky scandal, which brought down the then Socialist government and threatened to foment a civil war.

The Stavisky Affair revolved around Alexandre Stavisky, an embezzler who used his political connections to sell worthless bonds and devise other illicit money-making schemes. Stavisky maintained the façade of legitimacy by using his connections to high-level members of the Socialist government as well as to other influential businessmen. Faced with exposure in December 1933, Stavisky fled Paris to a chateau in the village of Chamonix, where police reported they'd found him dead from a gunshot wound. He was officially determined to have committed suicide, but there was persistent speculation that police officers had killed him.

Members of the French right believed that Stavisky had been killed to prevent revelation of a scandal that would involve liberal ministers and members of the legislature. Accusations led to the resignation of left-leaning Prime Minister Camille Chautemps. He was replaced by the socialist Edouard Daladier. One of Daladier's first acts was to dismiss the prefect of the Paris police, Jean Chiappe, who was notorious for his right-wing sympathies and suspected of encouraging anti-government demonstrations. The dismissal of Chiappe was the immediate cause of the crisis of February 6, 1934, which many saw as a possible right-wing putsch. That night, demonstrators from both political sides were set to gather in what looked likely to erupt in an explosive clash.

Carroll had discussed the situation with Heinzen, and they determined that Carroll should cover the event. They decided the socialist government supporters, mostly students, would be coming past the Arc de Triomphe down the Champs Elysees, while the right-wing supporters would approach from the west. The best place to be was the Place de la Concorde, where Carroll positioned himself shortly after noon. As the crowds began to gather, the atmosphere grew increasingly tense and rough; two city buses were stopped and set on fire. But to Carroll it appeared the police—seemingly friendly to the socialist sympathizers—had the mob under control.

About 3:30 p.m., however, right wing mobile guards from the provinces—apparently called in by President Daladier—"on beautiful horses, in full cavalry gear with helmets and breastplates" descended on the square to break up the crowds. The mounted soldiers swept around and around, trying to clear the square. Carroll ran while being attacked by a guard with a saber, and as he started to move away, he heard shots behind him. A mobile guard had fired point blank into the crowd. Carroll saw that a young man had been shot in the chest; blood pouring out of him. Carroll picked the young man up and carried him to the American embassy, where he was declared dead, shot through the heart. The student had been doing nothing but shouting "Vive Chiappe" when he had been shot, according to Carroll. Ever the UP reporter, Carroll "ran like hell" to a telephone and phoned in a bulletin to Heinzen. The police fired upon and killed 15 demonstrators, and Daladier was forced to resign.

The next day his story ran across the front page of dozens of U.S. newspapers. "Horrors of Paris Riots Told by Correspondent" was the headline in the *Los Angeles Times* on February 7, 1934:

> *A dying French youth collapsed in my arms here tonight shot down by the police and Republic Guards during frenzied, hysterical rioting by thousands of men and women in the historic Place de la Concorde, seeking the overthrow of the Daladier government.*
>
> *I was standing in the swaying mob when the first volley crashed into the shrieking rioters....*
>
> *The volley cracked across the square, near the new United States Embassy. The police and guards fired when other efforts to break up the mob attempting to force the bridge and gain entrance to the Chamber of Deputies failed.*
>
> *A French youth about 24 years of age staggered back and I caught him in my arms.*
>
> *He was killed instantly.*

Again, Carroll's was the only eyewitness account to run in papers across the United States.

The violence he had witnessed in France would further convince him that trouble was on the horizon. He would later describe the political warfare in England and France in the 1930s as portending Hitler's and Mussolini's rise. The disparities between the "haves" and the "have nots" were a powder keg that the diplomatic community would prove incapable of defusing.

His five years in Europe also left him with something more important. He would never forget the haggard faces of the hungry Welsh miners who had made their way to Trafalgar Square in search of a square meal; the brazen exercise of power against unarmed students in the Place de la Concorde; the fragility of the French government; or the underlying discontent of many. He would never again take government proclamations at face value or fail to question those in authority.

Carroll's time in London and Paris had expanded his professional credentials as well. He was now well-recognized across the United States and respected by UP's head, Hugh Baillie. His reward—a plum new assignment. At age 27 he would move to Switzerland, to become UP's diplomatic reporter covering the League of Nations in Geneva. There was no better place on the continent to observe and report on the diplomatic controversies and failures that would lead to the Second World War. He was ready to cover them.

Chapter 3

Love, War, and the League of Nations

"The League is very well when sparrows shout,
but no good at all when eagles fall out."
　　　　　—Benito Mussolini, Fascist dictator of Italy

Geneva in that serene spring of 1934 was, simply put, a very pleasant place to be, a "postcard perfect world of the Swiss Alps and leafy quays," according to travel brochures circulating throughout Europe. Entertained by sailing regattas, air shows, and marches by the American Legion Drum & Bugle Corps, the international community enjoyed what seemed an idyllic existence. Delegates to the embattled League of Nations picnicked leisurely along Lake Geneva. Americans tuned their radios to performances of *Amos 'n' Andy* and regularly attended Shirley Temple movies.

But the calm of daily life belied the reality of a world steadily marching toward war. While Geneva seemed untroubled, the rest of the world continued to reel from economic depression and widespread unemployment. The League's efforts at peace fared no better. The world's first international Disarmament Conference, held in Geneva in February 1932, had ended in stalemate. A year later the conference had reconvened only days after Adolf Hitler assumed power in Germany. In February

1933, Japan, outraged at being formally blamed for invading Manchuria in China, had abruptly marched out of the assembly. Eight months later Germany withdrew completely from both the Disarmament Conference and the League of Nations. Negotiations sat at a standstill.

Delegates assuaged their frustration by regularly attending cocktail parties and playing the roulette tables in nearby St. Moritz; reporters were bored. The League had been set up in 1920 as the first international organization whose principal mission was to maintain peace. But by 1934, it was becoming increasingly clear that the League lacked the power to do so.

▪ ▪ ▪

Nonetheless there was some hope on the horizon. The United States never formally joined the League of Nations, but when Carroll arrived in 1934 it had begun to play a more active role in the organization's work, and the Soviet Union, which had previously obstructed and ridiculed the political rule of the organization, had changed its attitude. The Soviets had joined the assembly that year and were continuing to give it steady support—in no small part from fear of Germany and Japan. The League had also attracted new member countries from Latin America and the Middle East and established the first genuine international peacekeeping force of 3,300 men, culled from the armies of Great Britain, Italy, the Netherlands, and Sweden.

But then again, in the spring of 1935, Adolf Hitler blatantly ignored the League's efforts at disarmament by launching his "Saturday Surprises," announcing, first, the creation of a German air force; second, complete repudiation of the military clauses of the Versailles Treaty; and then, institution of universal military service in his country. None of the Western nations pushed back, and in fact Britain would six weeks later willingly authorize him to disregard the treaty's naval clauses as well, permitting Germany to build submarines virtually without restriction.

While Hitler was rising to power, Italy was already in the hands of dictator Benito Mussolini, and in October 1935, he invaded Ethiopia, breaking with all covenants it had agreed to as a member of the League. The assembly, led by Britain, imposed sanctions on Italy in the hope that the economic consequences would drive Mussolini out of power. But in May 1936, without consulting other members, Britain and France agreed to a negotiated peace settlement that gave Italy almost all it had requested. One month later, the League withdrew its sanctions. Mussolini had won a decided victory. Even so, shortly thereafter Italy withdrew from the League entirely.

Carroll had reported on these events with growing frustration, compounded by the fact that his readers in the United States seemed little interested in the growing military aggressions of Germany and Italy. A particularly chilling example was a speech given to the General Assembly in June 1936 by Ethiopian Emperor Haile Selassie. As the emperor entered the assembly hall to speak, whistles and catcalls from Italian newspapermen and spectators silenced him; officials dimmed the lights twice to quell the disturbance until police could wrangle the protesters from the hall. Leaning over the railing in the reporter's gallery overhead, Carroll watched Selassie, standing calm and proud in a flowing black robe, declare in his native language that he was "here to claim the justice that is due to my people." Selassie recounted how sprayers placed on planes had "vaporized" his people, "scattering fear and death over the Ethiopian countryside," and that Italian newspapers had reported how clusters of Ethiopians were "bursting open like a rose" when bombed from above. Selassie went on to say that because his "confidence in the League of Nations was absolute," his people were now being slaughtered. His speech would later establish him as an icon for anti-Fascists around the world, and in 1936 he would be named *Time* magazine's man of the year.

Carroll had warned his readers in advance that the speech would rule out a "tame, routine League of Nations assembly," and that the outburst "was the climax of a series of Italian efforts to prevent the Emperor from addressing the assembly." Any "non-recognition of Italy's conquest" would need to be carefully phrased by the British and French delegations," Carroll reported, to eliminate "the embarrassing possibility of having representatives of [Selaisse] appear indefinitely at the assembly." As a result, British foreign secretary Anthony Eden, refusing to even recognize the conquest of Italy, called for a review of the League's "collective security" commitments (for the countries of Western Europe, but not Africa). The review called for economic sanctions against Italy to be rescinded. Although he reported on the results of the study, Carroll knew Great Britain and France's actions marked an effective collapse of the League's authority and further empowerment of the Fascist governments of Italy and Germany.

"I sat in the press galleries and prowled the corridors of conferences on disarmament and conferences on rearmament," wrote Carroll later, increasingly aware of the League's inability to be more than a shadow organization. He had identified only one delegate he felt was interested in peace—Maxim Litvinov, the Soviet Union's chubby Commissar for Foreign Affairs. Litvinov "treated Geneva to a display of magic such as the world had never seen," Carroll wrote early in his time there. "He used every device of the League, every technicality in its Covenant, to maneuver the British and French appeasers into a position in which they would have to be firm and courageous in spite of themselves."

Litvinov had advocated strongly for diplomatic agreements leading toward disarmament since the late 1920s, and he had been a leading voice for the official Soviet policy of collective security with the Western powers against Nazi Germany. In

1933 he was instrumental in winning a long-sought diplomatic plum: formal recognition by the United States of the Soviet government. Litvinov had also played a key role in the Soviet Union's acceptance into the League of Nations, where he would represent his country from 1934 to 1938. Internationally, he was greatly admired as a diplomat. "Nothing in the annals of the League can compare with Litvinov's frankness, [his] debating power, in the acute analysis of each situation. No contemporary statesman could point to such a record of criticisms justified and prophecies fulfilled," wrote one historian. Carroll agreed.

Litvinov—and Russia's—support for the collective security system was shaken by England and France's appeasement of Italy's actions in Ethiopia. Therefore, the Soviets felt, Italy's transgressions against Ethiopia had to be condemned, especially by England and France. This was not the position taken by Britain's Prime Minister Stanley Baldwin. Making apologies later, he told the House of Commons following the Italian invasion of Ethiopia that collective security "failed ultimately because of the reluctances of nearly all the nations in Europe to pro-ceed to what I might call military sanctions"—the reason being that no country except for the aggressor country was ready for war. But Carroll felt this was a weak excuse, and he reported it as such. Britain and France, unlike Litvinov and the Russians, would abandon the concept of collective security in favor of appeasement in the face of growing militarism under Hitler.

Litvinov's presence was to later figure importantly in Carroll's reporting on the Soviet Union. "I saw the magic of Litvinov and the other Soviet diplomats," Carroll would recall, "but I knew little of what lay behind it. Whether the influence of the Soviet Union was for good or for evil, I was convinced that it could not be ignored." When the Munich Agreement between Adolf Hitler and Neville Chamberlain was signed on September 30, 1938, Carroll knew Litvinov's efforts had been in vain. Litvinov would be recalled to the Soviet Union, where he would be dismissed by Stalin. Many would later say his dismissal gave the green light to Hitler to agree to the German-Soviet Nonaggression Pact months later. His replacement as Commissar of Foreign Affairs, Vyacheslav Molotov, had less of an orientation to the West and thus steered Stalin toward the pact with Germany and away from alliances with Britain and France.

Several years before this, however, in a prescient piece he had written in 1936 soon after Emperor Selassie's speech, Carroll warned that "Fear of war broods over Europe these mid-summer days like an ominous hush heralding a violent storm. Two dictatorships in Germany and Italy whose leaders have openly glorified war are playing the music to which Europe is dancing." The article, published throughout the United States, lambasted the British and French for their appeasement of Italy's invasion of Ethiopia, their weakness hobbling the League's authority, and their leaving the door open for Hitler's aggression. "The League has been so badly shaken by the conquest of Ethiopia that it can hardly be expected to deal with another problem of such magnitude for years to come."

His was not the only warning given to a still unsuspecting American public of the international crisis on the horizon. Winston Churchill, a former Member of Parliament at the time and a strong supporter of the League, felt the same way. He later commented that the League failed "largely because it was abandoned, and later betrayed; because those who were its best friends were until a very late period inflicted with a false sense of pacifism."

That same summer of 1936, walking along Lake Geneva, Carroll recalled and wrote about an encounter he'd had with a young Austrian. "You are lucky to be an American," the young man said. "In a few years I and all my friends will be killed in war."

■ ■ ■

For Carroll, however, the grim global outlook was offset in Geneva by perhaps the most influential event of his life. In the winter of 1937, he would meet—on a mountaintop—the brilliant, sophisticated woman he would marry. Carroll was skiing with expatriate friends when he met twenty-four-year-old Margaret "Peggy" Sawyer, who was working as an assistant to John "Gil" Winant, who was then the U.S. representative to the International Labor Organization (ILO). Peggy, petite and vivacious, was with a young Canadian diplomat, but that didn't stop Carroll from, as he later remembered, "moving in" and engaging her in conversation.

Peggy was one of several impressive young women recruited by Winant to help run the newly launched ILO. A graduate of Vassar College, she had grown up living all over the world, spoke French fluently, and provided inestimable help to Winant, who gave her an array of assignments, from drafting correspondence to preparing a study on food price regulations. Her father, Dr. Wilbur A. Sawyer, as head of the Rockefeller Foundation's Public Health Laboratory Service, had developed and refined the first effective vaccine for yellow fever. The Sawyer family had traveled extensively throughout Peggy's childhood; they had spent seven years in Australia, where she had attended the local public girls' schools and become familiar with the Australians' British habits and friendliness. From Australia, the family took frequent trips across Asia, to Indonesia, Sri Lanka, and the Philippines, and later to Egypt. By the time she met Carroll, Peggy was well-traveled, adaptable, and possessed of a remarkably adventurous spirit. She knew much of the diplomatic corps in Geneva and had an intelligence and personality that drew people to her.

She had also long demonstrated a strong social consciousness. In high school, while at the family home in Hastings-on-Hudson, New York, she had set up informal soup kitchens with her mother and siblings in their backyard to feed hungry neighbors and others who appeared on their doorstep seeking help. One summer she badgered one of her teachers to take students to France to learn the language and culture, an endeavor she funded through bake sales and other activities. After graduating from college, she had served a stint with the Department of Labor in Washington, D.C., where she conducted a tour of the Depression-era South, studying the nutrition of those laid low by the economic disaster. It was during an international conference hosted by the Labor Department that she had met Winant, who was so impressed by her he would offer her the job in Geneva.

Despite her world travels and sophistication, Peggy was only 24 when she met Carroll, who was six years her senior. She described him in a letter to her mother informing her of their engagement, telling her "he is not very good looking, but is a very good journalist and the nicest person in the world and I like him as much as I love him, which is a lot.... He did the best reporting at the Brussels conference, and always scoops everybody (I'm not being funny, it's true) because all the diplomats trust him implicitly and tell him everything.... You know, I never believed that I would ever <u>really</u> fall in love—thank heaven it was mutual!"

The usually reserved Carroll was also smitten, not the least by her outgoing personality, keen wit, and joie de vivre. They were perfectly matched in many ways; both enjoyed hiking and skiing in the mountains, as well as weekend trips to Mt. Blanc and Chamonix. He would remember one of their first evenings together, when they played the slot machines in a casino at nearby St. Moritz, and Peggy won the night's jackpot. As Carroll reminisced, "I thought this was a good sign and that—maybe—she was a keeper."

Carroll made good on that thought. On May 23, 1938, he and Peggy married in a civil ceremony conducted in French at the U.S. consulate. The judge conducting the ceremony stopped in the middle to ask Peggy if she understood what was happening. Of course she did, she responded. He didn't know she was the most fluent in French among all the participants. Following the ceremony, they hosted a reception for more than 100 fellow journalists, diplomats, and friends at the Le Clos Fleury, Chambesy, a restored castle in Geneva. The invitation list was a who's who of the pre-war diplomatic community, celebrating the first American wedding to be held in Geneva in four years. Photos show an elegant gathering in a world soon to be lost in global war.

More than a "keeper," Peggy helped define Wallace Carroll's life. Their love story would last 63 years. She was instrumental in both his happiness and his further development as a world-class journalist. Effervescent where he was dignified, outgoing where he was quiet and observant, Peggy adored him, and he adored her back. For the normally reticent Carroll, his love was deep and affectionate. Boarding a plane for a war-zone assignment shortly after they were married, he wrote that leaving her was "so painful I couldn't speak … and the hardest thing I've ever done. I wish you were coming with me." Years later when acquaintances remembered Carroll's event-filled life, they would remark on how Peggy's life might be the real story to tell. She was never in the background, always out front or standing beside him—and with nerves of steel to match his own.

▪ ▪ ▪

Besides finding the love of his life in Geneva, Carroll found a world of opportunity. And through Peggy's acquaintances and his own hard work and integrity, he had managed to garner contacts and friends who would help him immeasurably in his future personal and professional life.

The first was Llewellyn "Tommy" Thompson. A long, lean, and graceful man, Thompson was Carroll's roommate when he first arrived in Geneva in 1934 and, later, best man at his wedding. Thompson at the time was the U.S. representative to the ILO, appointed two years after President Franklin D. Roosevelt agreed to join the organization in 1934. After 15 years on the sidelines of the League of Nations, the United States had finally agreed to join the ILO due to pressure from Roosevelt's first female cabinet member, Frances Perkins, secretary of labor. Created with the mission of promoting social justice, fair wages, and humane working conditions, it was one of the very few international organizations America participated in during the 1930s.

During his three-year stint at the ILO, Thompson would hone his political skills and be recognized for his "shrewdness and tact." But he was never one of the "old boys" then prevalent in the Foreign Service. Already in the service for five years, his advancement had been slow in part due to his non-Ivy League background and his reputation as a playboy. (Carroll would later call him Geneva's "most eligible bachelor and redoubtable ladies' man.") But he and Carroll were cheery companions. They skied and hiked together, Carroll remembering Thompson going down the slopes "with grace and wild abandon" and climbing the Swiss mountains "with the elan of a mountain goat." They shared a Midwestern background and thoroughly enjoyed the cosmopolitan life offered by the city.

In 1941 Thompson would finally be recognized for his skills and be sent to Moscow as second secretary in the U.S. embassy, where he would play a pivotal role during the Second World War. He would later become ambassador to Russia during the Cold War and serve as chief adviser to President John F. Kennedy during the Cuban missile crisis. He and Carroll would remain friends for life, until Thompson's death in 1972.

Another close friendship developed with Rifat Tirana, Albanian ambassador to the League, and Tirana's American wife, Rosamond, whom Carroll would later call "the most beautiful woman in Europe." Both were young, cosmopolitan, and very much in love. Rosamond, a recent graduate of Swarthmore College, had grown up in an affluent and politically ambitious family in Greenwich, Connecticut. Both her parents were well-known socialists—her father helping to launch the National Association for the Advancement of Colored People and her mother supportive of the Russian Revolution as both an advocate and a novelist. Rifat, a Muslim, had developed a reputation at the League for his acuity as an economist. At the time he met Carroll, his country was under threat of invasion from a Fascist Italy, and he had a deep understanding of the dangers of Fascism spreading throughout Europe. In 1941, he would publish, under the pseudonym Thomas Reveille, *The Spoil of Europe*, which outlined in grim fashion the evils of Nazism, then still largely unknown or underestimated in the United States. After the war, he became head of the Export-Import Bank in Washington, D.C.

In Geneva, the three had become inseparable. They hiked and skied in the Alps, held casual picnics by the lake, and sipped coffee in the numerous cafes. When Peggy joined their party in 1937, their friendship continued to flourish. No doubt Carroll was influenced by their worldly sophistication, and it's likely he listened thoughtfully to their socialist perspectives. Rifat, who emigrated to the United States and became a U.S. citizen during the war, would die in 1952 at the age of just 44, but Rosamond would go on to become a well-known abstractionist painter and live for another fifty years. She kept a photo of the three of them—Carroll, Rifat, and herself—on her desk until she died. After her death her son sent it to Carroll; he would keep it on his desk until he too passed away.

Carroll at that time also became good friends with Richard C. Hottelet, the UP correspondent in Berlin, who on occasion showed up in Geneva to gain insights on the negotiations there. Born in New York to German immigrants, Hottelet had moved to Germany in 1937 to get a law degree from the University of Berlin, only to drop out when his professor, dressed in a brown shirt and Nazi armband, demanded that his students salute with a "Heil Hitler" at the start of each class. In March 1941, the Nazis arrested him on suspicion of espionage, and he spent four grueling months in jail, "the hardest and longest I ever spent," he would later admit. He was unexpectedly released from jail and turned over to the American Embassy, later returning to London where Carroll recruited him to join the Office of War Information. Hottelet later became one of Edward R. Murrow's "boys" reporting on the war, covering some of its bloodiest battles.

Carroll and Hottelet's friendship lasted for another fifty years. Despite their acknowledged expertise and experience covering historic events, they shared a reluctance to talk about their exploits and a commitment to the news as a public service. Hottelet was famous for articulating his approach to the news: "Don't tell them what you think. Don't tell them what you feel. Just tell them what you know." He would spend over 40 years reporting for CBS news and died in 2007 at the age of 97.

And finally, in 1937, Peggy also introduced Carroll to Gil Winant, who had just begun his second stint at the ILO, and would soon become the agency's new director. A former progressive governor of New Hampshire, Winant was known for his strong support of liberal causes and was seen by some as a potential political threat to then President Franklin Roosevelt. Roosevelt, who had dubbed Winant "Utopian John," first appointed Winant as representative to the ILO in 1934. After five months in Geneva, Winant had been called back to become chairman of the U.S.'s new Social Security Board, where he had worked tirelessly to implement sweeping social legislation. Frustrated by Republican resistance to the Board, he resigned, and Roosevelt sent him back to the ILO in 1937 as director. Winant would go on to become the U.S. Ambassador to Great

Britain in 1941, where he would be both a friend and a valuable source of support for the Carrolls, while working tirelessly himself to change American public opinion toward support of the war.

Winant was a brilliant leader, able to inspire through his selfless actions and empathy for those he saw as less fortunate. Tall, distinguished, and from an old, established New York family, he made every effort to connect with the common man. He strongly believed in the ILO's mandate, and spent his time in Europe as director traveling throughout the continent assessing the political currents and growing tensions. More than any other American, wrote the journalist William Shirer after lunch with Winant in Berlin in 1938, "he understands the social forces at work in the past decade."

Winant took both Carroll and Peggy under his wing. A warm, slightly disorganized man, he served in many ways as a father figure to Peggy, and their friendship would last until Winant's death in 1947. He would both seek to take care of Peggy during the war years and open the door for Carroll among the diplomatic elite. His mentorship would prove essential to them both.

▪ ▪ ▪

Sooner or later everyone who was anyone—prime ministers, ambassadors, financiers—had come through Geneva in those pre-war years. Carroll had witnessed the appeasements of the West and the heartbreaking pleadings of the leaders of conquered nations. The city had exposed him to the cosmopolitan and educated society of Europe, and he had absorbed it all. He was no longer a rather "breathless" reporter, but someone steeped in the ins and outs of diplomacy. And the contacts he had made would help him immeasurably in the years to come.

By 1938 most agreed that the League—or any foreign or international power—lacked the power to stop Hitler, although few imagined the scale of his aggression. Carroll early on questioned the policy of appeasement toward Hitler. He proved to be right. The world was headed toward a cataclysm, and he had an insider's view of the road paved to get there.

Nonetheless, after four and a half years as diplomatic reporter for UP in Geneva, and with the growing realization that the real news was a taking place elsewhere, Carroll was becoming restless. He questioned the relevancy and usefulness of his reporting, and safety notwithstanding, wanted to move where his coverage would be more worthwhile to the American public.

Just as he was contemplating leaving the Swiss capital, in the summer of 1938, he got a call from Harry Flory, European news manager of UP. The action was in Spain, Flory believed, where a destructive civil war had been in progress since 1936, and the tide had begun to turn against the left-leaning Spanish Republic. The Nationalists—an alliance of monarchists, conservatives, and traditionalists led by General Francisco Franco—were rapidly gaining ground, aided by air power provided by Germany.

The raging conflict was viewed by the American left at the time as a class struggle between dictatorship and republican democracy, between Fascism and Communism. In hindsight it would come to be seen as a dress rehearsal for World War II, as Franco's Nationalists were heavily backed by Adolf Hitler. The Spanish war would be a testing ground for Hitler's armaments, then being produced on a mass scale in Germany. It would be remembered for its atrocities, one of them the bombing of Guernica in 1937, grimly immortalized by Pablo Picasso. It was also, although less well known, a testing ground for Josef Stalin, who was the only world leader at the time willing to back the Republican forces.

Given this, how could Carroll not go to Spain? A wide array of foreign journalists and writers—among them George Orwell, John Dos Passos, Pablo Neruda, and Ernest Hemingway—had traveled to the war-torn country, despite the danger, to aid the Republican cause and to report on the war. Carroll discussed the trip at length with Peggy, his bride of only three months. Peggy was supportive of the Republican cause and appalled by the horrors unfolding. She was also privy through her diplomatic connections to reports of Hitler's firm backing of Franco and the Nationalists. If Carroll had anticipated reluctance on her part to have him go, he was wrong. As adventurous as her husband, if not more so, Peggy fully supported his efforts and understood a journalist's need to see the action before it was too late. She did in fact write to her mother that she wished she could go with him. She enlisted Gil Winant's help in arranging air transport for Carroll to Barcelona, the Republican stronghold.

Catching a flight out of Geneva, Carroll landed on August 2, 1938, in the battered Republican-held Barcelona. Four months earlier the Nationalists had broken through to the Mediterranean Sea, cutting the Republican-held territory in two. The Republicans were fighting back, but Franco, with the help of Hitler's Luftwaffe, had begun systematic, sustained bombing of Republican cities, Barcelona included.

His very first night in Barcelona, Carroll recalled, the Germans flew over in their Heinkel He 111 bombers. "They came in V-8 formation out of the West, over the mountain, and never deviated," he recalled. "I sat on the front porch and watched them. They went up the coast and hit the power stations north of Barcelona. The anti-aircraft fire didn't stop them." It was Carroll's first experience of German bombing. On August 5, 1938, he reported on the city's defenses, which consisted largely of underground air-raid shelters and tunnels built to shelter the civil population. According to Carroll, 1,500 air raid refuges had been constructed, with 500 more underway. Some 9,000 workmen burrowed through the earth night and day under almost every city block. When completed, they were to provide shelter for 600,000 persons.

With Barcelona seemingly secure for the moment, Carroll was determined to get close to the fighting going on west of Madrid, where the Republican Army was barely holding out against the Nationalist onslaught. With the help of the British foreign secretary, Carroll managed passage on a broken-down DC-3 flying over Franco's lines to the closest Republican-held town. The story of the flight is best told by Carroll himself in an artfully crafted dispatch:

> *MADRID—U.P. (August 23)—There are two ways to get from Barcelona to the other side of loyalist Spain if one is willing to take the risks of war. One is to slip down the coast by ship through the rebel sea and air blockade; the other is to fly over the area where Generalissimo Francisco Franco has amassed 500 warplanes.*
>
> *I chose the latter.*
>
> *After waiting 10 days in Barcelona, I received official authorization to fly. My instruction sounded like a page out of an adventure story. I was told to be ready to depart at an hour's notice, taking no more than 25 pounds of baggage.*
>
> *The exact destination of the plane was kept secret. Two nights later I received notice to depart, packed a suitcase and hurried through darkened streets to the meeting place.*
>
> *Searchlights combed the sky to detect possible raiders as we groped our way slowly across the city, by automobile, then, with increased speed along a country road lighted by a half moon. Road patrols halted us frequently until we reached the airdrome. We bounced across the field past planes under whose wings riflemen slept.*
>
> *A sentry wrapped in a blanket stopped us and examined our papers. Then we alighted and felt our way into a big monoplane. Motors roared. Red ground lights outlined the field for a moment as we hurtled through the darkness.*
>
> *The plane climbed until my aching ears told me it was the highest I had ever been. Below us the coast lay in darkness. Not*

a single light pierced the night to guide rebel bombers. In darkened towns and villages along the coast, babies were being born and men and women were dying without benefit of electricity....

A red streak in the east forecast dawn and the eastern sky began to brighten. Just as the last star faded in the west, we headed sharply downward and landed at a secret airdrome whose hangars were cleverly camouflaged to prevent detection from the air. We drove in a carabinero's car past fields where sturdy peasant women were winnowing wheat in Biblical fashion, past acres of tall sunflowers whose seeds are roasted and eaten, past vineyards, watermelon patches and olive groves until we reached Madrid, one-time Spanish capital which has held out against the longest siege of the war.

Once Carroll landed on the outskirts of Madrid, he realized he had no means of identification since he had been forced to hand in his passport to the Republican Foreign Office when he arrived in Spain. He nonetheless managed to secure a ride to Madrid on a truck full of conscripts headed to the front lines. Riding all day in the transport and sleeping that night in a haystack, he arrived in the capital city with a bad case of dysentery after drinking well water and eating fruit by the roadside.

By this time, the Nationalists had pinned the Republican-held Madrid under siege for two years. Its population had suffered increasingly from a lack of food, warm clothes, arms, and ammunition. As a result, distrust had risen within the Republican forces, who proceeded to make random civilian arrests and accusations of disloyalty. Franco had given up on another frontal assault on the city and was happy to constrict the siege gradually, to continue to bomb Madrid, and to let the civic unrest continue.

By the time Carroll arrived, the battle lines on the outskirts of Madrid had gotten dangerously close. Still suffering badly from the dysentery and doubled over, he was trying to get closer to the front when he ran into a doctor who stopped him asking if he could help. The doctor told him about a pharmacy in nearby Puerta del Sol where he could get some medicine. Weak as a kitten, he went looking for the pharmacy, feeling his way along the sides of buildings, when a Republican intelligence officer stopped him asking for his credentials. "I am an American journalist and am trying to get back to the hotel Victoria," he said. The officer ordered him to get into a nearby bus, which was randomly collecting what were perceived to be Republican subversives.

As Carroll stepped on the bus, "it was like a scene out of Goya," he recalled. "Everybody was praying to every saint and the Virgin and all that. And I realized this was the bus that took suspected fifth columnists out to be shot in the evening. All these guys were on the floor praying, and I was so damn weak I could hardly move."

Miraculously, just then an acquaintance Carroll knew from the British Foreign Office randomly walked by the bus. Carroll stuck his head out the window and yelled to him. The man, turning around, did a double take, hesitated for quite some time, then walked over to the officer who had ordered Carroll onto the bus and said something to him. Reluctantly, the officer waved Carroll out of the bus. He had been saved.

After his narrow escape, Carroll, still sick, made his way back to his hotel, and a couple of days later he caught a ride back to the coast near Barcelona, where he secured a spot on a plane that would fly out through North Africa to Geneva. While he was waiting for the plane to arrive, the Italians dropped bombs on the area, including on a boat he had previously hoped to take. Carroll, with others, piled into a deep air raid shelter nearby where they stayed until the plane to Africa landed to pick them up.

When Carroll finally landed back in Geneva, Peggy was shocked at his appearance. "I shouldn't have recognized him at the station," she wrote her mother, "if I hadn't seen a picture of him when he was in the gangly adolescent stage. He must have lost 20 pounds." For his part Carroll lamented that he had gotten so little out of the trip because he had been so sick. "I did, however, get a damn good story on the bombing of Madrid," he later recalled.

In truth he had gotten a lot more. He had seen firsthand the horrors of the conflict and its effect on an often-innocent civilian population. His dispatches, written with precise powers of observation, painted a picture of sacrifice and fear, of surprising fortitude coupled with physical devastation. "Food is strictly rationed on what appears to be an equitable basis," he wrote in one of them. "Almost every block has long lines of women waiting in front of food shops for the day's rations of bread and chickpeas.... Some buildings are completely wrecked. Others mere skeletons. Roofs are torn off, windows blown in.... With nightfall artillery fire increases. Little groups gather in unlighted streets near the Puerta del Sol and gossip as they used to do in gay cafes. A headlight of an occasional car casts weird shadows on walls or momentarily lights the faces of Madrileños wending home to sleep through a night of artillery fire."

After years of fearing its onslaught, Carroll had finally seen war. His reporting had taken on an almost poetic quality and had whetted his appetite for more adventure. It had also demonstrated to the UP brass that he was a reporter worth promoting. By the end of the year, his old mentor Earl Johnson, now head of UP's international division, called Carroll up to offer him a coveted assignment—management of UP's London bureau.

His job, Carroll recalled, was to "get it ready to cover the war."

SECTION II

CATACLYSM

Chapter 4

London 1939: On the Brink

*"War reporting is essentially the same—someone
has to go there and see what's happening."*
—war correspondent Marie Colvin

It's hard to imagine the degree of confidence Earl Johnson must have had in his 33-year-old correspondent to assign him to manage London's UP office. In early 1939, the world was on the brink of a global conflagration, and London would be central for much of what was to come. Many British—as well as the rest of the world—were worried what the coming months would bring. Hitler continued to ramp up his production of weapons of war and to annex territories, and it seemed that England might finally have to take a stand.

Hardly any journalistic assignment had a more integral need for reliable and accurate reporting. Yet Carroll had never managed a large office and had not even spent any length of time in London since leaving in 1931 for Paris and then Geneva. It was also a hugely stressful job. "Writing for a news agency, when a two-minute beat by the AP means disgrace, is the most nervously wearing occupation imaginable," Peggy would write her mother. "Not to mention highly irregular hours and meals. The man who had this job before Wally has been laid up for over six months with a nervous breakdown." But Johnson held an unshakeable faith in Carroll as the only one of his overseas crew with the steadiness of mind and manner, as well as the diplomatic contacts, to trust with the assignment.

The UP bureau operated out of the News of the World Building, on Bouverie Street, just off Fleet Street and about 150 yards from the Thames River. Home to the widely circulated tabloid of the same name, the building and its surroundings had become a mecca for seasoned journalists, many eager to find a respected place to cover what seemed the inevitable coming conflict. Carroll oversaw the work of about 75 journalists—25 in London, and the remaining 50 strung out around the British Isles.

The impending war had also attracted a wide array of young reporters eager to make their reputations, many driven mostly by adrenaline more than seasoned reporting experience. They came from a cross-section of society, some well-educated and rich, others undereducated but smart; some could speak several languages, while others had no linguistic ability at all. But they all shared a sense of adventure and curiosity, a strong sense of patriotism, and a willingness to undergo extreme hardship, including extended periods of risking death. Of the 1,800 correspondents accredited to Allied Forces at one time or another, 69 died during the war, by combat, accidents, or disease. The news agencies—AP, UP, and Reuters—were hardest hit, each losing five men.

Carroll, unlike many of the reporters inhabiting Bouverie Street, had both experience and a deep understanding of the causes leading up to the war. He also had the skill of recognizing talent. He immediately began to pull together an impressive staff. His first hire was Edward Beattie as his deputy. Beattie had reported for UP from its Berlin bureau in the early 1930s and covered the Italian invasion of Ethiopia. A Yale graduate, he was fluent in German and later covered General George Patton's Third Army advance toward Germany and Austria, where he was captured and held for more than eight months in a prisoner-of-war camp. Beattie would become a reliable second in command and stand in for Carroll when he went on assignment.

Another hire was Ferdinand "Ferdie" Kuhn, who had worked for UP from Germany and then with the *New York Times*. Kuhn took over diplomatic reporting from Carroll when he was made manager of the bureau. Covering the embassies, he developed what Carroll recalled as "excellent sources," including within the Soviet Embassy. Another staffer was Frederick Oechsner, who had been brought into London from the Berlin bureau. Oechsner, said Carroll, was "absolutely honest and fearless and went up against the Nazis in his reporting, something not so true of the Associated Press's correspondent (Louis) Lochner." According to Carroll, Lochner was in bed with the Nazis, even though he won a Pulitzer Prize in 1939 for his reporting from Berlin and later was held prisoner by the Germans.

Carroll would also recruit two recent Rhodes Scholars straight out of Oxford: Charles Collingwood and Howard K. Smith. Collingwood had a flair for the dramatic, having acted in plays in both high school and college. Although inexperienced, he showed an aggressiveness that was appealing. Carroll also probably liked his academic bent, which was not necessarily an attribute of many UP reporters. Smith, unlike Collingwood, was innately reserved and courtly but could also be aggressive and outspoken. Both demonstrated what was most needed in a newly hired Unipressor—chutzpah. They would later go on to have distinguished careers in journalism, two of many reporters who got their beginnings under the UP umbrella and would make the jump to become broadcast journalists.

Carroll's most well-known colleague was Edward R. Murrow, a former Unipressor, whose CBS News office was directly across from Carroll's. Murrow had become the new patron saint of journalism by leaving UP to join CBS, and his graphic coverage from London during the Blitz would come to be considered a milestone in the evolution of American journalism. His collection of radio journalists would become famous as the "Murrow Boys," who made their early careers by reporting on the war. Tall, dark, and handsome, Murrow had both moral and physical courage, according to Carroll, and he charmed his way into getting permission directly from Prime Minister Winston Churchill during the war to bypass the censors in airing his nightly broadcasts. Murrow used every trick he could imagine in the medium to make his broadcasts come alive, including holding his microphone to the ground to catch the sound of bombs hitting the pavement, and of the unhurried footsteps of London residents walking—not running—to underground shelters.

The battle between the print news services and radio was on. In 1935, UP had become the first service to supply news to radio stations. Unlike AP, it realized that the broadcast market was the lucrative wave of the future and began tailoring newswire for broadcasters.

Until then radio had been known primarily for entertainment rather than hard news. But by the late 1930s it had become increasingly the source Americans went to for information. News commentators such as a young Walter Cronkite, who had been trained as a print journalist by United Press, began to describe news over the air with "style or authority, or both, and then to editorialize lightly upon it." Radio also had the advantage of reporting events in real time, something a newspaper could never do.

Murrow, who had worked previously for UP, began adding correspondents to his team in the spring of 1939, with support from CBS headquarters in New York to expand his operation. His recruiting drew many reporters away from print and into on-the-air reporting. Carroll resisted this, for reasons that are still somewhat unknown. Most likely it was because he believed that the more serious reporting was still being done by the written press. But he remained good friends with his radio colleagues.

Carroll and Peggy would join Murrow and his wife, Janet, at the Murrows' apartment on Hallam Street, where CBS broadcasts turned into de facto clubhouse parties for the Bouverie Street cadre of journalists and an assortment of international political exiles and friends.

There is little doubt that Murrow's extraordinary broadcasts from London became a major means through which Americans received news of the impending war. By the end of the war, his broadcasts, described as "like hearing an old friend describe the threatened destruction of other friends and their entire world," were the most trusted coverage of the war.

Both Carroll and Murrow had long argued that the future of news lay in on-the-scene reporting, not in an announcer reading wire copy in New York. He later remarked of Murrow's newscasts that "Ed was doing what I was doing, except he was broadcasting it on the radio." And, as Murrow would often admit, his broadcasts were greatly enriched and informed by the eyewitness reportage from Carroll's UP bureau.

▪ ▪ ▪

Early that year, Carroll also made the acquaintance of a young journalist who became a lifelong friend and colleague. The Associated Press had sent James "Scotty" Reston to London in 1937 to cover big sporting events, including Wimbledon tennis, international golf tournaments, the Irish Sweepstakes, and championship prizefights. Two years later, on September 1, 1939—the day Hitler invaded Poland—the *New York Times* hired him to cover the war.

Reston was born in Scotland, and his parents emigrated to Dayton, Ohio, with their daughter and son when Reston was eleven years old. With little money, but unflagging energy, he worked his way through college at the University of Illinois and up through the journalistic ranks, first as a sportswriter for the

Springfield Daily News (Ohio), then with the Associated Press. Plucky, congenial, and with a light humorous tinge to his columns, he would become one of the most respected journalists of the century.

Carroll and Reston had many things in common—a solid Midwestern upbringing in which money was scarce, being first in their families to complete college, their early beginnings as sport writers, and their happy marriages to intelligent and accomplished women. Both saw a journalist's role as going beyond just reporting facts to encompassing analysis of the news, which required a thorough understanding of the issues. And they enjoyed each other's company. Serious but with a keen sense of humor and an inherent optimism, each believed unshakably in the role newspapers should play in accurately and objectively reporting the news and in informing the American public of the coming conflict. They also believed that the press provided an indispensable public service, and could have a profound effect on the outcome of events. Together they covered almost a full century of news for their readers.

■ ■ ■

While Carroll claimed to have given over his diplomatic reporting to Ferdie Kuhn, he still pursued his own stories and followed closely the diplomatic blunders—particularly on the part of British Prime Minister Neville Chamberlain, Carroll thought—that were leading Britain to war. At the end of 1938, the British were divided over the signing of the Munich Agreement several months earlier. In the agreement, Chamberlain had ceded the Sudetenland of Czechoslovakia to Hitler in exchange for a promise of no further aggression. While Chamberlain had returned to jubilant crowds in London, many—including Winston Churchill and Duff Cooper, who resigned as Chamberlain's First Lord of the Admiralty in protest—saw it as a humiliating surrender.

Carroll and most of the foreign press covering the subsequent discussions in Parliament tended to side with Churchill. Churchill had also watched with alarm Britain's years of acquiescence in the League of Nations to Germany's rearmament and questioned how any further concessions could aid the cause of peace.

Although he continued to report on Chamberlain's reluctant commitment to rearmament, Carroll's skepticism about the prime minister would later be clear. Carroll, who had a more nuanced view from his time at the League of Nations, believed Chamberlain had inherited his distrust of Russia from his father, who had made a fortune producing screws in Birmingham and had what Carroll called "a businessman's fear of Communism." Carroll reported that even as late as April 1939, Chamberlain was "making cautious soundings in Berlin to determine whether there is any ground for an attempt to improve relations." Carroll's frustration at Chamberlain's reluctant outreach to Russia was echoed by former prime minister David Lloyd George, whom Carroll interviewed at length in early 1939. Lloyd George, "who knew something about war," remembered Carroll, "was convinced that the British and French could not stop Hitler. Therefore, he wanted the British Government to move aggressively to line up Russia on the side of the British and French." But this advice, too, was ignored.

As Carroll had predicted, it took only six months for Hitler to renege on his Munich promise. On March 15, 1939, he moved his armies into Bohemia and Moravia and invaded Czechoslovakia, exploding the Nazis' claim that they only wanted to bring racially Aryan Germans into their reach. Alarmed and sensing decreasing support for appeasement at home, Chamberlain, without conferring with his senior staff or Parliament, on April 1 issued a guarantee to Poland that Britain would come to its aid should Hitler invade, a move that could easily pull Britain into war. At the same time, he stalled negotiations with the Russians that could have led to a united Allied front against Nazi aggres-

sion—a policy of alliance heavily supported by Churchill and
Eden. Even Lloyd George—who had long supported easing
reparations against Germany—came to oppose Chamberlain's
appeasement.

Making the rounds of government departments and foreign
embassies in those spring days of 1939, a skeptical Carroll wrote
that he "could not convince myself that Chamberlain's supposed
negotiations with Russia had a basis in reality," adding, "I could
feel there was something questionable about Chamberlain's
intentions and tactics." He was sure Chamberlain fervently
wished to form another bilateral agreement with Hitler, on the
pretext that the Poles were unwilling to enter an alliance with
Russia. Chamberlain and his Cabinet "were getting scared and
wanted to appease Hitler," he later wrote.

The British paid a price for their obfuscation. On August
23, 1939, Stalin, frustrated at Chamberlain's repeated delays in
forming a united buffer zone against Hitler in the East, signed
the German-Soviet-Non-aggression Pact with Germany, opening
the door to the Nazi invasion of Poland. Churchill, in a speech
on October 1, admitted, "I cannot forecast to you the action
of Russia. It is a riddle wrapped in mystery inside an enigma;
but perhaps there is a key. That key is Russian national interest."
Carroll, more forthright, had a different take. "The Soviet-
German pact was," he later wrote in his book, *We're in This With
Russia*, "the bitter and inescapable fruit of Chamberlainism."

Less than two weeks after the German-Soviet pact, early
in the morning of September 1, some 1.5 million German
troops invaded Poland all along its 1,750-mile border with
Germany. The journalist Clare Hollingworth, a friend of
Carroll's whom he had met at the League of Nations, had
noticed the German buildup along the border several days
earlier, and was the first to report the invasion when dawn
broke on that Sunday. To convince doubtful embassy officials
in the capital city of Warsaw that the invasion had begun, she

held a telephone outside the window of her room to capture the sounds of German soldiers' boots hitting the cobblestone streets as they marched. By the end of the month the Nazis had captured Warsaw.

"My job," Carroll later recalled about the morning Poland was invaded, "was to find out if the British government was going to face up to this now. Were they going to appease Hitler again?" Following a tip from his sources, he headed to 10 Downing Street that Sunday morning, one of only two correspondents around. As they waited, both journalists mulled over the idea that Chamberlain could very likely persuade the Cabinet to stand down.

After a while, Minister of Health Walter Elliot came out of the meeting "in a daze," according to Carroll. He told Carroll the British were going to deliver an ultimatum. "If Hitler doesn't get out of Poland in three days, by Sunday, September 3, we are going to declare war," Elliot said. Carroll, after interviewing Elliott about the deliberations inside, rushed to a telephone and called in the story that the British had decided to "face up to it." That same day the *Chicago Daily News* ran Carroll's story, saying England would go to war. Next to it was a dispatch from Louis Lochner in Berlin, an AP story, saying the British were going to appease Hitler again. Three days later, on September 3, 1939, at exactly 11 a.m., the British, Poles, and French, having received no response to their ultimatum, declared war on Germany. Carroll had been among the first foreign correspondents to give the American public a correct accounting of the negotiations, and then of England's commitment to go to war. As such he'd beaten out all of UP's rivals, as well as the British press.

Chamberlain, in a radio address to the nation that solemn Sunday morning, delivered what James Reston referred to as "a sad and painfully personal speech." Failing to accept any blame for the upcoming conflagration, he cited what a "bitter blow" it had been to him personally that peace had failed. He went on to say, "I cannot believe that there is anything more or anything different that I could have done that would have been more successful."

Later that day King George VI, who had supported Chamberlain and hoped peace could be maintained, struck a more courageous and principled tone. If no one stood up to the Nazis, he said in a radio speech free of his serious stutter, "the peoples of the world would be kept in bondage of fear, and all hopes of settled peace and of the security of justice and liberty among nations would be ended.... It is unthinkable that we should refuse to meet the challenge."

When the air raid sirens began to wail in a false alarm at 11:27 that morning, they struck home—this time the country really was at war. Carroll was walking across Green Park when a passing bobby told him to find shelter.

"Where?" responded a dismayed Carroll. There was no protection to be found. The closest air raid shelter was at St. James Park, almost a mile away.

▪ ▪ ▪

Like most of the British, Carroll had expected the war to begin with massive bombing attacks targeting the country's key cities. He immediately began to think how he could best cover the coming onslaught. The News of the World Building on Bouverie Street was four stories high, with a tall tower rising from it that went up another two stories. The day after war was declared, Carroll, climbing to the top of the tower, saw that the view enabled him to see "all of South London up to the Thames, the Houses of Parliament, and down past St. Paul's (Cathedral) to the London bridges and London docks." He could even see the center of London on the other side.

Carroll had a telephone installed in the tower, with a line going down to a copy desk on the third floor, where one of his reporters could put on a set of earphones, sit at a typewriter, and take dictation from up on the roof. The reporter would type it out and send it to a cable operator who would tap it out in Morse code, then send it to the cable office where the censors were. With any luck, Carroll conjectured, it would make it to New York for printing. A firsthand account of any attack was assured.

He and Peggy also began to think about how safe the city was likely to be. "The tension is of course almost more than we can bear," she would write her mother. "People here are having the jitters (except Wally of course). We have it on high authority that London is to be suddenly bombed in the night very soon. And still they do nothing about their air raid shelters, which are full of stagnant water and wouldn't protect against anything but shrapnel even if they finished them." She was four months pregnant with their first child and had been working in the U.S. Embassy under Gil Winant. They decided she should return to her parents' home in Hastings-on-Hudson, New York.

But such a trip was treacherous, too. German warships were already at sea, along with most of the U-boat fleet. The Germans had immediately begun attacking British and French shipping. The ocean liner SS *Athenia* had been sunk by a U-boat hours after war was declared, and a month later a U-boat had slipped into the supposedly impenetrable British Naval Base at Scapa Flow in Scotland and sunk the HMS *Royal Oak*. Together these attacks had resulted in the loss of more than 300 civilian lives and crew. The Luftwaffe had also begun to launch air raids on British warships in the Atlantic.

The British public knew little of this information, but Carroll heard it from his many contacts in the British government. Nonetheless, Gil Winant helped arrange passage for Peggy, and she set sail in early September from Liverpool. Unable to negotiate the rolling decks, she spent most of her time in an upper bunk in her cabin, reached with help from the porter on duty, who had to lift her up. After safely reaching the United

States, she gave birth—two months early—in early November to a baby girl, Margaret, named after a long line of maternal mothers and grandmothers, including Peggy herself.

"I am so very proud of you," Carroll wrote when he heard the news. "The two of you have given me the biggest surprise that I have ever had—and the most pleasant!" For the first time he began to wonder if he shouldn't leave his job and return to the United States in an effort to bring them all together. Peggy, safely ensconced in her parents' home in Hastings-on-Hudson, looked eagerly to London for news; torn between wanting to be with Carroll and staying with the new baby, she for the first time fell into a mild depression. For baby Margaret it was to be her home for the next four years. She would be two years old before her father would see her red-haired curls.

CHAPTER 5

ANTICIPATION

"If we're going to have a war, I wish they'd get on with it."
—the character Dawn in the movie *Hope and Glory*

With Peggy's departure, Carroll, along with the rest of the British public, waited. An eerie stillness seemed to settle in. Barrage balloons anchored with nets to impede enemy aircraft dotted the London skyline like a fence around the city and millions of sandbags lay at the entrances to shops and public buildings. Nightly blackouts were in full effect. Terrified parents sent their children off to relatives or boarding schools in the country. In the first four days of September, more than 500,000 children were tagged and placed on trains to take them away. An article by journalist Storm Jameson called "City Without Children" described London on September 6: "London looked as it would look if some fantastic death pinched off the heads of all those under fifteen." In all, more than 3 million people evacuated the city. The London Zoo put down all its poisonous snakes for fear they might escape during a bombing raid.

People were baffled, according to Carroll. And still the British government was unsure what to do. As James Reston wrote, "The phony war gave everybody time to think, but few officials took advantage of the opportunity." Chamberlain ordered an inventory of assets and estimates of what was needed based for a war lasting three years, seemingly unaware of the need to institute a crash program of rearmament. Some believed he was still secretly trying to negotiate a deal with Hitler and that the whole thing would be called off. When Stalin invaded Finland in November, the Cabinet dithered further, unsure of how to respond to the hostility.

Perhaps most disturbing was the lack of information, as most Britons were kept in the dark about what was going on. The British Expeditionary Force of approximately 390,000 troops, more than 21,000 vehicles, and 36,000 tons of ammunition was sent to France at the beginning of September, soon after war was declared. It assembled on the Belgian-French border, dug in, and waited. As did the rest of the country. Nothing happened. One member of Parliament described what he believed to be the feelings of the average British citizen about a "phony" war that never came: "We are told nothing. We know nothing. Nobody seems to want us, and we hope that [the government] will soon finish with it."

Conscription, food rationing, and the diversion of public transport for military use made civilian life increasingly difficult. A cold winter set in, freezing the Thames and bursting pipes. Britons dealt with the blackouts, which "transformed conditions of life more thoroughly than any other feature of the conflict." During the first month of the war, the dousing of all sources of light after nightfall led to 1,130 road deaths. Everybody carried gas masks, even for infants, some "in the form of an envelope, big enough to carry an entire baby."

Frustration over the "twilight time," as Churchill coined these seven months, did not last for long. As the cold winter turned to spring, melting the Thames and bringing forth a profusion of flowers, Hitler struck. On April 9, 1940, he launched Operation Weserübung, the invasion of Norway and Denmark. Denmark capitulated to the Nazis in six hours. On May 10, the German Wehrmacht launched its "blitzkrieg" against France, Belgium, Luxembourg, and the Netherlands.

That same day, with confidence in Chamberlain finally destroyed, Winston Churchill, then First Lord of the Admiralty, was named prime minister. As the German army streamed out of the Ardennes forests to overrun Belgium, Luxembourg, the Netherlands, and northern France, Churchill felt as if he were "walking with destiny" and "that all my past life had been but a preparation for this hour and this trial." Destiny notwithstanding, Churchill faced the prospect of complete annihilation of the British Expeditionary Force, as well as the French, Belgian, and other forces fighting on the Continent.

The Germans began their assault against the Allied lines and quickly broke through the forces assembled on the France-Belgium border. With the Belgian army's surrender on May 28, the British commander, Viscount Gort, John Vereker, made the decision to order the British and French troops to retreat to the French port of Dunkirk, where they were pinned down against the sea. French troops bravely set up a line to defend against the on-coming Germans. Even then, the British War Cabinet debated whether the country should fight on or try to pursue a compromise peace with Hitler, as the French had done. But Churchill insisted the fight continue, and he, finally, won the day.

■ ■ ■

The miracle of Dunkirk, in which the Royal Navy and hundreds of small boats piloted by civilians rescued more than 330,000 British and Allied troops, saved Great Britain from what Churchill feared would be a colossal military disaster. Carroll, wanting to see for himself, rushed down to Dover on May 30 and wrote of the Tommies landing "bloodstained, muddy and walking like men asleep." Citing several soldiers, he described the bombs constantly raining on the men, and how some had used the bodies of their fallen comrades to protect themselves from the fire. Even in his worst nightmares, "I have never imagined anything like it," said one exhausted soldier. "How I got back, God only knows."

Churchill, in an attempt to seize victory from defeat, addressed the nation several days later on June 4. Summoning his unique power with words, he stated he had "nothing to offer but blood, toil, tears, and sweat." His aim? "Victory." Cigar in hand, turning to one of the radio technicians after the address, he chuckled as he marched out of the room, "We may have to hit the buggers over the head with beer bottles."

■ ■ ■

Carroll had long believed that Churchill would be the determining factor in whether the British stood up to Hitler. After several lunches with him in early 1940, Carroll commented, "You could tell the man was saturated with British history.... He knew what Britain had to do and he was going to do it." More important was his ability to tell the British public exactly what they needed: the truth. "Listening to Churchill and the British people, you could see a tremendous change taking place," Carroll later remembered. "The British people had been uncertain, now they knew they were going to resist. It was a tremendous transformation, say in 48 hours."

He continued to report to the American public on Churchill's resolve, and on his prodigious use of the English language. On June 16, 1940, in an article published across the United States, Carroll quoted Churchill's declaration that Great Britain was prepared for "continuous battle," and that there were "good and reasonable hopes for victory." One day later, on June 17, he filed a dispatch that reemphasized Churchill's power with words, citing him as announcing to the world that Britain and its far-flung empire will "fight until the curse of Hitler is lifted from the brow of man.... What has happened in France makes no difference to our actions and purpose. We shall defend our island home and, with the British Empire around us, shall fight on unconquerable."

■ ■ ■

Carroll also knew enough, however, to question whether, rhetoric aside, the British *could* resist militarily. Churchill's claims had been in contrast to what Carroll had reported after visiting the British Ministry of Home Security that spring—the only journalist to be allowed to do so—to examine reports of the country's existing war machinery. So, he set about finding out. He knew that the Germans had been amassing landing barges all along the estuaries, rivers, and ports of Belgium and Normandy for an invasion. What was left of the British Army to resist, should a land invasion come?

In late June 1940, he and several other journalists, including Quentin Reynolds of *Collier's Weekly*, a renowned practical jokester, commandeered a car and driver and journeyed down to visit the headquarters of the British Third Division, stationed near Brighton and charged with defending the southeast coast, where it was almost certain the Germans would land. The only defenses they saw on the way down were members of the Home Guard, dressed in old khakis and congregating in villages and crossroads. Soldiers too old for the regular army, they had been recruited to take down road signs to confuse the invading Germans, identify strangers who might be fifth columnists, and shoot any parachutists that might come tumbling down from the sky. Success, they were told, would be to kill just one parachutist. In some cases, they armed themselves with broomsticks and later old Lee-Enfield rifles left over from World War I. Journalists joked about the small Home Guard being Britain's only line of defense.

The scene of such rustic volunteers standing up against the German Wehrmacht was too much for Reynolds, who was perched in the back of their open convertible. When they came upon a dozen or so members of the Guard leaning on their rifles, he called out using his best German accent, "Pardon me, please, but can you tell me where we can get our parachutes pressed?" As he said it, several Guardsmen scrambled to reach their rifles. The panicked driver flew down the road.

"Britain's finest," Carroll later recalled with a laugh, "at that point, just stood there, dressed in their khakis and holding broomsticks, dumbfounded."

Chamberlain's reluctance to ramp up production of armaments over the previous years—with the exception of fighter planes and a sophisticated radar system, Carroll discovered—left the country almost completely defenseless to invasion. To compensate, Brits hastily constructed emergency coastal batteries and pillboxes on the east and south coasts, armed with whatever weapons were available. As an aged H.G. Wells told James Reston during a meeting in June 1940, "We were plainly drifting toward world catastrophe, yet hardly anybody was talking frankly, modestly, or unreservedly about where we were going." The only hope was that Hitler would forestall his planned invasion.

Britain's biggest fear was a lightning-fast channel crossing of massed German forces in which they would establish a foothold on the island. The army's ability to resist such an attack was paramount. Britain had left behind nearly 64,000 vehicles at Dunkirk, 76,000 tons of ammunition, and 2,500 guns. It had lost 70,000 men, a massive dent in its forces.

So, when Carroll and his mates finally reached the Brighton army base, they were dubious about what they might find. The men asked to see the commanding general, who was none too anxious to talk to American journalists. But, Carroll remembered, "The order was that anyone who could play a role in potentially bringing the United States into the war was to be treated kindly and given access to all information." So the general took him and his colleagues to lunch. An irascible character with hawk-like features and thinning hair, dressed in corduroy trousers, he refused notwithstanding to give up any information, defensively repeating, "We took no nonsense from the Germans. When we saw them in the lines, we took them out." The general shuttled reporters out for a grand show by the British infantry, which ended with a platoon lining up to demonstrate their use of American-made Tommy guns, which had somehow made their way over to Great Britain. Carroll counted 16 guns among the infantry. When he got back to London that night, he called the American military attaché, General Raymond Lee, to check something out and mentioned what he had seen that day.

"Man," Lee said, "you saw the only 16 Tommy guns in the British Isles." Sixteen guns against the might of the German army.

Carroll also mentioned the nondescript general they had met, citing his colleagues' view that the general "had a rather narrow idea of what warfare was about" and wondered if this was the best the British had to offer.

"It very well may be," said Lee.

The nondescript general was Field Marshal Bernard Montgomery. Notorious for his lack of tact and diplomacy, Montgomery, Churchill's favorite, would later lead the British Eighth Army to victory in Tunisia and command all Allied ground forces during the D-Day landings five years later.

■ ■ ■

Following his trip to Brighton and based on his well-placed sources, Carroll knew that if the Germans could get ashore, the British could do very little to stop them. So he focused on finding out if the Royal Air Force was up to the task of holding back the Luftwaffe, which to this point had only moderate success in bombing military installations and towns across the country.

In late June 1940, he began visiting aerodromes to assess the quality of the fighter planes and pilots who would be the first line of defense against the Germans. According to his count, he later recalled, his intelligence had told him the Germans had about 1,400 bombers, 900 Messerschmitt 109s (ME109s), and another 150 slower fighters. On the British side, he counted about 650 fighters. Most of these were Hurricanes and Spitfires, small single-engine, single-seat craft. The Spitfire could go almost as fast as the ME109, the Hurricane less fast, but both planes were more maneuverable than the German fighters. And he saw other advantages. If a fight came, the British would be defending their own territory; pilots could bail out and know they would be safe. British aircraft factories were producing more planes every day and could likely keep pace with the loss of planes shot down. What couldn't be replaced were the pilots.

Making control of the skies a first priority, after some initial skirmishes, Hitler on July 10, 1940, unleashed his bombers and fighters over the Channel to destroy Britain's airfields and radar stations, 50 of which were scattered all along the southern coast and up to Scotland. Hitler and his military leader, Hermann Goering, had recognized the advantage these radar stations gave to the RAF, despite its smaller staffing and equipment. The Germans had developed a form of radar but saw no need for it on the French side of the Channel. Hitler sidetracked its use, which in time would prove to be a crucial error.

British radar was a well thought out and controlled operation. Radar towers peppered along the coast would pick up the flight of German bombers as soon as they launched and send a signal to Fighter Command headquarters at Bentley Priory, an eighteenth-century mansion and deer park on the northern edge of Greater London. Headquarters would forward information on through fighter command stations across the country. The signal would tell pilots how many and what kinds of planes were coming, their altitude, direction, and exact location. The radar stations relied on tens of thousands of volunteer spotters on the ground, many of them women, to keep lookout, mark the planes as they appeared, and relay this again to Fighter Command headquarters. If the German planes changed direction, the British pilots knew. They could go out to meet the Germans without wasting gas on finding them.

Despite their overall lack of preparedness, the British, in addition to building the radar system, had upped the production of fighter planes during the phony war. What worried British Air Chief Marshal Hugh Dowding was that the rate of training new pilots was slower than planned, a fact Carroll relayed to Hugh Baillie, UP's head, who disseminated the information broadly. In terms of numbers of fighter planes, the Luftwaffe had only a small advantage over Britain's Fighter Command, but Goering's men had an enormous numerical superiority. Dowding kept his forces well spread, knowing that Germany could choose when and where it attacked.

In July, the Germans accelerated their attacks. They launched an air blockade, with the Luftwaffe targeting the radar towers, coastal shipping convoys, and shipping centers. The resulting dogfights between British Spitfires and Hurricanes and the Luftwaffe's ME109s and bombers are legendary. British pilots, numbering around 2,300 in total, flew as many as four or five sorties a day, responding to calls from command headquarters about approaching aircraft. On August 1, Goering directed the Luftwaffe to abandon targeting the radar towers to achieve air superiority over the RAF, with the aim of incapacitating RAF Fighter Command; twelve days later Germans shifted the attacks to RAF airfields and infrastructure. As the battle progressed, the Luftwaffe also targeted aircraft production factories. On August 15, "The Greatest Day," the Luftwaffe mounted the largest number of sorties of the campaign, with the British inflicting 20 percent losses on German bombers and BF110s, demonstrating that the British meant to defend their island. On August 18,

"The Hardest Day," the greatest number of casualties among the British was reached. In total British Fighter Command lost 26 percent of its pilots in the month of August, the Germans 15 percent. In September, British losses climbed to 28 percent, while the Germans lost over 23 percent. Both sides were losing experienced fighter pilots and having to rush untrained crews out of operational training units.

Watching the dogfights overhead became a regular assignment for the public. "People in towns, villages and fields of southern England watched the aerial battles with a sense of excitement and wonderment," wrote one observer. "Swirling contrails were left high in the deep blue summer sky, and occasionally what had been a glinting pinprick one minute would become a thrillingly low-level chase the next."

The dogfights also made good copy for journalists, including Carroll, who ventured out from London to watch the aerial acrobatics, which somehow seemed divorced from the horrors of war. James Reston watched planes battling in the sky as he lay in green fields and contemplated what people hiding in their summer cottages by the sea must be feeling.

Carroll meanwhile spared no drama in reporting on the action. "Along the southeast and south coast British fighter patrols were engaged with the Nazi raiders in constant dogfights over a scattered area of hundreds of square miles," he wrote in an article appearing in the *Dayton Herald* on August 16. "Reports of air battles and the downing of Nazi planes flashed in so rapidly that it was difficult to tabulate them. In many places, it was reported, planes fell at the rate of one a minute, fluttering down like broken birds or plummeting in flames."

The young British pilots, whose average age was about 20, deeply impressed Carroll. In visiting the airfields, he "would watch the boys take off in formations of eight, and we would wait. Soon, somebody would say here they come, and we would count four, five, and six, then we'd wait, and seven and eight wouldn't come home. Already the six who had come home were being briefed for their next flight. These boys were going up two, three, four times a day and taking a lot of punishment."

He also marveled at their ability to retain a sense of humor despite risking their lives daily. On one trip to the airfield at Biggin Hill on the outskirts of London, the action had slowed down, and many pilots were milling around the makeshift medical unit set up close to the barracks. A Nazi pilot captured after bailing out over the southern coast lay injured in the unit, arrogantly bragging that the Germans were coming, and the British didn't have a chance of beating them. Two pilots, also injured, told him with all due seriousness, that luckily during his recent surgery, he had received blood from a Jew that had probably saved his life. Infuriated, the pilot tried to tear off his bandages and had to be subdued from doing himself further harm. Antics aside, Carroll later noted, the next day the Germans "blew the daylights out of Biggin Hill." More than 200 people were killed.

By the end of August 1940, the British had only 800 pilots left, as Churchill later noted, "on whom the fate of Britain depended." It was touch and go. British production of Hurricanes and Spitfires couldn't keep up with losses and there weren't enough experienced pilots to replace those that had been killed.

But then Hitler's impatience got the better of him. With faulty intelligence telling him the RAF was near to defeat at the hands of the Luftwaffe and enraged by British bombing of German cities, he decided to give up on Fighter Command targets and draw the last remnants of the RAF Fighter Command into a battle over London. On September 6, Goering sanctioned the change. The next day German bombers were ordered to hit London and other cities.

The Blitz had begun.

CHAPTER 6

STAYING ALIVE

"There was something inspiring just in the awful savagery of it."
—Ernie Pyle, Pulitzer Prize-winning
journalist in WWII

*"I never thought I should live to grow blasé about
the sound of gunfire, but so I have."*
—George Orwell

C arroll, as did much of the world, marveled at the resilience of the British people during the bombing of their country. "By every test and measure I am able to apply, these people were staunch to the bone and wouldn't quit," he later remarked about the Blitz. Peggy, who had returned to London in March 1941, leaving four-month-old Margaret with her parents in Hastings-on-Hudson, also persevered. The trip across the Atlantic that spring was the second of five harrowing trips Peggy made during the course of the war, a feat that was much more hazardous than that faced by most of the reporters covering the war and even by many bombed-out Londoners. Peggy was one of the few wives of American journalists who joined them in London. "I realize I would be better off at home," she wrote her mother, "but I think this is the place I belong now. It's no use pretending that London is as safe as one's own bathtub in America, but safe or not I'm going to stay with Wally until he leaves."

When she made this second voyage, the "Battle of the Atlantic," as it was dubbed by Churchill, was still in its early stages. But by June 1940, with the fall of France, German U-boats began attacking merchant convoys in packs, sinking more than 270 vessels through early 1941. Peggy had narrowly missed this onslaught. Her nomadic upbringing had steeled her to the challenges of travel, and she wanted to be back in London with Carroll, recognizing the strain he was under. "Often during the night I wake up and put my arm around Wally and I am so happy to have him with me still," she wrote her mother from London. "In these days when you don't know whether everything may be changed before the next sundown you appreciate to the full the common routine of living."

And as with most Londoners, once Peggy arrived, the couple kept up their daily routines despite the nightly raids. Peggy rejoined Winant, who was working at the American embassy, to support his efforts at better educating the British public about the United States. She arranged a series of displays and information sessions throughout the countryside on what it meant to be "American" and found those attending remarkably uninformed. Among the most frequently asked questions was "What do Americans think of England?" or "Do you find us too restrained and old fashioned?" In particular, they wondered about the treatment of Black people and the fact that so many Americans were "foreigners," not speaking English at all. "We are not a democracy like you," one British woman explained. "We have an aristocracy here, and a few families control everything."

Carroll, although happy to have Peggy back with him, was working sixteen-hour days, seven days a week. Despite the strain, he and most of the other reporters found ways to ease the tension. One night he and fellow correspondents met for a late supper at The Strand Hotel with Bob Casey, a combat veteran of World War I who had been a flamboyant and well-known police reporter for the *Chicago Daily News*. Casey had covered gangsters Al Capone and Dean O'Banion during the 1920s and was well-versed in writing about bloodshed and violence. As they were having supper, Carroll later recalled, the air raid sirens blasted on. Carroll could tell German planes were approaching by the sound of their two engines, which were desynchronized, making a particular hum to throw off the detection system on the ground. All of a sudden, it sounded as if a "freight train had fallen off the moon and was coming straight at us," he recalled. "As they instinctively fell on the floor and covered their heads and faces, a bomb hit outside and the windows blew out, plaster coming down from the ceiling. They lay there for a few minutes, and Casey raised his head and said casually with a smile, 'This will make nice small talk in our old age … if we have an old age.'"

The Carrolls had shunned the luxuries of the Savoy Hotel, where many journalists were living, and were renting a flat near Kensington High Street at the Stafford Court, among the largest block of flats in London. It had been constructed with steel, which Carroll hoped would stand up better under the bombing. Like most Londoners they were slow to use the air raid shelter in the basement, preferring to sit out the bombings in their own dwellings. Joining the building's fire brigade, they took turns two or three times a week with other residents to watch on the roof for incendiary bombs, which were dropped in a breadbox-type casing that opened 300 to 400 feet above ground and flung small magnesium-filled bombs over several hundred square yards, setting numerous fires. "We watched a good deal of the night bombing of London from that roof," Carroll recalled.

Their task, once they saw a small bomb landing on the roof, was to run over with a bucket of sand and a shovel and throw sand on the incendiary before it caught on fire. When the Germans began to put explosives in the incendiary bombs, things became even more dicey, according to Carroll. "If we didn't get there fast enough with the sand, they would explode and fill your body with shrapnel." Despite several close calls, they both managed to put out all the bombs that landed on their watch. In this, they joined thousands of Londoners, who formed brigades that took pride in being the first to stamp out the ensuing flames from incendiaries.

In their apartment block, an Indian colonel took charge of the brigade, and after each night watch he would invite the Carrolls to his apartment for tea. A bomb fragment in World War I had hit him, and he felt, according to Carroll, that as a survivor he should take firm command of the attempts to outlast the bombing.

On another night, when the couple were cooking over an oil stove, they forgot to close their blackout curtains. The air warden posted on the corner quickly ran up to their apartment on the eighth floor and "practically had Wally arrested for being an American," Peggy recalled. When things had calmed down, and the warden had left, a bomb just missed the Carrolls' roof, landing to the right of the building and blowing the warden's apartment to smithereens. Fortunately, the warden survived. The next morning the Carrolls saw him waving up to them, standing on the corner where his apartment had once stood. "That's how it was during the blitz," Peggy recalled. "There was no rhyme or reason, so people just did their best to go about their normal business."

Peggy wrote frequently to her mother about what life was like, at this stage even reveling in the excitement of it all and the unreal nature of a raid: "The night is black. Then a searchlight leaps up all around it making a shifting criss-cross in one part of the sky," she wrote. "Then they all lean a little further in one direction and slowly and waveringly cross the sky. It is more like the Northern lights than anything else I have seen.

She, too, wrote of the British spirit, "You cannot imagine how well people are taking this. I interviewed yesterday two boys who are going to America. Their mother told me that the house behind them was completely destroyed on Saturday, and that the police thought a delayed-action bomb had fallen near them and made them stay in the bedrooms at the back; the boys had bits of shrapnel in their pockets, yet they were not in the least panicky. The mother thought it really was time for them to go on to America now, that is all."

In early November, in an effort to escape the nightly tension, the Carrolls flew to Ireland, which Carroll recalled was "belligerently neutral" at the time. Once there, they slept for a full 24 hours, not realizing they had been living on their nerves for months. No one had checked their passports when they had arrived, and Carroll decided to try to get an interview with Ireland's Prime Minister Éamon de Valera. The prime minister had been a commander in Ireland's 1916 Easter Rising against British rule and a political leader in the Irish War of Independence and the anti-Treaty Irish Republican Army opposition in the Irish Civil War. He was vehemently in favor of Irish neutrality during World War II.

Before Ireland had won her independence, the British had three naval bases on the west coast of Ireland, which would be useful in fighting the German submarine blockade. Churchill had wanted those three bases when war was declared; de Valera was not going to let Churchill have them or to allow British troops on Irish soil. It occurred to Carroll that de Valera might let the Americans have them, since the United States was still neutral at that time.

So he went to see "old Dev," he recalled, who was a "remarkable man."

"The first thing he did was reach down into his desk and hand me a map showing the six counties of Northern Ireland. With a shaking finger he pointed to the map and said, 'There will never be peace in Ireland until we have those six northern counties.'"

Carroll asked him about letting the United States use the bases. "No, I will not give those bases to anyone," de Valera replied. "Ireland is going to be the Switzerland of the North Atlantic."

Carroll wrote up the interview, which appeared on November 20, 1940, in the *New York World-Telegram*, confirming that de Valera would not give the bases to either Britain or the United States. Gil Winant was in New York when the story came out, on his way to Washington to brief Franklin Roosevelt, who had wanted to launch talks with de Valera. "Well, that settles it then," Roosevelt said. Roosevelt knew he wasn't going to get them, Carroll recalled. But, he commented, "Sometimes journalists can help out on the diplomatic front, too." De Valera never changed his mind about allowing U.S. bases in the Republic of Ireland. It was only in Northern Ireland that U.S. air bases were established, charged primarily with refueling and overflight agreements.

When Carroll and Peggy arrived back in London that December, they witnessed one of the city's worst raids. Peggy's father, Dr. Sawyer, who was then head of the International Health Division of the Rockefeller Foundation, was staying at the Savoy. On the night of December 29, he stood with them and journalist Ernie Pyle on the hotel roof and watched as bombs fell for one square mile around St. Paul's Cathedral. The Thames was at its lowest tide of the year, so fire hoses could not pull up enough water to put out the flames. They could see fire eating up vast areas of the city behind St. Paul's. When the all-clear sounded, they decided to walk up to the devastated scene, where the neighborhood's fiery ruins still engulfed the cathedral.

"It was a spectacular sight," he recalled, to see the statues that had survived with flames all around. Taking notes, Carroll was almost arrested by the police who questioned his American clothes and were convinced he was a German spy. The next day he summed up his response to the scene:

"Beyond the fire we could see St. Paul's Cathedral. I had never seen it looking so serenely beautiful. As the smoke and flames swirled around its dome it seemed to rise higher above them. So far as we could tell there was no military objective to what was destroyed, but what the Germans are destroying during the night can never be restored—beauty, serenity, grandeur, history in stone."

Carroll later wrote of Churchill's walk through the ruins:

LONDON—U.P. (Dec. 30)—Standing amid the ruins littering the ancient "City" of London after German bombs had all but wrecked it, Prime Minister Winston Churchill today snapped a grim rebuke to a woman who shouted, "What about peace?"

"Peace?" the heavy-jowled, bull-dog-visaged leader of the nation asked in a tone of incredulity after staring hard at her as if he failed to comprehend.

"Peace. When we have beaten them."

Then he walked on through scenes of devastation left by what the British said was a deliberate attempt to burn London without regard to military objectives.

"They gave us something last night, didn't they Winnie?" a man called.

"And we'll give them something back," Churchill retorted.

A great crowd collected at the heels of the Prime Minister and his wife as they walked through the debris that a few hours earlier had been some of the most hallowed shrines in the world. The people cheered and waved hats as they received repeated assurance that the capital's blisters had not weakened the popular will to fight.

"We won't crack up, sir, we won't crack up, sir; we won't crack up," a flustered little man cried as he ran up to Churchill, taking comfort from the grave rejoinder:

"No sir, we won't crack up."

Regardless of the tension and constant fear, Peggy believed she was right to have traveled back to London to be with Carroll. But the stress of the raids in April 1941 convinced them they needed a break, so they went down to Stratford-upon-Avon, where Shakespearean plays still were performed nightly. On May 10, Carroll got a telegram from Ed Beattie, who was managing the UP office while he was away. "Come back immediately," it read. Rushing back, Carroll discovered that his offices at the News of the World Building had been burned down, with unexploded bombs still littering the surrounding streets, threatening their inhabitants. Beattie, at the Savoy when he heard that flames surrounded the building, had rushed over to salvage records. The enormity of the destruction shocked Carroll, particularly the damage to St. Clement Danes, one of Britain's great churches, which lay just beyond Fleet Street and the News of the World Building.

"London was in flames," wrote Quentin Reynolds of *Collier's Weekly*. "Across the river a solid sheet of leaping, maddened fire banked the river for nearly half a mile.... There were flames on every side. I looked toward Fleet Street and winced. Two large fires were reaching up into the night. I had a lot of friends working down there."

Fortunately, Carroll learned, none of his staff had been hurt; his reporters quickly moved offices to the building where the British Ministry of Information was housed and continued to file dispatches despite the loss of all their records and equipment. That night they received a note from a stringer in Glasgow, saying that a German aviator had flown over Scotland and bailed out of his fighter plane. He had asked for the Duke of Hamilton and been taken to the duke at his castle. At the time, the aviator said only that he was an official of the German Foreign Office. Just as Carroll was reading the dispatch, the phone rang and a spokesman from the Foreign Office announced that the pilot was Hitler's Deputy Fuehrer Rudolph Hess.

By the time Carroll had learned of the story it was already public, which angered Carroll, burned-out offices notwithstanding. But several days later, British censors allowed Carroll to file a story that questioned Hess's true motivation. "The big question," Carroll wrote, "is whether Hess is what he claims to be—an apostle of peace—or whether he is the instrument of a Hitler plot." Hess proved to be neither. Disowned by Hitler and shunned by Churchill, he was imprisoned for the remainder of the war. Hitler ordered him shot if he ever returned to Germany.

■ ■ ■

The bombing of May 10, 1941, had been the most brutal single night of the war for London. It had lasted nearly seven hours and destroyed the House of Commons, whose roof caved in from the raging fire, along with much of Hallam Street, whose history dated back to the eleventh century, and Bond streets, famous for its retail stores. The District Railway Line and parts of Westminster Abbey had also been destroyed. More than 1,400 Londoners lost their lives, and 2,000 were seriously injured.

"Life never seemed so unreal, so like a chapter from a novelette," wrote one British journalist on the morning of May 11. "When I get up in the morning I have actually to look at the damage before I can believe that so many of the buildings and places that I most treasured in London have just disappeared off the face of the earth."

Londoners, sifting through the detritus of their city, felt a new level of hatred for the Germans. As he walked around the city that morning, journalist and screenwriter Quentin Reynolds saw streets "filled with grim-faced, sullen-looking men and women" who "were through with 'taking it.' They wanted to give it. The steel had entered the soul of the Briton."

Peggy remembered Carroll's assessment of the British and quoted it in a letter: "Their strength lies in their complete inability to understand when they've lost. In the last war they lost for three years and never knew it, in the Napoleonic Wars for

15 years. You can't defeat an Englishman because he wouldn't believe it as long as he lived."

Several months later, on October 20, 1941, Peggy recalled one night of the bombing:

> *We came home by underground early last evening. The air was too thick to breathe and the faces of people coming off the trains glistened with the heat. Every inch of platform and stairs was claimed by the people who waited, resenting the travelers, until they could sleep. Some of them squinted at newspapers in the smoky light, some knitted, most of them just sat. A little girl with dirty bare legs and her hair in curling rags stretched in her sleep across the aisle cleared for travelers. Her mother smacked her back onto her gray blanket.*
>
> *After we got home some bombs fell pretty close. Wally went on telephoning [in his story] lying flat on his back and I heard him say, "Can you hear the building shake?"*
>
> *Half an hour later an express train [a bomb] swished through the air right on us and cracked wide open at a thousand miles a minute. Bricks could be heard dropping down again outside for an interminable time, and it rained glass. The lights went out. "Wally," I said from the kitchen floor. Then another one whanged at us. The floor was shaking and ready to slither down with all the other falling masonry.*
>
> *"All right, boys," I thought, "You've got me now, go ahead and hit me."*
>
> *"Stay on the floor!" called Wally from the other room. Another one came.*
>
> *The building shook itself quiet. We groped for each other and Wally for a flashlight. Red light flickered around the edges of the blackout curtains. The end of the building seemed to be on fire. "Hold on," said Wally. "Get your helmet and your best coat and anything you want to save." With a few things in hand we went down and waded through the glass to see that one bomb had*

*hit the gas line main beside the end of the building and a great
flame reached toward the sky. I went back in and sat with the
other tenants on the stairs. The next morning, we had no gas, no
electricity, and only the water that remains in the tanks on the roof.*

■ ■ ■

Such sacrifices were made by Carroll and Peggy in part
because they saw his reporting as an almost desperate effort to
help the British people. Both understood that the survival of
Great Britain depended on changing American attitudes toward
supporting the war. Hemmed in by a Republican and isolationist Congress, Roosevelt had only managed to send fifty aging
destroyers as military aid to a besieged Britain in the summer
of 1940. The passage of the Lend-Lease bill in March 1941,
which enabled the U.S. government to lease (but not sell) war
supplies to England, would not supply much relief to a desperate
Britain, but it signaled an evolution in Americans' thinking. Polls
indicated in the summer of 1941 that a majority of Americans
supported continued aid to Britain, even if it meant that such
aid might lead to a war with Germany. The media coverage, by
both radio and written journalists who had risked life and limb
to report on the Blitz as well as the Nazi threat to the world,
had helped to turn the tide.

The reporting of the Blitz by newspaper correspondents and
broadcasters represented one of the most significant achievements of the American media during the entire war. Getting
the story out was not easy. Every piece written passed through
the hands of the censors, many of them untrained and often
quixotic in their decisions. Correspondents fought endless, often
losing battles with men wielding a blue pencil, largely impervious
to the challenge. What the reporters, including Carroll, had in
common was a strong sense of patriotism and a willingness to
undergo extreme hardship, including risk of death.

Carroll had succeeded in both managing the UP office and continuing his eyewitness reporting. He had recruited many outstanding journalists who would go on to cover the major military campaigns of World War II. He also developed friendships with a who's who of star reporters—Ernie Pyle, who frequently came to dinner at the Carrolls' apartment, and William L. Shirer, whom Peggy described as similar to Carroll in his near-sightedness, Midwestern roots and enjoyment of fine wine. By developing trust among his highly placed friends, and especially with U.S. Ambassador Gil Winant, he had skirted the censors and reported the truth to the American public. His background covering pre-war Europe, combined with an ability to see the broad picture, continued to garner him respect among his colleagues. In this he stood out. And by toughing it through the worst of the Blitz, he developed an even more compassionate understanding of the suffering of others.

Peggy Carroll, when asked years later what it was like to live through such fear and destruction, said, "The funny thing was that when you woke up in the morning you always felt so good to be alive." Her husband, seldom if ever prone to exaggeration, said he had "never seen any Englishman who showed the slightest sign of cowardice. They all lived up to the ideal Churchill set up for them."

It was a remarkable example of the power of the English language to induce heroism and self-sacrifice in a nation—and hardboiled evidence of Carroll's belief in the power of words.

What the citizens of London didn't know that May was that their resilience had already won victory. Hitler had turned his attention east, toward the Soviet Union. The May 10 bombing was the last great raid of the Blitz. The conflagration had cost the lives of 43,000 civilians, with almost 140,000 injured and more than a million homes damaged or destroyed. As the days proceeded, people began to believe it was finally at an end.

On June 22, Hitler launched Operation Barbarossa, unleashing a million German troops along an 1,800-mile line of destruction aimed at the Soviet Union.

Exhausted and at the end of their nerves, the Carrolls began to think maybe they had made it through after all, when a cable arrived from Earl Johnson in New York.

It asked Carroll: "Can you get to the Russian front?"

CHAPTER 7

THE ROAD TO MOSCOW—
AND BACK

*"It's dangerous as hell, and the fight will probably
be over by the time you get there anyway."*
— Edward R. Murrow, 1941

On June 22, 1941, U.S. Army Chief of Staff General George
C. Marshall summoned the heads of the major news
bureaus in Washington, D.C., to a secret meeting at his office in
the War Department. At dawn on that cloudy Sunday morning,
Hitler had launched the largest military attack in human history,
Operation Barbarossa, the invasion of the Soviet Union. Marshall
wanted to know what the newspapermen thought. Could the
Soviets hold out against the Nazi onslaught? His intelligence,
not always the most reliable, predicted a minimum of one
month, at most four months. The British were less sanguine at
a mere six weeks.

According to sources in the U.S. Embassy, the Russians were
primitive in their production capacity, lacking in leadership, and
mired in endless bureaucracy. Marshall was worried the invasion
would be over before the Russians even had a chance to mobilize.
Based on the material at hand, it promised to be brutal and unstop-
pable, but he wasn't sure he could trust his military intelligence

about the Russians. Did the editors have any further details from their news sources? He needed to know.

Earl Johnson, the soft-spoken head of United Press's international bureau, along with others in the room that afternoon, had no choice but to concur with Marshall. Their press reports from Russia, heavily censored, held little information, and government intelligence was notoriously unreliable. Stalin had refused to let any foreign observers near his army for five years, and no one seemed to know or understand the Soviets' military capacity. What Johnson did know was that he had to get the story before the conflict was over. And more important, he had to beat the AP in doing so. Time was of the essence.

But who should go? Rushing out of Marshall's office that late Sunday afternoon, Johnson thought through his options and decided to send Carroll.

"Brilliant decision," Carroll later remembered thinking after accepting the Johnson's offer, "but how?"

■ ■ ■

By late June 1941, when Carroll got Earl Johnson's cable, Adolf Hitler controlled the whole of continental and Eastern Europe, as well as the sea lanes up the coasts of Norway and Finland. Germany was striking everywhere at will. Its bombers were still hitting London; its submarines wreaked havoc and death in the Atlantic and North Sea; and the Afrika Korps threatened to seize North Africa and all of the Middle East. More important for Carroll, Hitler's forces had smashed through the Russian border along a two-thousand-mile front, encircling Soviet forces at Minsk and Smolensk. The only possible open route into the Soviet Union was up to Iceland, around to Greenland, past the German bases in Norway and Finland and through the Arctic Circle, a route heavily patrolled by German U-boats. Even if Carroll could get into the Soviet Union, he mused, no foreign correspondent had been permitted to see the Red Army in action. Would the Soviets give him access to the military and enable him to report on the strength of the Russian Army?

Carroll got to work. Through his contacts in the diplomatic community, including those with U.S. Ambassador Gil Winant and the British Foreign Office, he learned that a single Catalina flying boat, ungainly but with long range and equipped for water landings, would be making the flight up a few days after the invasion and over to Archangel in Russia. The British, somewhat remarkably, agreed to allow Carroll a spot on the boat, but a day before he was scheduled to leave, Harry Hopkins, President Roosevelt's personal envoy, bumped him from his spot. The president was sending Hopkins to discuss directly with Stalin what the Soviets most needed from America.

Undaunted, Carroll went back to his well-cultivated friends in the British Foreign Office, who assured him they would find him a way to get into Russia. They meant what they said. Several days later they called to say they could get him on a convoy, leaving from Liverpool several days later. He would have to leave immediately for the port city by train out of Euston Station.

Carroll returned to his apartment in North Kensington to confer with Peggy, still working for Winant at the American Embassy and seven months pregnant with their second child. Unflinching, Peggy encouraged him to go. "I don't think other women would have put up with this," Carroll later recalled, "as it seemed a rash thing to do, but Gil Winant assured me he would take care of Peggy no matter what happened. I guess this eased my mind." Peggy was worried but told Carroll he had to go.

Before leaving for Euston Station that August night, Carroll called Ed Beattie, his most experienced correspondent, and left him in charge of the 75-person UP operation. Armed with a typewriter, suitcase, backpack, helmet, gas mask, and some concentrated food, Carroll boarded the train for Liverpool.

Just before boarding he ran into an old friend, Vernon Bartlett of the BBC, who was making the same journey. Bartlett was England's foremost broadcaster and one of her best-known diplomatic correspondents. "If I had to name one man of whom it could be said, 'This is an Englishman,'" Carroll later wrote, "I would pick Vernon Bartlett. He had the honesty, the quiet sense of humor and the love of good beer which are the marks of the true Briton." Together they were off on a grand, if perilous, journey.

Both wondered what they would find in Liverpool. Two months earlier the Luftwaffe had dropped 870 tons of high-explosive bombs and 112,000 incendiary bombs on the city, which, as the port of entry for incoming convoys, was providing a lifeline to a starving and ammunition-poor Britain. As the train finally made its way toward the docks it passed one after another bombed-out warehouse. But waiting at the docks when they arrived was the *Llanstephan Castle*, an eleven-thousand-ton passenger ship of the Union-Castle Line, which would be the first ship to leave Britain for Russia following the Nazi invasion. Carroll and Bartlett boarded the *Llanstephan* and stood on deck as the ship left the dock, heading north along the Scottish coast. Soon six merchant ships and two warships joined the passenger vessel to protect its sides, forming a small convoy.

For three weeks the *Llanstephan Castle* sailed up past Iceland, around to Greenland, and up beyond German bases in Norway through to Archangel on the Russian coast. Carroll and Bartlett amused themselves by getting to know a contingent of RAF pilots who had been brought on board to teach the Russians how to assemble British Hurricanes and American Curtiss Tomahawk fighters that were lashed to the decks, the first Allied war materiel for the Soviets. They were joined by an American pilot and Polish and Czech officers who were going to join the fight against the Germans and by a host of international luminaries, including Charlotte Haldane, who was going to Russia for the *Daily Sketch*, a national British tabloid.

Several days into the journey as the boat drifted past Iceland, they were summoned up to deck to be assigned to lifeboats. Carroll and Bartlett were instructed to stand in the middle of the afterdeck as the RAF pilots, considered the most valuable passengers, received the first lifeboat assignments, then the Polish and Czech officers, with the rest assigned to rafts along with the crew. No space in the lifeboats would be assigned to them. Bartlett and Carroll forlornly made their way over to the side of the ship, glancing down to see two great basking sharks swim up to the ship with their jaws opening and closing. Bartlett, turning to Carroll, remarked with a laugh, "The one on the left is calling out 'Wally, Wally.'"

As the *Llanstephan* neared the Arctic Circle, Carroll, to keep himself busy, began Russian lessons. "By the time we reached Archangel I had a vocabulary of more than five hundred Russian words and phrases.... I became convinced Russian is not the difficult language it is generally supposed to be," he later recalled. He paced the deck with the crew and other passengers and listened to an impromptu Chopin recital by an RAF corporal in the passenger lounge. Later the British, Czech, and Polish pilots put together a party and vaudeville show.

Two weeks into the journey the weather had grown colder as the ship moved northward, plunging in and out of fog banks. Boats trailed fog buoys a hundred yards behind, raising a feather of foam to guide the next boat in line. When the fog cleared, the threat of attack from planes overhead became so great that the captain of the ship "wished the fog would settle down and stay with us all the way from now on," Carroll later recalled.

The Arctic solitude enveloped the ship—no bird, fish, plane, or other vessel in sight. As he walked the deck, the fog cleared, and night descended. Carroll marveled at the glass-like sea, which appeared to run uphill to the north and then curve off over the horizon into seemingly limitless space. Though marveling at the beauty of the northern skies and snow-touched distant mountains, Carroll was relieved when they finally reached Archangel. "The most beautiful three weeks with the sun shining every minute," he recalled. "Not a moment of darkness. Somehow the German submarines never found us."

Carroll, Bartlett, and the passengers of the *Llasntephan Castle* indeed turned out to be the lucky ones. Two convoys later, 22 of 29 ships were sunk, with the loss of hundreds of lives. The "death route" chartered by this first convoy later became the burial ground for thousands of American and British personnel who were making their way to help the Soviet cause, along with tons of war materiel being sent predominantly by the Americans.

"And we never got any thanks for it," Carroll later recalled. "All we got were complaints that things weren't getting to them any faster."

■ ■ ■

The low gray hills of the Russian coast greeted Carroll and his shipmates as the *Llanstephan Castle* made its way through the White Sea to dock at the mouth of the Northern Dvina River near Archangel. Awaiting Carroll was a Russian-piloted Douglas transport sent to take him and a few other passengers to Moscow. Flying low over the forests of pines and silver birches and wooden hamlets, they reached the Russian capital, where a representative of the British Embassy took them into town. Waiting for Carroll was Henry Shapiro, UP's Moscow correspondent.

Shapiro, fluent in Russian and a graduate of the University of Moscow's School of Law, had been the leading correspondent in Moscow for years, covering Stalin's purges of the late 1930s and the events leading up to the Soviet-German collaboration at the outset of the war. Carroll referred to him as "the best correspondent in Moscow and a prince of a fellow," and Shapiro lived very well in Moscow indeed. Carroll settled into his large apartment, tended to by Shapiro's staff of a cook, a maid, two assistants, and a Russian driver, all put at his disposal. The surroundings, he later admitted, were far more comfortable than anything he had lived in during his two years in London.

He promptly set about his task, which as he saw it was "to tell the American people whether the Russians were going to last or not." But how to do it? "You're one miserable reporter," he later lamented, "coming into a huge country. Everything is censored. I quickly found out that nobody in Moscow knew anything."

But Carroll had contacts, and he began to use them. Chief among these was the British Ambassador Sir Richard Stafford Cripps, and, of perhaps more importance, Noel Mason-MacFarlane, the head of the British Embassy's military mission, who Carroll believed was one of the few "really smart" intelligence officers around. U.S. Ambassador Laurence Steinhardt was "a total loss," and the military attaché in the embassy also knew nothing. "He hated the Russians and couldn't believe anything good about them," Carroll recalled. Even Carroll's good friend Tommy Thompson, an officer in the U.S. Embassy, didn't know very much, but he offered to help Carroll in whatever way he could.

Carroll also turned to the Polish officers he had befriended on the *Llanstephan Castle*, who were set to rejoin the Polish Army being formed in Russia to liberate Poland. They connected him with other Poles who had made their way into Russia to fight the Nazis, and who also had "all kinds" of contacts in the country.

■ ■ ■

By this time, it was early September and the German Army had advanced far into Russia, in a blitzkrieg that resulted in a line of occupation stretching north to south from Novgorod in what is now Estonia down to the Sea of Azov. With lightning speed, they had encircled Kiev in the north and Smolensk, which commanded the road to Moscow. In less than three months, an estimated 800,000 Soviet soldiers had been killed, captured, or wounded, and nearly 4,000 tanks destroyed.

But the victory at Smolensk had come at a cost to the Nazis. Despite huge losses, many Soviet soldiers had escaped through a gap left open for more than three weeks due to fierce Soviet resistance. This, along with overstretched supply lines and logistical problems, caused the Wehrmacht to realize that it had perhaps underestimated Soviet strength. It also persuaded Hitler to turn his attention north to Leningrad and south to the industrial center of Kharkov. He ordered his commanders to halt the advance toward Moscow.

And in early September, just before Carroll's arrival, the Soviets had met with a small victory. The Red Army had managed to push back German-held territory at Yelnya, 200 miles southwest of Moscow and a staging area for their intended advance. The German retreat was the first setback for the Wehrmacht and came with a surprising loss of men and materiel. Wanting the world to know of this victory, Stalin, for the first time since the purge of the army in 1937, decided to allow foreign correspondents in Russia to visit the front. Carroll was among them.

Carroll was well aware that the Soviets were staging the visit and would heavily censor any reports he would file. Nonetheless, he knew that "all I had at my disposal were my eyes, my ears, and my brain," and he was determined to make the best assessment he could. Their convoy would be the first formal visit ever paid to the Red Army by any foreign correspondent, a precedent that would establish the rules for future trips that gave the world its eyewitness accounts of the war on the Eastern Front.

■ ■ ■

On the morning of September 15, 1941—the same day the Nazis began their siege of Leningrad—six M-1 cars, the Russian version of the 1936 Ford, pulled up at the British Embassy in Moscow. Ten correspondents, five British and five American, climbed in, all eager to see the front. In Carroll's car were Henry Cassidy of the Associated Press, Cyrus Sulzberger of the *New York Times*, and Margaret Bourke-White, a photographer for *Life* magazine. Bourke-White had been invited, despite her lack of press credentials, as a favor to her husband, Erskine Caldwell. His novel *Tobacco Road*, with its grim portrayal of the American South and of capitalism, had been translated into Russian and widely circulated, positioning Caldwell as a favorite of the Politburo. As such, his wife was spared no favors. She appeared that warm autumn morning in a flowing red cape, as Carroll recalled, "suitable for a night at the opera." In another car were Caldwell; Mrs. J.B. Haldane of the London *Daily Sketch;* Alexander Worth, special correspondent for Reuter's; Philip Jordan of the London *News Chronicle;* A.T. Cholerton of the London *Daily Telegraph*; and A.T. Steele of the *Chicago Daily News*. Each car had a Russian driver and Russian guide from the foreign office. They started out on the great four-lane highway going from Moscow to Smolensk, part of which the Germans had already captured. Their destination: a town called Vyazma, about 145 miles away.

Years later Carroll recalled the scene:

There was a steady flow of military traffic on the highway. Cars creeping along at about 20 miles an hour. Trucks loaded with all kinds of military equipment, guns, light artillery, munitions. Some of the trucks had big tanks, like hot water tanks you have in some houses. The tanks had in them charcoal, or wood chips, or peat, or pressed straw, which was ignited and used as gas to fuel the engines to make the cars run. Because this gas was very hard on the engines the drivers weren't permitted to go more than 25

miles an hour, and we found out later that if a driver was caught
going over 25 miles an hour he was taken off and shot on the spot.
So we didn't see any drivers going along over 25 miles an hour.

In the fields as they rode, they saw labor battalions, with
as many women as men, as Carroll recalled, digging tank traps
along the way, or small foxholes about five feet deep. The aim
was for a soldier to burrow down, wait, and then try to pop a
grenade into a tank's treads or throw grenades at the German
infantry as it came by. "It was a suicide job," said Carroll, "but
they had these foxholes all along the road."

Henry Cassidy would later write of his impression of the
Russian soldier, a "silhouette, against a mournful, gray autumn
sky, of a husky figure, wrapped from head to foot in a water-
proof cape, and carrying a rifle from which protruded the
long wicked-looking bayonet. All along the road they stood
thus, vigilantly on guard." According to Cassidy's estimate, five
million men formed the active fighting force. For each man at
least two were waiting to take his place, on the basis of a total
mobilization potential of nineteen million men, one-tenth of
the entire population.

"It is no heel-clicking army, no army of blistering top ser-
geants and rasping colonels who stopped learning about war
20 years ago," Carroll wrote from the field. "Above all it is a
young army."

Carroll had another observation, which he relayed through
a letter to Peggy back in London, "As a feminist, you will be
glad to know that Russian women share the dangers of the
front with the men. There are women soldiers, surgeons, nurses,
waitresses, all in army uniform, working with front-line units. It
seems some of the soldiers take their wives with them—you see
women seated beside the drivers in army trucks and tractors."

As the cars of journalists rolled along the highway, a German
reconnaissance plane spotted their car along the road and

dropped a few sticks of bombs, forcing them out of their M-1 automobile to hide in a ditch. Although they emerged unharmed, the Nazis had been alerted that somebody worth noting was likely headed toward Vyazma, which at that time was being used as a base for the Soviet air force. When they arrived in the town, the Soviets treated them to a generous lunch before the journalists reboarded their cars to continue on lesser unpaved paths toward the front.

As they rode along, Carroll recalled, a tank came up behind them moving across the fields. Carroll estimated it was a 30-ton tank, traveling about 30 or 35 mph, much faster than their car. Carroll didn't think the British or Germans had a 30-ton tank that could go that fast. They also saw fighter planes, which hadn't been in evidence around Moscow. The planes had liquid-cooled engines; in the Spanish Civil War, Carroll recalled, Soviet planes had air-cooled engines. "These planes were very slick. They looked like British Spitfires, the best planes in Western Europe." As they drove into one field, they were met by Major General Georgy Zakharov, a burly young man in a fleece-lined flying suit and blue-banded cap, who volunteered to show them some planes close up. Carroll noted that the wings were made of plywood "because they're easier to repair up here at the front than metal wings," General Zahkarov told them.

To Carroll's surprise, one of the planes had three rockets underneath each wing, something he had never seen before. "We use them against tanks on the ground, or against armored columns or against infantry," said a young pilot who met them. "I'll show you." He proceeded to take a plane up, where it circled and headed toward a far end of the field. It swooped down and unleashed a rocket, blowing a bunker to smithereens.

That night, on their return to the International Hotel in Vyazma, 43-year-old Lieutenant Vasily Sokolovsky—later Field Marshal Sokolovsky—joined Carroll and the other journalists for dinner. Two months later, Sokolovsky was named Chief of

Staff of the Western front, where he would help coordinate
the Soviet winter attacks that pushed the Germans away from
Moscow. Sokolovsky had led the Russian offensive to push back
the Germans outside Vyazma. That night at the dining-room
table, on which cups of tea and platters of sandwiches had been
stacked, Sokolovsky quietly described the battle in detail to the
correspondents, ending with a prediction, "The blitzkrieg is
over. From now on it's going to be a war of attrition. It will
be a long process, but we will grind them down bit by bit."
Sokolovsky went on to outline reasons for the failure of the
blitzkrieg and the stabilization of the western front: the will of
the Russians to fight, increased production of arms, the weak
rear of the Germans, and the loss by many Nazis of faith in
the invincibility of their own army.

That night, Carroll went to bed at the hotel, in a room
shared with Henry Cassidy. At 7 the next morning, the sound
of air raid sirens and approaching planes that sounded like
bombers woke him. "We've got visitors," Carroll told Cassidy,
and seconds later the anti-aircraft guns began to bark, and the
bombs came whistling down. Carroll heard cries on the street,
then a loud "swish" outside the building. He climbed back into
bed, pulling the covers over him. Cassidy, terrified, jumped on
top of Carroll. Moments later the window next to the bed was
blown in by a bomb. And then everything went quiet.

Carroll pushed Cassidy off him, got dressed, and went out
to the street. Townspeople were picking up bodies in the road
and putting them on a flatbed truck. Then, he later said, he witnessed "among the most callous thing I saw during the entire
war." Margaret Bourke-White appeared, dressed to the nines
again, in crimson slacks and white blouse. She went up to the
correspondents' Russian guide, a Cossack named Alurof, and said
to him, "Will you have them take the bodies off the truck and
put them back on the ground so I can photograph them being
put *back* on the truck?" Alurof demurred, but knew he was to

do as Bourke-White pleased, so he ordered the townspeople to do it, Carroll recalled. "These were the neighbors, maybe even the cousins, brothers of the dead people, but they obeyed orders from Moscow and began to take the bodies off the truck and lay them down on the ground. As they started to pick them up again, Bourke-White would say, 'Tilt them a little bit this way, or that way,' so she could see their faces."

"I was sickened," recalled Carroll. "And this was done by an American woman. She was not greatly loved by the rest of us."

Later, Carroll and his colleagues were taken to "see a lot of things," he recalled. One place they visited was an underground hospital, very neat, clean, "with white cheesecloth on the walls and all instruments laid out." The chief surgeon was a 31-year-old woman. "I sensed this may be a show put on for our benefit," he recalled—but this thought was dispelled when, caught under artillery fire later in the afternoon, they took refuge in another underground field hospital where they weren't expected, and it was just as good.

From this latest field hospital, they drove to a dugout where a club had been established for non-commissioned officers and men. In one room the troops were dancing one of the traditional Russian soldier dances to a spirited folk song played by an orchestra of piano, accordion, and violin. They were ushered through a tunnel into a library, where the books on the shelves were, of course thought Carroll, the works of Lenin, but he also saw novels by Tolstoy, Dostoevsky, and Mikhail Sholokhov, and the plays of Ibsen. The group were told that there were thousands of these clubs along the front and that the average Russian soldier was very well-educated indeed.

Carroll and his colleagues spent six days at the front. The Russians told them of their success at night fighting and the cooperation of the partisans, or guerrillas, who were working behind the German front armed with airdropped weapons and responding to orders from the Soviet high command. They would attack the Germans from the rear while the regular army attacked from the front. They saw Russian artillery "firing as if the war might end tomorrow," with apparently limitless supplies of ammunition.

But perhaps what influenced Carroll the most was what he learned on his return to Moscow from a Polish pilot and an American pilot he had met on the *Llanstephan* on the Arctic crossing. Both had been stationed up north with the Russian Air Force, where they had been brought in to help the Soviets learn how to assemble planes coming from England and the United States via the Lend-Lease program. They had lived with the Russians, Carroll later wrote, so they "could not be bamboozled; they saw what was really going on." Both had been tremendously impressed, "first, with the mechanics." The Russian mechanics had looked at the new planes coming in and questioned some British gadgets on the planes that cost the planes about 15 mpg. Without being told, the Russian mechanics insisted they had to come off. And, said the Polish pilot, "they were assembling British planes, which they had never seen before, as fast as the British were assembling Hurricane Fighters that they had been working on for years." The pilots were good, they said. And morale was high.

Harry Hopkins, who had bumped Carroll off the Catalina Flying Boat, had also learned something, Carroll reported, when Hopkins met with Stalin about what he wanted under Lend-Lease. Just one thing—trucks, Stalin had said. Judging by what Carroll had seen on the road to Vyazma, he was right. Hopkins told Carroll when they met in Moscow, "Stalin has plenty of weapons—guns, tanks, ammunition—or he would have asked for these."

Carroll put together everything he could to get an answer to the question, "Are the Soviets going to survive?" and came up with a "pretty confident *yes* at the time."

▪ ▪ ▪

But less than a month later Hitler struck again. He turned his attention away from Leningrad in the north and Kharkov in the south and directed his armies to take Moscow before the weather turned bad. On September 30, he had launched Operation Typhoon, the massive drive to Moscow. The assault consisted of two pincer attacks, one to the north of Moscow, which would cut off the Moscow-Leningrad railway, and another to the south. Simultaneously the German 2nd Panzer Division would advance directly from the west. The Germans intended to commit up to 2 million troops, 1,000 tanks, and 14,000 guns to the all-out assault, but the summer campaign had weakened their air strength. The Soviets by late October had amassed a formidable concentration of 1.25 million men, 1,000 tanks, and 7,600 guns.

The Germans initially broke through to the north at Vazyma, where more than 500,000 Soviet soldiers were killed or captured. But then rain and melting snow turned the ground into a muddy quagmire, halting German tanks and supply lines. Meanwhile the Soviets continued to counterattack, taking advantage of their T-34 tanks, the same ones Carroll had seen earlier, that were more heavily armored than their German counterparts and also, due to their wide tracks, more mobile in the mud. Nonetheless, the German advance continued.

Carroll could feel that the war was drawing closer to Moscow. More soldiers appeared on the streets, with military trucks rolling frequently out of the city down the Smolensk Road. Labor battalions of men and women with spades on their shoulders marched out of the city to dig trenches and anti-tank ditches. The Soviets ordered compulsory military training for men and also for boys who were not of military age. Over the loudspeaker system, a voice told workers, "The Fascist aggressors will never see the streets of our city." Rumors ran high, bolstered by leaflets dropped by the Germans warning the people of Moscow that unless they surrendered immediately the capital would be devastated.

Covering the offensive was almost impossible, as Carroll and other correspondents were not allowed to go to the front, and communiqués from the government became terser. Despite this, Carroll was able to file several reports from Moscow about subjects that were integral to the fight. Writing about the role of political commissars in an article published September 26, 1941, in the *Los Angeles Times*, he described them as ever-present "fighters, teachers, publicity men and sentinels for the Soviet government and the Communist party," whose chief mission was to raise morale and, in many cases, to urge soldiers on to their death in defense of the motherland. Another article outlined the Russian resurgent belief in the church and the sudden relinquishment of government power to prohibit attendance. Moscow was tense but not panicky, according to Carroll. Carroll's stories were among the very few that made it through the censors and were published broadly in papers across the United States. Little, if anything, was known by Americans about the Soviet Union, so his dispatches were eagerly read.

On October 15, Carroll and the other foreign correspondents were summoned to the U.S. Embassy by his old friend Tommy Thompson, who was then second secretary at the embassy, and told the Soviet Foreign Office was moving to Kuibyshev, a forlorn port 650 miles away on the Volga River. Stalin would remain, as would all other government departments, and Moscow would be defended, "street by street" if necessary. But the diplomatic corps and journalists would move to Kuibyshev. Thompson, however, would remain in charge of the embassy and stay in Moscow no matter what happened. Carroll, remembering their close friendship in Geneva, shared a quick drink with his former roommate, wishing him the best before departing.

Carroll rushed back to Shapiro's apartment and packed his bags. Embassy cars arrived to take him and Shapiro to the railway station. Tension in the city had increased, with pedestrians swarming the streets, as buses and taxis were commandeered to carry troops. "By that time, it was dark outside," recalled Carroll, "and there was a heavy snowfall coming down. It was blacked out, but there was anti-aircraft fire that shot big star shells which made enough light so that the snow could be seen falling down." Carroll was assigned a car with an embassy officer, Charlie Thayer. They drove around the corner and onto the B Circle, a wide avenue leading to the station.

The following description, in his own words, describes his harrowing escape:

> *Careening around the corner we almost hit a woman carrying a little baby in a blue blanket," remembered Carroll. "As we started down the wide avenue, the other way we saw trucks loaded with munitions for the front, some troops, and then came a contingent of troops marching and carrying their rifles and bayonets. The dimmers were on the trucks with blue filters over the headlights, so everything shone blue. Blue lights picked up the bayonets of these troops marching to the front, behind them came a labor battalion of men and women carrying shovels, and marching along in step. As they came abreast of us, we heard them singing a marching song.*

Along the way, Carroll saw many women with bundles over their backs, some with babies, trying to reach the railway station. People were waiting patiently for the trolleys that came along, green sparks going. "There was no panic," he recalled. "Nobody was in a hurry. It was all very orderly."

As they neared the railway station, Carroll, seeing a long line ahead, jumped out and ran through the snow to the station. Inside, he came into a waiting room with "dozens and dozens of these poor women with their bundles, lying on the floor with their heads on the bundles, and one contingent of troops that looked completely worn out, lying down asleep with their rifles by their sides." Moving into another room he sat at the side on the floor; a wooden bench next to him had been reserved for nursing mothers, with other women on the floor and troops all around. Fortunately, a heavy snow was falling, preventing German Heinkels flying overhead from dropping their bombs on the railroad station, an event that would have wiped out countless Russians and the entire foreign colony assembled near the platforms.

Suddenly an officer of the Red Army appeared and asked Carroll if he was with the embassy. "Yes," he replied and was taken into a brightly lit restaurant, where the whole diplomatic corps was assembled. He saw Shapiro and a new man who had just come out from London, Charlie Handler, and teamed up with them again. They told him they had been assigned a "hard compartment," the lowest class of train ride, meaning they would spend the night sleeping on hard wooden benches. At 1 a.m., they boarded the train, slowly pulling out of the station. They could hear anti-aircraft guns firing from behind a half hour later.

■ ■ ■

The trip to Kuibyshev that normally could be done in 24 hours took five nights, Carroll recalled. The train would go a little way, then pull over to let other trains go by—a troop train traveling the other way into Moscow, or a train filled with artillery and munitions passing them by, or a train carrying factory machines from Moscow to a safe place, followed by a boxcar with the factory's workers. "The Soviets had a principle that if you dismantled a factory you had to take the workers with it," Carroll recalled.

In Kuibyshev they were assigned to the Grand Hotel. The city's population was swollen by half a million Moscow refugees, and correspondents plunged into despondency. Shapiro, "as smart as could be," according to Carroll, thought of getting to the town baths. He and Carroll headed downtown, where they came along a line of some 200 people waiting to get into the baths. Shapiro, moving through the crowd, asked to see the manager. "These are two very illustrious journalists who have come from America, to tell Americans about the glorious fight of the Soviet citizens against the Fascist aggressors," he told the manager in perfect Russian. "In!" the manager said, pointing and leading them to the best room in the house, a steam room with slate walls and four taps of water, two of them steaming hot. The two threw basins of cold water against the walls and "scrubbed, and scrubbed and scrubbed, then sloshed water over ourselves. We felt great." The next morning, walking past the bathhouse, they noted the lines of ambassadors and generals trying to get in. They had made it first.

But Kuibyshev was neither a place for a war correspondent nor very inviting to anyone. According to Larry LeSueur, one of Ed Murrow's reporters who had made his way there, "drunks curled up in the gutters to escape the howling Siberian winds, and camel trains from Turkestan plodded through snow-packed streets." There was nothing to be learned about how the war was progressing, and even if so, no way to get the information out. Unbeknownst to the journalists, the Germans, mired in mud and already suffering from the bitter cold, had made their way to the gates of Moscow, where Soviet counterattacks would stop them in early December. It was not until December 12 that they received a communiqué from Moscow that said German armies around the capital were in full retreat.

■ ■ ■

In the end, Hitler's delay in attacking Moscow was a major cause of his defeat. It had enabled Stalin to bring in troops and materiel from Siberia and the Far East and to mobilize every last man, woman, and child in the defense of the city. By December the unrelenting Russian winter was freezing the German troops, who lacked cold weather clothing; machinery failed to work; gas lines became blocked; roads were impassable. The Battle of Moscow was, according to Henry C. Cassidy, won by "sheer strength, courage and sacrifice." By constructing three lines of defense, deploying reserve armies, and bringing in troops from Siberia and the Far East, the Soviets had driven the German army back from the gates of the city, and from a mere six miles from the Kremlin. The battle had lasted six months, and more Soviet soldiers died in the battle alone than all the British, French, and American forces in World War II combined. Hitler became so enraged on hearing of the defeat that he fired his chief of staff, Walther von Brauchitsch, and took personal control of the military—a decision that was eventually to be the undoing of his elite army.

Carroll would later write, in *We're in This With Russia*, a detailed account of the battle of Moscow, remembering the almost surreal calm with which the Muscovites marched out to defend their city. Others who had witnessed it would also remark of its historic significance. Carroll, who had managed to file several eyewitness reports from his time at the front, had been right in his assessment of Russian strength, but at the time he, like others, had no idea if the Russians would be able to hold on to Moscow. Now he decided it was time to head for home. But again, the question arose, "How?"

▪ ▪ ▪

Carroll's only possible way out of Russia was through the East, and it would require him to literally circle the world in whatever route he could put together. He faced nonexistent communication, and his mode of travel would include everything from airplane to rowboat to taxi. The journey would require every last ounce of resourcefulness the self-contained journalist could muster, as he would be relying entirely on his own devices.

His first order of business was to get a visa from the Soviet Foreign Office so he could leave the country. Remembering that "the only way to get things done in the Soviet Union is to ask a woman," he made contact in Kuibyshev with a Russian woman who he knew had worked in the American Embassy. The saying about women was true, Carroll recalled; she came back to him with his passport stamped with an exit visa.

Then once again, he relied on his contacts with the British. The head of the British Ministry of Foreign Affairs had come to Kuibyshev in a Red Army plane from Tehran, to consult with the Russians. Carroll knew the plane was going back to Tehran. Drawing on his friendship with Sir Richard Stafford Cripps, the British ambassador to the Soviet Union who had also been evacuated to Kuibyshev, Carroll won permission to get a seat on the plane and was assigned a young British officer, Jeffrey Wilson, to help him.

"I'll never forget what Cripps did in getting me out of that hell hole of Kuibyshev," he later recalled.

In the meantime, he had been joined by a young reporter from the *Chicago Sun-Times*, Dennis MacAvoy, who Carroll believed "had never written a word, but was just bumping around Russia." MacAvoy was also given a seat on the plane. Together the two took off on a journey that would take them across the Asian continent.

They flew at no more than 100 feet above Ukraine, staying low so that the Russian anti-aircraft batteries, which had no communication among them, would not fire at them. "So we stayed down and went over that black earth which is as rich as anything in Iowa, hour after hour," said Carroll. They finally touched down

CARROLL'S TRIP (Oct. 15–Dec. 25, 1941)

1. **Kuibyshev, Soviet Union** (now Samara)
2. **Makhachkala, Soviet Union**
3. **Baku, Azerbaijan**
4. **Teheran, Iran**
5. **Ahvaz, Iran** (100 miles from the Persian Gulf coast)
6. **Basra, Iraq**
7. **Baluchistan, Pakistan**
8. **Karachi, Pakistan**

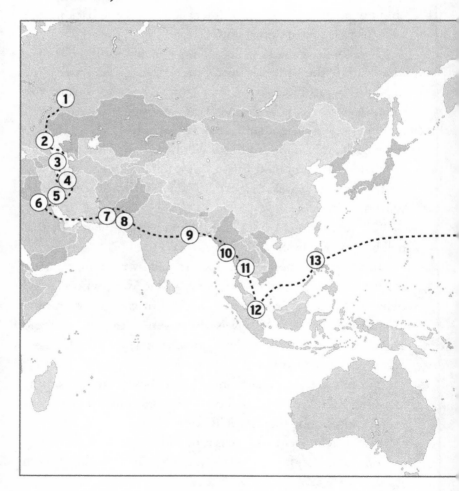

9. **Calcutta, India**
10. **Rangoon, Siam** (now Myranmar, Burma)
11. **Bangkok, Thailand**
12. **Singapore**
13. **Manila, the Philippines**
14. **Pearl Harbor, Hawaii**
15. **San Francisco**
16. **New York, New York**

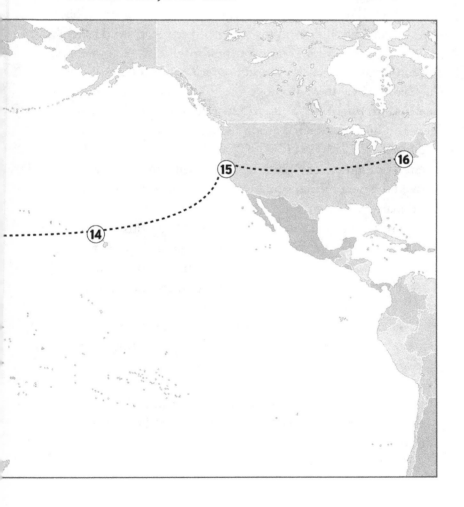

at the city of Makhachkala on the west coast of the Caspian Sea, where they were unexpected but still treated with a dinner and a room in a hostel for members of the Communist Party.

The following morning, they took off across the Caspian Sea for Baku, Azerbaijan, then the great oil center of the Caucuses, with "oil derricks all around." Some girls were waiting at the airport for the three Soviet airmen flying the plane, so the crew got out and kidded around, piling back in to put on a show for the girls. As the plane got off the ground it went around and around, the tips of the wings scraping the ground, before they headed south toward the Caspian, giving the passengers "a roller coaster ride that I never in my life hope to repeat," said Carroll.

The plane went up and over the foothills of the Caucuses, landing in an Iranian town where MacAvoy and Carroll spent the night, then flew the next day to Tehran. There, Carroll realized he might get a flight out if he could make it to the Persian Gulf. He scouted around and found a rail line, built by the Swedes, called the "Line of 200 Tunnels," that would take them overnight to the Gulf. Securing seats, he and MacAvoy arrived the next morning at Ahvaz, which was then the British headquarters in Iran.

Here, the visa became an issue again. "The British were very sticky about anybody coming out of Russia and going toward India because the Russians had tried to stir up trouble in India," Carroll recalled. "We came upon a very stuffy councilor in the embassy, who refused to issue us a visa."

Sizing up the situation, Carroll spruced up his look and went in to ask the councilor about sending a telegram to the British Foreign Office to a man whose name Carroll concocted. The bluff worked.

The councilor picked up his stamp and approved both his and MacAvoy's passports. "The councilor didn't know him from William the Conqueror, but, being British, he didn't want any trouble from 'a big fellow in London.'"

With their visas, the two were still 100 miles from the Persian Gulf, with the South Iranian desert in their way. "I found a taxi driver who was willing to drive us across the desert," remembered Carroll, but he warned them that they would most likely be stopped by nomads. Twenty minutes into the journey, the nomads arrived on camel, "wicked-looking characters indeed, stopping before us and not letting us proceed."

"Don't say anything," warned the taxi driver. Deciding the correspondents were not worth robbing, the nomads moved on. As they approached the Gulf, Carroll realized they had about three to four miles of water to cross before they could reach Basra, the British base in the region. Scouting around the docks he found two Arabian men with a boat who agreed to ferry him. After some time, they arrived and went to the nearest hotel.

By happenstance as they checked in, they met a doctor who worked with the Rockefeller Foundation and knew Peggy's father. When Carroll mentioned Dr. Sawyer, the doctor couldn't do enough for them. He arranged cholera shots, took them to dinner, and steered them to the British Airways office, where they managed to get two seats on a Pan American Clipper all the way to Singapore. The next day they started out flying over the Gulf, stopping to take up British mail pouches, each time surrounded by sharks gaping at the aircraft. They cut across the mouth of the Gulf and landed in Pakistan in Baluchistan, a forlorn spot, according to Carroll, then flew on to Karachi, where they spent the night, and then on to Calcutta, on a flying boat with no wheels, making it onward to Rangoon and then Bangkok and finally to Singapore. In late November 1941, the Japanese had not yet captured the city but were beginning to make their way down the Malay Peninsula. In Singapore, the two got a couple of seats on another Pan American Clipper flying to Manila in the Philippines, where they finally had a chance to rest.

■ ■ ■

Carroll used the time in Manila to write dispatches on what he had seen in Moscow. "After five months of the heaviest fighting in the history of the war, the Soviet Russian giant is battered but unbowed, still strong enough to hold the German Wehrmacht through the winter and to face a new campaign in the spring of 1941," he wrote on November 17, 1941. Two days later, another article published in the *New York Daily News*, captured a dinner he had attended at which Stalin had toasted Franklin Roosevelt in front of members of the American and British commission that had successfully concluded arrangements for sending supplies to the Red Army. Another recounted the Battle of Moscow. The story, he wrote, was of how the "iron will" of Josef Stalin had been imparted down to the humblest soldier, of how mothers and daughters shouldered picks and shovels and marched across the snow-covered plains west of Moscow to dig defenses for their sons and brothers. Carroll, like by now others, felt the Soviets would not only hold out but would have the strength to launch an offensive in the spring.

After a week in Manila, Carroll again pushed on toward home. Unable to get a seat on a flight to Honolulu, he booked passage on the SS *President Coolidge*, the largest passenger ship in the Pacific. The ship sailed out of Manila Harbor on November 27, scheduled to arrive in Pearl Harbor on December 7, 1941.

As they started, Carroll noticed the ship was not traveling east but instead headed south. He later learned that Admiral Thomas Hart, commander of the Pacific Fleet, had for some unknown reason ordered the ship not to sail directly to Pearl Harbor and Honolulu but instead to take a much longer route through the South Sea. The ship was somewhere near the Solomon Islands when passengers got the news by radio that the Japanese had attacked Pearl Harbor.

Carroll later commented on his luck. "If we had stuck to our original course—the biggest ship in the Pacific, completely defenseless, we would have been in the path of those Japanese bombers." The *President Coolidge* arrived in the bombed out naval base seven days after the attack, on December 14.

"I immediately went out to the Naval Headquarters," recalled Carroll. He met Captain Waldo Drake, the South Pacific Fleet's public relations officer, who had been an editor of the *Los Angeles Times*. Carroll and Drake knew of each other, and Drake, somewhat uncharacteristically, as he was known for keeping a tight lid on news, volunteered to ask Admiral Husband E. Kimmell, Commander of the Fleet, to let Carroll "go around Pearl Harbor." At that time no one from the press had been allowed to go in. The whole world knew that the Japanese had attacked Pearl Harbor, but nobody had learned what damage had been done. It had all been kept under wraps.

Drake came back and told Carroll, "The admiral said you can go on his launch. You can't print what you see. But when you get back to New York you can report to your superiors at United Press on a strictly confidential basis what you've seen." Carroll boarded a launch and saw the devastation. "It was the saddest, most depressing sight I have ever seen," he later commented. "Those great battleships on the bottom, with just the smokestacks and super structures above the water. And they were all there prow-to-stern like buses in a barn. The Japanese could have come in blindfolded and hit something."

Carroll couldn't understand how, after two years of ongoing war in Europe, nobody had been prepared for the attack. "Nobody was going to send letters to us saying, 'We're going to attack you in the morning,'" he wrote. Since their attack on the Russian Fleet in Port Arthur in 1904, the Japanese had never given any warning on any attack. "Yet our people had not taken any precautions."

When he got back from the ride, as he was coming around the dock, Carroll ran into Kimmel with his briefcase on his arm and his chin on his chest. After a long and successful career, he had just been relieved, on December 17, as commander of the U.S. Pacific Fleet for his refusal to act on warnings that a Japanese attack might be imminent. The dismissal was humiliating to Kimmel, who would go on to be subjected to numerous investigations and inquiries about the devastating attack, only to be exonerated by a Senate committee years later. "Maybe his order to put me in his launch to let me go around Pearl Harbor was the last order he ever gave," remarked Carroll, "because when I saw him he was fired."

■ ■ ■

Carroll wrote one more article from this trip on his way to the United States that later brought him much criticism for its effect back home and would haunt him in the years to come. In it he reported that Japanese spies had "paved the way" for the surprise blow at Pearl Harbor. Published on December 31, 1941, the article outlined several findings that, Carroll said, pointed to the existence of fifth columnists within the Japanese-American community who had "predicted when the bulk of the battle fleet would be in Pearl Harbor" and relayed this to the Japanese. He was told that, among other evidence, on the day of the attack huge swaths in the shape of arrows had been cut in the sugar cane fields, pointing toward the objective sought by the Japanese airmen.

Later the article was called into question, but the damage was done. Japanese and Americans of Japanese descent in Hawaii numbered one-third of the population—too many to round up entirely. But they were immediately put under suspicion by former friends and neighbors, their radios and cameras confiscated, and their communications closely monitored. Leaders of the Japanese community were brought together—without warrants—and detained, many for the entire length of the war.

It was worse on the mainland. The Japanese, already under suspicion following gruesome news reports of their invasion of China, were portrayed by the media as sneaky, dangerous, and in some cases inhuman. Such exaggerated reports grew more vociferous. Less than three months after Pearl Harbor, President Roosevelt issued Executive Order No. 9066, which forced 110,000 Japanese Americans to leave their homes in California, Washington, and Oregon to live in detention camps in desolate parts of the United States.

This was a case in which Carroll perhaps got it wrong—his reporting on Japanese-American residents of Hawaii spying and aiding in the Japanese attack. And since his stories were printed on the front pages of newspapers across the United States, its effect was not insignificant. He would later come to deeply regret the story, even though at the time he had had it confirmed by then Secretary of the Navy Frank Knox. But after seeing first-hand the destruction in Pearl Harbor, immersing himself for months before that trying to cover the largest military invasion in history to date—the Nazi onslaught into the Soviet Union—and before that enduring two years under German bombing in London, Carroll reacted in a way that is not so difficult to understand. He had traveled the countryside and reportedly seen indications that the Japanese had informants on the island. In addition, he had been hugely frustrated by Americans' lack of caring about the destruction he had seen in Europe. The problem, of course, was that innocent American and Hawaiian Japanese suffered the consequences.

After several days of intense writing, Carroll boarded the *Coolidge*, finally headed home. The ship sailed through the Golden Gate in San Francisco. Carroll immediately got a seat on a puddle-jumping United Airlines plane flying across the continent the next day. He had managed to get through to Peggy's parents at Hastings-on-Hudson and learned for the first time that she was not in London but was safe with them. Peggy, again, had made the dangerous Atlantic crossing, this time while pregnant with their second child.

"So I left word that I would be arriving at LaGuardia about 11:00 that night," Carroll later recalled. "The DC3 I took stopped at every milk route across the continent," delaying his return even more. When he finally arrived, Peggy was waiting with her father and mother, along with Earl Johnson, his UP manager who had sent him to Russia. Also waiting was little Margaret, his two-year-old daughter who he would meet for the first time.

It was Christmas Day, Carroll recalled, "and I had made it home."

THE ART OF PERSUASION

CHAPTER 8

WHAT NEXT?

"This is a people's war, and to win it,
the people should know as much about it as they can."

—Elmer Davis

On Christmas morning 1941, a tired and bedraggled Wallace Carroll stepped off the plane at LaGuardia airport to land, finally, in the arms of Peggy and her parents. After more than two months of desperate travel via plane, ship, taxi and rowboat, he was finally home. The Sawyer's house in Hastings-on-Hudson must have seemed like a land lost in otherworldly tranquility. Perched on a hill overlooking the Hudson River in Westchester County, New York, Hastings was home to a bevy of distinguished artists, writers, and performers, including Billie Burke, who had two years earlier taught the importance of home to a young Kansas girl as the Good Witch of the South in *The Wizard of Oz*.

While a bastion of liberal thinking, Hastings nonetheless mirrored the quiet nonchalance of most of the country regarding the European war. Peggy noted in a letter that December to Gil Winant that coming home to Hastings where her parents lived was "like going back to high school after you have been earning a living for a few years." While heartened by the town's efforts at supporting the war following Pearl Harbor, she was amazed at what little knowledge residents had of the conflict. Friends, she remembered, thought "blackouts were achieved by simply turning out the lights!" She wrote, however, that people seemed committed now that the United States was actually in the war:

> *You doubtless know what an excellent unifying effect the Japanese attack had on our people. In our village everybody has volunteered to do something—the only sad part is that there are not enough useful jobs to go around. I have been surprised at how little they knew about the air raids after all that has been written in the American press, etc....*
>
> *Of course many of the fumbling ways of approaching the war problems here are silly, but the spirit behind this is all right. There is far less hysteria and excitement about uniforms and titles than I feared. People are being very sensible indeed and they are trying their best to get information.*

Hastings-on-Hudson provided Carroll with a much-needed place to rest and think following the extraordinary events of the past two years. It also gave him the opportunity to witness the birth of his son in late January. "John Sawyer Carroll," he wired Winant on January 27, 1942, "wants you to know he and his mother are feeling grand." Peggy had crossed the Atlantic again in September 1941. Her cabinmate this time was the journalist Mary Welsh who three years later would marry Ernest Hemingway.

Shortly after her arrival, Peggy had been asked by First Lady Eleanor Roosevelt to give a talk at the White House on conditions in England. She gladly accepted, and delivered a speech that was widely praised. Rather than just discuss domestic affairs, she gave a realistic account of the economic hardships faced by the British during the war: the food privations and the challenge of maintaining any kind of productive ordinary life when faced by shortages everywhere. Her talk reflected her background as an economist as well as her skill in portraying with great detail and empathy her time in the British capital.

Although delighted to be together again with Peggy and his young family, Carroll still had an almost desperate desire to capture and consolidate his experiences for the American public. He began to work furiously on a book that would outline not only his experiences in Russia but also the diplomatic maneuverings he had witnessed leading up to the conflict while covering the League of Nations. Always a fast writer, he hunkered down in Hastings-on-Hudson for five months, consolidating his notes and churning out his first full-length book, *We're in This With Russia: How to do Business with Stalin and Why*. At the time it was the only book-length eyewitness account of developments in the Soviet Union and, more importantly, whether it could be trusted or not by the United States.

Carroll had returned from Russia confident in the spirit of the people, and in the country's ability to stave off the Nazis' attack. "Behind the government and the Red Army stand embattled workers and peasants as united in their resistance to the invader as are the British behind Winston Churchill," he had written in a piece published by the *New York Tribune* on November 18, 1941. He had been impressed by Josef Stalin's ability to mobilize Moscow's proletariat to fight the Germans and had acknowledged one diplomat's contention that the dictator, while often described as a "man of steel," could be perceived as well as "a nice old gentleman." His account of a diplomatic dinner he had attended with Stalin, Averell Harriman, Harry Hopkins, Lord Beaverbrook, and others while in Moscow referred to Stalin as "having a retentive memory, and a thorough knowledge of English, German and French literature." In a later dispatch Carroll would credit Stalin with the defense of Moscow: "It is the story of how the iron will of Josef Stalin was imparted to army and corps commanders, divisional and regimental leaders, down to the humblest soldier; how mothers and daughters shouldered picks and shovels and marched across the snow-covered plains west of Moscow to dig defenses for their soldier sons and lovers."

His years in Geneva covering Russia's diplomatic efforts at the League of Nations also colored his opinion. To Carroll, the Soviets, after Litvinov's efforts at collaborating with the West failed, had had little choice but to side with Hitler in 1939 through the Soviet Non-Aggression Pact. This ensured Russia would not be invaded by the Nazis, who were empowered by the "dishonorable" secret approaches made by Neville Chamberlain to appease Germany. Chamberlain, at the same time as he was appearing to appease Germany, had been publicly appealing to Stalin to join forces against the Nazis. The onus for the failure of the Western powers to make an ally of Russia prior to the war, Carroll believed, fell entirely on Chamberlain. The Russians had good grounds to conclude that Chamberlain only wanted to trap them into a war with Germany in which they would be left alone to do the fighting.

Carroll had been one of the few reporters to have witnessed Moscow prior to the Nazi onslaught on the capital, and his diplomatic connections—primarily with Tommy Thompson, who had been deputy ambassador in Moscow during its defense—gave his reporting great weight and credibility. At the time he had been billed as one of the best-known reporters in Europe; his picture and brief biography often accompanying his front-page dispatches. As a result, his opinion—that the Soviets did not have the internal economic strength to want to expand their boundaries following a defeat of the Nazis—was widely credited. Stalin, he thought, knew that Russia "must have a long period of peace in which to conquer its internal problems and build up its productive capacity." He therefore was not likely to seek out new Soviet states in Eastern Europe. "[The Soviets'] primary aim," he wrote, "must be to solve their domestic economic problems—to double, triple and quadruple their industrial output—they cannot allow themselves to be diverted by this urgent task by gambling on revolution in other countries."

Carroll also for the first time in his book articulated his long-held belief in America's need to reach out to other countries, including the Soviet Union, and to play a lead role in the post-war world. This was the only way to avoid future conflicts. "The events of December 7, 1941, shook the deep-seated American belief that peace could be had by staying at home and minding your own business," he wrote in *We're in This With Russia.* The United States should not refuse to work with any country that was sincerely interested in establishing peace, including the Soviet Union. "A country barred from the council table becomes a force for mischief and instability," he wrote. As such, he saw no future except one in which cooperation with the Soviet Union would be essential.

Carroll, through his earlier reporting, had been among the first to go on the record as believing the Soviets would be able to defeat the Nazis. In time he was proven right. At the same time, he also had fallen under the spell of Stalin and underestimated the ruthlessness of his regime. In this he was not alone. Larry LeSueur, a correspondent for CBS who spent a year in Russia, came back extolling the regime, writing of the steel and fire the Russians showed at Stalingrad, their vitality and fierce love of the motherland. Others were inspired by the Russians' grit, including General George Marshall. At war's close he credited both the Russians and British for their resolve: "The refusal of the British and Russian peoples to accept what appeared to be inevitable defeat was the great factor in the salvage of our civilization."

We're in This With Russia consolidated the reputation of a journalist who at the time was considered "one of the ablest young newspaper men the United States has sent abroad."

Rushed into print in October 1942, it was met with overall good reviews and nationwide publicity. The *New York Herald Review* ran a full-page review on the front page of its book section with a large photo of Carroll. The review was written by William L. Shirer, whom Peggy and Carroll had met in London.

"For twelve years Wallace Carroll, a quiet, shrewd and very intelligent young American correspondent sat in the council halls of Europe—at Geneva, Lausanne, Paris, London—and saw firsthand how the peace was lost," wrote Shirer. "No other correspondent that I know has had a better average in keeping both feet firmly on the ground at all times, both in his dispatches and in his book." Shirer went on to summarize Carroll's findings, including Carroll's suggestion that the United States be realistic and hard-boiled toward its Soviet policy. But he also believed that Russia would not try and see a Soviet Europe when the war was won.

Later, the book would prove to be somewhat of an embarrassment for Carroll in its glowing picture of Stalin and the Soviet Union. He felt it had been written too quickly, and "not very well." But the book, along with a series of articles he had written about Russia, which won him the National Headliners Club Award in 1942, had established him as a Soviet specialist, and one who had a largely positive view of the country. He had shown that he believed an alliance with Russia was necessary to win the war and to bring freedom and democracy to the peace. It was a labeling that would stick to him for many years.

■ ■ ■

The book finished, Carroll was feeling restless again and frustrated at the blasé attitude many took toward the war in Europe. In February 1942, he was invited to speak at a Convention of Engineers at the Waldorf Astoria in New York on his war experiences. He told the engineers gathered about his time in London during the Blitz and his narrow escape from Moscow, but later recalled that, when he had finished speaking, a fellow got up, the first to speak, and had asked, "Now tell me, did the Germans really bomb London or was that just newspaper talk?"

"If the waiters hadn't removed my plate, I would have beaned him with it," the normally calm Carroll recalled. American journalists, he believed, had taken all possible risk, used all their ingenuity to tell the American newspaper reader what it was really like in Britain during the air raids, yet the man had asked the idiot question of "whether I had faked it all."

Frustrated with America's sense of apathy, Carroll had decided to return to his UP post in London that spring with Peggy, when he got a call from Elmer Davis, who was at that time the most famous radio broadcaster in the United States. Davis, a former Rhodes Scholar and reporter for the *New York Times,* had leapt to instant success two years earlier as a news commentator at CBS Radio. By June 1941, he was broadcasting seven days a week to 95 radio stations and listened to by more than 12.5 million people during his popular 8:55–9:00 p.m. time slot.

Originally from Indiana, the fifty-one-year-old Davis, who boasted white hair, black eyebrows, and dark eyes behind horn-rimmed glasses, had a Hoosier accent that inspired confidence and endeared him to the heartland. *Time* magazine called him "clear-headed, sensible … one of the best newsmen in the business," while Norman Cousins in the *Saturday Review of Literature* pointed to the "fundamental clarity in his thinking," and the *New Republic* hailed him as "a liberal respected by conservatives, a man of broad appeal." Davis soon had the public's full attention, for he was, indeed, as one journalist noted, "solid American to the core—the sort of American that belongs to the heart of the country."

Because of his broad appeal and non-controversial reputation, Franklin Roosevelt felt Davis would be the ideal candidate to head up a new government agency, the Office of War Information (OWI), which would be tasked with informing both the American and foreign publics about the war. At the time most Americans saw the war as "a drama that, while interesting to watch, had nothing to do with their own lives." The public was also dubious about government efforts to inform them, in part due to over-arching attempts during World War I, instituted by the then Committee on Public Information, to use propaganda to influence public opinion. The committee, headed by the contentious journalist George Creel, had run an extensive propaganda campaign during the war that was designed to promote American ideals and persuade citizens to make sacrifices, its aim being to ensure that democracy would triumph worldwide as a result.

Creel's campaign had been all too effective. It had stirred up hatred of all things German, led people to believe that spies were everywhere, and generated unrealistic hopes for a better world. After the war, when Wilson's efforts at peace were less than successful, and his efforts at home to ratify his Fourteen Points were rejected by the U.S. Senate, Americans were left to grapple with the sharp contrast between unfulfilled dreams and the realities of world politics. They also learned of the unfair discrimination and fear tactics that had led to the destruction of many Americans' civil liberties. This left a bitter taste in the mouth for many regarding the duplicities inherent in government-led information campaigns. President Roosevelt, too, was dubious of such programs, preferring instead to be his own propaganda mouthpiece.

In January 1941, eleven months before the Japanese attack at Pearl Harbor, Roosevelt had outlined his potential U.S. war aims in what has come to be known as his Four Freedoms speech. It outlined four fundamental freedoms that he believed people "everywhere in the world" ought to enjoy: freedom of speech, freedom of worship, freedom from want, and freedom from fear. The speech provided a rationale for why the United States should abandon its isolationist policies and concluded with a list of the benefits of democracy. These beliefs were further endorsed in August of that year when he and Winston Churchill met at sea and signed the Atlantic Charter, which conceived a postwar world in which the self-determination of nations, equal trading rights for all, and a system of general security would prevail.

But Roosevelt had to be careful how his war aims were presented. Before Pearl Harbor, the non-interventionists on the right, led by Charles Lindbergh, still wielded a great deal of political power. Millions of Americans, convinced that survival of their country was at stake, were against the United States joining the war in Europe.

Among the pro-interventionists on the left were two well-known literary figures, Archibald MacLeish and Robert Sherwood. Both had played an early and active role in promoting the president's strong pro-democracy interventionist sentiments. MacLeish was a famous poet, whom Roosevelt had appointed in the fall of 1941 as head of a newly established Office of Facts and Figures, created to keep the public better informed about the national defense. A former Rhodes Scholar and editor of *Fortune* magazine, he had years earlier recognized the dangers posed by Adolf Hitler, and had incessantly lashed out about the evils of Fascism. Sherwood shared MacLeish's convictions. He had achieved outstanding success as a playwright, winning three Pulitzer Prizes within five years for his plays in the late 1930s and early 1940s, including the hugely popular *There Shall Be No Night* about the Soviet Union's invasion of Finland. He was also at the time Franklin Roosevelt's speechwriter, credited with coining the phrase that America would become the world's "arsenal of democracy," a frequent catch phrase in Roosevelt's speeches.

In a further effort to promote his war aims, in the summer of 1941 Roosevelt had appointed Sherwood to head a newly created Foreign Information Service (FIS), whose aim was to inform the rest of the world of the aims and objectives of the American government with regard to the European war. Under the FIS, Sherwood created The Voice of America, which soon gained popularity for spreading the gospel of democracy abroad over the radio. MacLeish was more interested in messages aimed at a home audience; Sherwood more interested in overseas propaganda.

By early 1942, however, and following the attack on Pearl Harbor, Roosevelt increasingly recognized that MacLeish's Office of Fact and Figures, Sherwood's FIS, and other various and disparate agencies, including William "Wild Bill" Donovan's newly created Office of the Coordinator of Information, which had been charged with analyzing material dealing with national security, had to be brought under one umbrella. After receiving advice from Milton S. Eisenhower, Dwight Eisenhower's well-known younger brother,[1] who had been brought in to make a survey of war information needs, Roosevelt signed an executive order on June 13, 1942, creating the Office of War Information (OWI). But he only agreed to do so after he had obtained Elmer Davis's commitment to head up the new organization. Recognizing the challenge before him in reconciling competing agendas, personalities, and messages, Davis soon after his appointment remarked that he sometimes "felt like a man who had married a wartime widow and was trying to raise her children by all her previous husbands."

Davis's discomfort was well foreseen. Roosevelt would give lukewarm support to OWI, preferring to balance competing people and agendas against each other rather than directly intervene in its operations. As the war dragged on, he would

---

1. Dwight Eisenhower's younger brother, Milton, held a series of high-profile jobs in the Roosevelt administration, including as director of information for the U.S. Department of Agriculture, where he was a chief spokesman for the New Deal. He would go on to direct the War Relocation Authority, even though he was strongly opposed to the mass incarceration of Japanese Americans during the war, and later served as president of Kansas State University, Pennsylvania State University, and Johns Hopkins University. At the time Roosevelt tapped him to advise on OWI he was better known to the public than his older brother.

show a reluctance to prioritize democratic ideals over victory at all costs, and MacLeish and Sherwood would see their efforts at promoting democracy gradually sublimated to achieving military objectives. Similarly, neither Elmer Davis nor Wallace Carroll, who at the launch of OWI were also inclined to promote the ideals of the Four Freedoms and Atlantic Charter over military objectives, were aware that Roosevelt would change his priorities. Thus, added to the administrative hurdles facing Davis and Carroll was a lack of direct support from the president, as well as what seemed to be ever-shifting priorities and agendas.[2]

▪ ▪ ▪

As created, the newly launched OWI was to coordinate a wide range of government information and propaganda efforts about the war. Yet it was not to be a central agency that would assume all information functions. Its mandate was to provide truthful information to the American public, as well as to develop campaigns—like bond-buying or salvage drives—to secure certain actions. The new organization would consist of two branches—the domestic branch, aimed at relaying information about the war to the American public, and the overseas branch, designed to influence the enemy as well as those under the enemy's control in conquered territories. In September 1942, Davis asked Carroll to work in OWI's Overseas Branch, taking charge of

---

2.   Roosevelt's treatment of OWI was little different from his treatment of scores of other organizations in the years he held office. The president was a master at using men. His penchant for making conflicting appointments, so evident before the organization of OWI, allowed him to play off his appointees one against one another. Having set men on their own, he could reserve the right to intrude if something really mattered to him, or simply allow his subordinates to work out their conflicting claims themselves. Even when officials came to him for support, he could put them off. See Warren F. Kimball, *The Juggler: Franklin D. Roosevelt as Wartime Statesman* (Princeton: Princeton University Press, 1991).

the London office. He would report to Robert Sherwood, who was made head of the Overseas Branch but would be based in New York. Sherwood's deputy was James P. Warburg, a strong interventionist, who would be heavily involved in "whipping the organization into shape."

Carroll, by now thirty-eight years old, later admitted he knew nothing about the job he was about to assume. He felt, however, that he needed to do more to support the war effort than to just continue working as a reporter, and Peggy supported his decision. But he also understood that OWI from its outset seemed fraught with conflicting interests, restricted power, and ambiguity over what was the American public's right to know. In particular, Sherwood, who had pulled together a spirited staff in New York from newspaper, theatre, and radio circles was often at odds with William Donovan, as well as with Secretary of War Henry Stimson, who both felt the liberal tendencies of Sherwood and his staff should be subordinate to military objectives. The State Department also resented the Overseas Branch's authority, making coordination of their activities difficult.

His doubts about the new job were confirmed when Davis took him to see President Roosevelt just prior to his departure for London in early September 1942. It seemed clear to Carroll that Roosevelt knew nothing, or pretended to know nothing, about much of the work of the new OWI, remarking that Carroll's job would be one of just "plugging holes in British censorship." When Carroll told him he was not supposed to have anything to do with censorship, Roosevelt seemed to brush him off, warning him nonetheless to tell the British to "tighten it up."

So, with no further clarification, Carroll began to pack his bags for London. Peggy would join him when she could, thus planning on making her fourth crossing of the U-boat-infested North Atlantic since the start of the war. It would also mean leaving three-year-old Margaret and one-year-old John with her parents in Hastings-on-Hudson. She was conflicted about whether or not to go, but in the end decided she could be more useful in London. "This straining between two continents is more painful than almost anything. If the waiting were over and I were in England it would be easier, but staying here and always having the opportunity of changing my mind and fulfilling my duty to the kids is driving me slowly to schizophrenia or some such," she would write Carroll. Her old friend and mentor Gil Winant had promised her a position in the U.S. Embassy. She, too, would be front and center as events unfolded across the continent.

CHAPTER 9

TO WIN HEARTS AND MINDS

"In war, opinion is nine points in ten."
—Jonathan Swift, eighteenth century essayist

When Carroll arrived back in a blackened London on September 10, 1942, he was met at Paddington Station by Winant and other friends from the American embassy, including James P. Warburg, who had been sent to London six weeks earlier to help set up their headquarters. London was a depressing place, all concerned agreed. Huge swaths of the capital lay in ruins, and "everywhere there were the marks of bombs and fires—rows of stately houses with one or two gone, like missing teeth; whole neighborhoods destroyed." The blackout was in full force, and although the Blitz was over, the Luftwaffe still managed to bomb the city frequently enough to keep people on edge at night, wondering whether or not to go down to the shelters when the sirens rang out. After three years of war, a noticeable shabbiness and fatigue had set in among residents; there was little fuel, and food was heavily rationed. The British people had been carrying on doggedly since September 1939, and opinion was divided as to how they would respond to the presence of a couple million American servicemen soon coming their way.

Carroll's mission in London, he had been told by Davis, was to be twofold: first, to conduct a straightforward information program in the British Isles to enhance British understanding of America, and second, to organize and direct American propaganda campaigns aimed at Germany and Italy and the captive peoples on the continent.

Peggy would finally join him four months later in January 1943. Despite the general air of despair among the population, she noted that there was a hint of optimism that the worst might be over. "There have been two days in which evidence of sunshine has come to the attention of an experienced Londoner," she wrote her mother. "Nothing to dazzle of course, but a luminosity in the clouds, and a pink glow on the breasts of the pigeons when they sail up into the sky from their home in the blasted-out house across the street, in which the only visible furnishing is a toilet in perfect repair."

Together again, they would take on their first task—to let the British know about America—something that was much needed because at the time there was an almost unbelievable lack of knowledge about the United States among the British public. Carroll later recalled that the average British citizen based his understanding of the United States "on a hundred gangster films and other Hollywood caricatures of American life." Peggy's work with Gil Winant in the U.S. Embassy would confirm this. One of her first assignments was to put together an exhibit entitled "America Marches," which was made open to the British public. Peggy oversaw the information desk at the exhibit and later wrote a detailed report summarizing the attitudes of those who'd attended. Many were unaware of the size of the United States, and when looking at a map, curious about the number of states; some wondered why Pearl Harbor wasn't on the map of the continental United States. Few knew anything about the American political system but remarked that they believed America was less class-conscious than Great Britain.

Interestingly, many questioned the status of African Americans in the country, indicating bewilderment about other

Americans' attitudes toward them, wondering "how the Negro problem will be solved." Peggy would write movingly about how difficult it was to explain the racial situation in the United States, remembering a concert by Black American soldiers that she had recently attended was "the most moving thing I have ever heard—the sadness, the patience and the hope of the race. They did 'Ballad for Americans' and I nearly wept. The contrast between what we always think we stand for and what the Negroes have gotten was almost too much."

Wallace's work mirrored Peggy's efforts. OWI's London Bureau was charged with not only dispelling myths about American domestic life, but also with building an understanding of Roosevelt's aims in the war and the post-war world, and with easing the irritants that were bound to come when "hundreds of thousands of rambunctious young Americans poured into that neat little island where resources and nerves were already strained by three years of war." To help him in his efforts, Carroll asked Peggy to summarize a report from the British Ministry of Information about how American soldiers were behaving when on leave. The results were rather desultory; the Ministry saw American soldiers as having "slouchy deportment, a lack of manners, untidy habits such as spitting and dumping chewing gum, drinking to get drunk, and with the attitude that they could get anything if they had the money to pay for it." In general, they were seen as having "a lower moral standard than ourselves," particularly when it came to young girls.

Eisenhower had also picked up on this issue—and particularly the fate of Black soldiers. He had written Roosevelt in September 1942 that "To most English people, including the village girls—even those of perfectly fine character—the Negro soldier is just another man, rather fascinating because he is unique in their experience, a jolly good fellow and with money to spend." The biggest problem arose when white soldiers saw English girls spending time with Black soldiers, which often led to violent fights. Eisenhower would spend a good deal of time during his short stay in Britain in mid-1942 preoccupied with the problem of keeping American troops "separate but equal."

Both the British Foreign Office and Chiefs of Staff in June of that year had warned that the likely presence of American troops on British soil could have serious effects on Anglo-American relations. The War Cabinet instructed the Ministry of Information to undertake a mammoth operation for liaison with American forces, and a large-scale official effort was made to smooth the path of relations between the British public and the U.S. Army. Winant, as U.S. Ambassador, was aware of this and had anxiously awaited the arrival of the Carrolls.

▪ ▪ ▪

Once settled in offices in the U.S. embassy, Carroll began to organize what he called OWI's British Division, which was strongly supported by Winant, and tasked with improving British understanding of America. His first hire was James Reston, who established a news service from America which gave the British newspapers a more complete daily report on the United States than they had ever had before. Reston was charged with countering the insidious Nazi anti-American propaganda drummed into Britain every night. The campaign centered on how the Roosevelt administration was planning to use British shock troops to do the fighting while it was plotting to relieve Britain of its economic resources after the war.

Carroll also brought in Ferdie Kuhn, who was now based in Washington and had worked with him covering the Blitz. Kuhn had a good grasp of what the British wanted and needed to know about America. He and a small staff began to send a flow of books for republication, speakers, photo exhibits, and other information materials to London. A new hire in London, Victor Weybright, who later went on to become a well-known publisher with Penguin books, took the materials and others he developed on his own initiative and fed them into British distribution channels. Eventually Carroll put the division under the direction of Herbert Agar, who had recently been the editor of the *Louisville Courier-Journal*. Under his direction, the British division did much to smooth the irritants in American contacts with the British people, and set a pattern for similar informational programs on the continent.

All in all, however, Carroll soon recognized, as did Reston— who left OWI after four months to go to the *New York Times*—that the Americans were novices at best at what they were trying to achieve, and that there was already disorganization among the lines of authority in the OWI.

▪ ▪ ▪

With the task of the British Division underway, Carroll began to turn his attention to his second priority, which he termed "psychological warfare." This "flamboyant term," as Carroll referred to it, was aimed at "winning over the hearts and minds of both enemies and friends across the European continent," but to Carroll, a seasoned reporter, it seemed a bit nebulous at best. No agency had developed any body of doctrine or tactics to give it effect. Nonetheless he jumped in, a "complete greenhorn in a field where the British, Germans and Soviets were already proficient."

The British in fact had long understood the importance of maintaining morale through using propaganda to influence public opinion. They had a powerful belief that British propaganda had contributed to the defeat of Germany in 1918 by undermining civilian morale. If the British had been able to do this, they believed the process could be reversed and turned against them, especially by an opponent possessing the formidable propaganda machine of Nazi Germany. They understood that managing public opinion, and thus keeping morale high, was crucial to winning the war. In this they were much more advanced than the Americans in informing the public of what was necessary to maintain the war effort. Throughout the war, through its Ministry of Information, the British Government would disseminate a vast number of propaganda films and radio broadcasts. The Ministry was also a major wartime publisher, producing books, illustrated magazines, pamphlets, leaflets, and postcards. A wide range of themes were addressed: everything from fostering hostility to the enemy and support for the Allies to specific pro-war projects such as conserving metal and growing vegetables.

What the British understood, and the Americans did less so at this point, was that their enemy—Adolf Hitler—believed that propaganda was central to the success of any political or military campaign. It had played a key role in the rise of the National Socialist German Workers' (Nazi) Party, and it would be given top priority once they reached power. Hence, Hitler and his cohorts were experts in the field. When Hitler became Chancellor of Germany in January 1933, he had promptly established the Reich Ministry of Public Enlightenment and Propaganda headed by Josef Goebbels. The propaganda ministry was responsible for ensuring that every means—from radio, film, and media to education, art, and rallies—was used to effectively communicate Nazi messaging. Propaganda was seen as essential to the war effort as the Nazis prepared for war in the late 1930s. It permeated every aspect of German life, using all available means of communication, and was carefully crafted in an effort to coalesce Germans around their government and to intimidate foreign rivals. These efforts would continue as the war raged on.

Carroll was perhaps still too unskilled in the field of propaganda to understand its overall importance to the success of the war effort, or that in his capacity as director of OWI he would be the Allied counterpart of such an accomplished propagandist as Josef Goebbels. He nonetheless knew enough to learn from the British and to coordinate his efforts with the British government. To provide communications support for military actions, his first step was to build a working relationship with Sir Robert Bruce Lockhart, who was the director general of the British Political Warfare Executive (PWE), a secret British agency created in 1941 to produce and disseminate propaganda. Its aim was to damage enemy morale and sustain the morale of countries occupied or allied with Nazi Germany. Their primary task was to "marry" the central directives of the OWI and PWE. Each week the PWE and Carroll's office at OWI would send Dwight Eisenhower a jointly prepared directive and back it up with staff who could carry out propaganda operations against the Germans and Italians. The aim was to forestall any differences in both agencies' propaganda output that the enemy might exploit to show that Britain and the United States were out of step. The process was grounded in careful coordination with actual activities being undertaken by PWE.

One of their first tasks was to assure the British and Europeans that, though bombed into war by Japan, the Americans considered the liberation of Europe to be their first priority. This meant the preparation of radio broadcasts to go out over the BBC and other stations that would maintain the hopes but not inflate the expectations of captive peoples on the continent.

OWI also prepared leaflets to be dropped by the RAF over Europe aimed at deceiving the Germans into believing an invasion of France was under urgent consideration (as it was for a time), when in reality Eisenhower was planning a critical strategic move to land Allied forces in Africa. It was later acknowledged that if the Germans had learned of this African expedition, they could have easily had it aborted by sending divisions through Fascist Spain to Gibraltar and through France to the Mediterranean coast. All sorts of military feints were employed to keep the Germans pinned down in the north, and Carroll's work would play a large part in this effort to gain time and position.

▪ ▪ ▪

Carroll's arrival in London coincided with the U.S. and British militaries' decision to invade North Africa, which he soon found out about from James Warburg, Sherwood's deputy who was then visiting London. Warburg informed him that an Allied force under American command would land in North Africa in late October or early November. The essence of the plan, called "Torch," was to persuade the French in North Africa to welcome the Allies as friends and to cooperate with them in throwing the Germans and Italians out of Africa. Propaganda would have an important part to play, and OWI was to be asked to draw up the appropriate plans.

The relationship was complicated, however, by U.S. relations with the French Vichy government. Vichy had been established following the German occupation of France in the summer of 1940. A line had been drawn: to the north, the Nazis would control government operations; south of the line, French Fascist sympathizers, led by Marshal Philippe Pétain, would have control. The United States had formally recognized the Vichy government and sent an ambassador, William D. Leahy, to undertake negotiations. Back home, many in the United States wondered why America would maintain friendly relations with a Fascist regime that was known to persecute Jews and to throw opposition members into concentration camps. Privately, Leahy's aim was to use American influence to encourage Vichy to work in opposition to Germany. But for public diplomatic purposes, the U.S. government—and Leahy as its representative—had to reckon with the fact that Vichy was in control of the North

African countries—Morocco, Algeria, and Tunisia—that would be invaded by the Allied forces under Torch.

General Eisenhower, who would be in charge of Torch, was well aware of the delicate public relations surrounding the situation, and sympathetic to the need for the kind of psychological warfare, or propaganda, that OWI and Carroll were offering. He gave Carroll an office in his headquarters at Norfolk House where he could work in absolute security on plans for the North African landings. Carroll remembers Eisenhower at the time as "not yet at ease with his new authority, but obviously intelligent, refreshingly youthful, and, above all things, direct." His only requirement of Carroll was that he report directly to Eisenhower and no one else. Carroll took this to mean that while he would keep his boss in New York—Robert Sherwood, who had been made head of the Overseas Department—informed of his actions, the ultimate decision-maker would be Eisenhower.

In cooperation with PWE, Carroll drew up the general propaganda directives for the North Africa offensive and arranged for a team of French language specialists to go from New York to London and then on to North Africa with the Allied forces to take control of the radio stations in Algeria and conduct all other propaganda operations in support of the invasion. This propaganda operation would consist of encouraging both the French and the native populations of the benefits of the Allied cause, and to persuade them to support Allied efforts during the invasion. These first "psychological warriors," as Carroll called them, became the nucleus of Eisenhower's Psychological Warfare Branch and later Eisenhower's Psychological Warfare Division, which would play a key role leading up to and during the D-Day landings in 1944.

When the Allies launched their invasion of North Africa in November 1942, they had expected, because of the U.S.'s friendly relations with Vichy, to be met with open arms. However, Marshal Pétain, under the German gun in Vichy, called for resistance against the Allies; the French troops in most of North Africa began to put up a furious fight. Eisenhower, facing unexpected military resistance and with backing from Roosevelt, then—after only a few days of fighting—suddenly agreed to make a deal with Pétain. He agreed to the appointment of Admiral Jean François Darlan, the notorious vice-premier of the Vichy Fascist government in metropolitan France, as "High Commissioner" in North Africa, in charge of all French forces. The quid pro quo was that Darlan would pull the French forces back from fighting against the Allies and would no longer interfere in the Allied invasion of North Africa. But it also meant that officials appointed by the Vichy regime would remain in power in North Africa. No role was provided for Free France, which deeply offended General Charles de Gaulle, its leader in exile. It also offended much of the British and American public, who regarded all Vichy French as Nazi collaborators, and Darlan as one of the worst. Eisenhower insisted he had no real choice if his forces were to move against the Axis in Tunisia, rather than fight the French in Algeria or Morocco.

This was startling news to those on the home front. Even Carroll was puzzled and initially unbelieving. In short it created a public relations nightmare. How could the United States make such a deal with the Nazi collaborators? Weren't we fighting to save democracy, and to stamp out the evils of Fascism? Even worse, the agreement also put all the channels of communication—predominantly radio and the press—into the hands of the Vichy French, who had been spreading anti-Allied propaganda for two years. This, of course, alarmed Carroll, who thought the American military underestimated the effect such propaganda would have on the local population. Darlan in particular was seen as a shady character. He was well-known to be in bed with Hitler through the Vichy government, and had been working both sides of the conflict.

One outspoken critic in the United States was William "Wild Bill" Donovan of the newly created Office of Strategic Services (OSS), who would go on to be one of the founding fathers of the Central Intelligence Agency (CIA). Donovan wrote to Roosevelt that, "Our great influence with the people of France has been due not only to our strength but to our straight dealing." For many this had been shattered by the Darlan deal. Robert Sherwood also weighed in, noting that to people everywhere "It seemed to confirm the impression that while the Americans talked big about the principles of the Four Freedoms and the Atlantic Charter, they actually knew nothing about Europe and could be hoodwinked by any treacherous gangster who offered them collaboration."

Carroll knew he had to act quickly to try and salvage what he could from the public relations disaster. He began to immediately press for the release of information that would help break the shock in America, in Britain, and throughout the world. He wrote a memorandum to Davis and Sherwood outlining the uneasiness the Darlan agreement was causing among the Allies and, in particular, how it would harm British public opinion of the Americans. Davis forwarded Carroll's message to the White House, where it coincided with a similar message from Winston Churchill.

Finally, on November 18, Roosevelt in a statement to the press reiterated that the arrangement with Darlan was "temporary," and only justified based solely on the stress of battle. He went on to lay down the principle that in the future the French government would be established only by the French people themselves after they had been set free by the United Nations. To Carroll, the President's words fell "like a welcome rain at the end of a sultry day." Nonetheless, protests continued pouring forth from political leaders on both sides of the Atlantic. OWI's New York office, led by Sherwood, continued to be outraged, as was Sherwood's deputy Warburg. Their reaction formed an early wedge between Carroll, Sherwood, and Warburg, tension that would continue to escalate. The tension was not helped by the weighing in of Donovan, who also continued to speak out strongly against the alliance with Darlan. The firestorm was not put out until Darlan was assassinated on December 24, 1942, by a member of the Free French.

Although Carroll felt the Darlan affair had been a political defeat, he eventually came to understand that the decision was made for military reasons that perhaps were justified. Eisenhower's forces had met with unexpected hostility from the French in Algeria, and hence had no choice but to deal with Darlan, who was the only French leader who had Marshal Pétain's support and could guarantee an end to the resistance. After researching cables from Eisenhower and garnering as much military intelligence as he could, Carroll concluded that without Darlan, Eisenhower would not have been able to seize Tunisia, lure the French fleet out of Toulon, or bring Dakar over to the Allies. He considered that the Darlan arrangement was the lesser of two evils. To ensure military success, it had by all appearances "cast principle aside and struck a bargain with one of the most despicable of Hitler's foreign lackeys."

Carroll together with PWE had managed to paper over the cracks to some extent, but the incident still festered, especially with General Charles de Gaulle, leader of the Free French, based in London. In retaliation for the American recognition of Darlan, de Gaulle stopped all cooperation between the OSS and the Free-French's intelligence service. The fallout of the Darlan affair caused the British and the pro-Allied French to rally around de Gaulle, leaving the United States, at least temporarily, out in the cold.

It also heightened Carroll's sense of the importance of propaganda to the Allied cause. He considered the Darlan affair a major political defeat for the Allies, despite the military success of the North African invasion. Confidence in the motives of the United States had suffered a severe blow, he thought, and the incident was a classic example of the folly of ignoring the reality of public opinion in war or in politics, a theme he would later call on in writing about the Vietnam War.

▪ ▪ ▪

The Darlan Affair caused such an uproar that Roosevelt sent Milton Eisenhower over to North Africa to talk with his brother about the propaganda nightmare. Milton conveyed to Ike the need to explain the military decisions that were being made, and left recommendations in North Africa for ensuring a smoother flow of news back to the United States. General Eisenhower, for his part, asked in turn to be better informed about adverse political comments. A month later he lifted the veil of censorship and allowed editors and columnists to visit North Africa to see what was happening.

The incident also set a pattern of Carroll working with Eisenhower's Psychological Warfare Branch (PWB) in North Africa and later Italy that would keep Carroll in good stead with the Allied commander. Drawing on this, at the beginning of 1943, Carroll set about to further organize the London branch, a staff of about 30, to press forward on longer-term projects. He established a small policy and planning unit to work on ideas and campaigns, to coordinate those with the British, and to feed them to Washington. He then created an intelligence unit to collect information that might shed light on the state of mind and morale among the enemy and captive nations. This unit gathered information from British intelligence sources and interviewed new arrivals from the underground forces on the continent. A third unit, the propaganda analysis unit, sifted through hundreds of thousands of words brought in by monitoring enemy and other broadcasts and boiled them down to fifty thousand words a day for Washington.

He also beefed up leaflet bombardment of the continent, which had been ongoing since early in the war. British bombers had been dropping leaflets at night on their flights over France, the Low Countries, and Germany. OWI's small publications unit, eager to get into the action, now began producing prototype leaflets in French, German, Dutch, and Norwegian. Essentially these were miniature newspapers containing brief news items that the German censors would not have allowed to appear on the continent. The overall aim was consistent: to fortify the will of those under occupation and give them hope, to undermine the will of the enemy, and "to create a base from which the psychological assault could be launched together with the military thrust across the Channel." Stymied by the U.S. Air Force's resistance to dropping the leaflets, Carroll turned again to the British, who arranged for their air force to drop hundreds of thousands of OWI leaflets each month. Stung by the success of Carroll's solution, Eighth Air Force Commander General Ira Baker soon assigned an entire squadron of Flying Fortresses, using special equipment, for leaflet dropping. By the end of 1943, OWI's delivery of leaflets to the Continent had risen to more than eighteen million a month.

Also crucial was the construction of six medium-wave radio stations based in Britain designed to override the jamming stations set up by Hitler's Propaganda Minister Josef Goebbels. All over Germany, Italy, and the occupied countries, Goebbels had multiplied these stations so that voices from the world outside could be heard only against a pulsating staccato sound that soon discouraged the listener. Carroll's new stations were far more powerful than the short-wave medium being used by the Voice of America. The new stations, known as the American Broadcasting System in Europe (ABSIE), were able to put out a powerful signal into Germany, France, Italy, and other parts of Europe, and rebroadcast programs from New York as well as programs originating in British studios.

By the end of 1943—16 months after Carroll's arrival—the London office of OWI had grown to 300 people and was working well with the British propagandists. Several members of the Truman Committee of the Senate, established in part to review the operations of OWI, had flown to London to inspect the office's operations and quizzed Carroll thoroughly before going back to Washington and writing a favorable report. Colonel Harold Kahn of the Joint Chiefs of Staff had also inspected every aspect of the office's activities and given it, despite frequent criticism of OWI at home, the "equivalent of the Good Housekeeping seal of approval," Carroll later noted in his papers. In general the Overseas Branch had proved itself as effective as the Domestic Branch, if not more so, in no small part due to Carroll's efforts and his close working relationships with both Eisenhower and the British.

■ ■ ■

But in truth all was not well with OWI, not the least because of tensions among the cast of characters working within the organization, where internal squabbling was constant. Especially problematic was Robert Sherwood, who headed the New York office and was Carroll's supervisor. Sherwood—according to James Reston, who joined the London office for a few months in late 1942—while a great playwright, was "vague, unpunctual and protective of his close ties to the president." Sherwood had lapsed into a blood feud with William Donovan, head of the Office of Strategic Services, that ruled out any cooperation with Donovan's intelligence gatherers, and he often refused as well to take direction from his own supervisor, OWI director Elmer Davis, based in Washington. Sherwood would also fall into black moods where he would withdraw into himself and stuff important cable messages into his pocket or let them lie unanswered on his desk. His secretary later recalled that "piles of correspondence went into his office in the morning and came back at the end of the day untouched." Carroll had frequently been frustrated by the lack of support shown the London office from New York. To compensate for this, he had increasingly turned to the British to help in both the production and the funding of propaganda materials.

Sherwood's lack of support created acute problems for Carroll, who was trying to reach agreement with the British on all that OWI was doing in preparation for D-Day and thereafter. Week after week the PWE representatives, flanked by their military advisers, would present their proposals. And week after week, with his own military looking over his shoulder, Carroll would have to say his instructions had not yet arrived, but no doubt would be coming along soon.

When Carroll would at last hear from Sherwood, he would be rebuked for failure to communicate, lack of cooperation, and other perceived shortcomings. He had also been angered by Sherwood's sending over Warburg, his deputy in the New York office, to oversee Carroll's work. Carroll had been working sixteen-hour days, had suffered two attacks of jaundice, and was both exhausted and frustrated. Knowing that he could not carry out his mission without Sherwood's confidence, in December 1943 he resigned. Three of his deputies resigned with him, and another fifteen offered to do the same before Carroll persuaded them to stay on.

Sherwood's assistant would later remark that Carroll left London, "as bitter a man as I have ever encountered." The failures of the OWI, Carroll would assert, turned on the inadequacies of New York. Warburg, Carroll added, "was unacceptable to the British, to the American Embassy, and to military leaders on both sides of the Atlantic." But there was more to Carroll's fights with Sherwood and Warburg and to his resignation than personality and the inevitable tensions of running a three-thousand-mile coordinated effort under wartime conditions.

Carroll believed that the role of propaganda was to explain and support American foreign policy, not to make it. He did not always like or approve of American policy. He disliked Darlan, for example, and thought Eisenhower and Roosevelt had made a dreadful mistake in recognizing the former Vichy minister. But he did not believe it was his role to change that policy. Rather, he believed, the propagandist's job was to ameliorate relations and to sell American policy, regardless of the difficulties that policy created. During his tenure he had concerned himself more with immediate military victory than with long-range consequences of peace. And his disagreements with American policy, unlike those of Warburg—who was a strong supporter of Sherwood—were never so deep as to bring him into harsh conflict with the State Department. Carroll got along well with the State Department, which offered him a job in March of 1944, a job he unhesitatingly turned down.

For Elmer Davis, who also was not at war with American foreign policy, Carroll's discontent and resignation would have much wider implications, reaching all the way through Davis, to the White House. Davis had been frustrated with Sherwood's running of the Overseas Branch, and Carroll's resignation would prove to be the last straw. As Carroll recalled, this latest tempest "increased the frustration on Davis's part and his awareness that the Overseas Branch was not running very effectively." For the Carrolls the situation reinforced their frustration with bureaucratic life. As they reluctantly packed their bags to journey home, they recognized that a bright light would be in reuniting with their children at Peggy's parents' home in Hastings-on-Hudson.

On January 25, 1944, the London *Daily Telegraph* ran a brief story entitled, "Dynamic Couple." "Mr. Winant has lost one of his personal assistants and the American Office of War Information its director, Mr. Wallace Carroll," read the article. "Mr. Carroll did outstanding work when he was head of the United Press here during the Blitz of 1940–1941. Mrs. Carroll, who is no less dynamic than her husband, accompanies him back to Washington."

Without doubt, many believed, they would be sorely missed.

CHAPTER 10

UP AGAINST GOEBBELS

"The truth is the enemy of the state."

"If you repeat a lie often enough, people will believe it, and you will even come to believe it yourself."

"Think of the press as a great keyboard on which the government can play."

—Josef Goebbels

By the time the Carrolls arrived back in the United States in January 1944, the Office of War Information was under attack from all sides. As Carroll had predicted, the administrative failures of Robert Sherwood, coupled with increasing skepticism of OWI's efforts by the State Department and top military brass, had put the organization in crisis. Added to this was Roosevelt's reluctance to face the growing tension between Sherwood and OWI Director Elmer Davis. Roosevelt had repeatedly sidelined Davis, not inviting him to important meetings to bolster his standing internally and with the Allies, and had refused to rein in Sherwood, who several months earlier had demanded full control over all overseas operations. Davis, in part bolstered by Carroll's resignation, had had enough.

The showdown came on February 2, 1944, when a determined Davis met with Roosevelt and Sherwood at the White

House. Davis demanded that OWI be drastically reorganized and that he be given total control over the Overseas Branch, currently based in New York under the supervision of Sherwood. Davis recalled that the president, finally realizing he had to take a side in the controversy, "wished he had a good long ruler, the kind that schoolboys' hands used to be slapped with when he was in school," in referring to the meeting between Davis and Sherwood. "He was good and God-damned mad at both of us for letting a thing like this arise and get into the papers at a time when he had a war to think about," recalled Davis. Unable to face disappointing either, Roosevelt ordered the two men to go off into a side room to iron out their differences.

Several days later, "in order to promote harmony of operation and to avoid misunderstanding," both Davis and Sherwood reached an agreement that gave Davis complete authority over the operations of the Overseas Branch. Sherwood would move to London to theoretically take up where Carroll had left off, thereby saving face but effectively removing him from power. In the meantime, Davis promptly hired Edward W. Barrett, a former writer and associate editor for *Newsweek*, to serve as deputy under Sherwood. In effect, Barrett assumed all of Sherwood's authority, and several months later Sherwood resigned from OWI to work on Roosevelt's reelection campaign. Warburg would also be asked to resign.

With his newfound power, Davis quickly moved to re-hire Carroll as deputy director under Barrett to head up OWI's European Operations, responsible for all propaganda going to conquered Europe, leading up to and during D-Day and beyond. Carroll knew Barrett and understood that he could work well with him, but was skeptical at first about overseeing European operations from afar. Moreover, he had been furious with Sherwood and Warburg when he resigned from his London post and was still dubious that the disorganization he had witnessed in the New York office would in truth dissipate. After four long years in the trenches in London, he made it clear that he would only take up the post if it was based in Washington. He checked with his contacts in the State Department—notably, H. Freeman "Doc" Matthews, who had become the chief of the Office of European Affairs in the State Department—to ensure that there would be a free flow of information from the department to OWI so that efforts could be coordinated. Matthews assured Carroll that he would get all the intelligence he needed to do the job properly.

The shakeup within OWI was met with mixed reaction by the public. Critics charged that, with Sherwood's departure, there was no longer any independent thinking about war aims within the OWI; that it was now totally under military control. For the most part this was true. The Overseas Branch quickly became more strongly attached to the Psychological Warfare Division of the Supreme Headquarters Allied Expeditionary Force (PWD/SHAEF) based in London. Moving forward, few decisions were made without the approval of PWD/SHAEF or the Joint Chiefs of Staff.

By this time, Carroll was even more convinced that propaganda could be most effective when it was married to military objectives, and while OWI would not always be in internal agreement about what its messages should be, they seldom acted without the knowledge and authorization of the military brass. The early idealists who had argued for the creation of OWI as an independent organization dedicated to articulating the liberal principles behind the war had no choice but to be guided by the military conduct of the conflict. OWI became devoted to ensuring that their activities were in line with military objectives.

▪ ▪ ▪

For Carroll, the new OWI assignment meant a move from Hastings-on-Hudson to Washington, D.C. Peggy set up house on 4612 Drummond Avenue in Chevy Chase, and both parents began the process of getting better acquainted with five-year-old Margaret and two-year-old John—whom they had seldom seen, in the course of the war, since the children were born. They remained in close touch with Gil Winant, whom Carroll wrote in March after accepting Davis's offer: "It may not surprise you that I took your advice to 'stick with Elmer,' but it did surprise me," he wrote. "I had practically made up my mind to return to newspaper work in London when Elmer got what he wanted from the President. With many misgivings, I finally decided to accept his offer. I believe now that I made the right choice—provided the circumstances which compelled me to resign in London do not repeat themselves."

For her part, Peggy was delighted to be reunited with the children and was finding that "being a mother is a much more strenuous job than working for Gil Winant.... She likes it, however, and is developing into quite a hausfrau," wrote Carroll in a letter to Winant. No doubt she was relieved to be out of the pressure cooker of London, which at the time was still under sporadic bombardment and suffering from a lack of most amenities, including food. They would live in the residential, leafy neighborhood of Chevy Chase, just north of the Washington, D.C., line, which was home to a wide array of diplomatic and military families. Peggy would finally have her own house, complete with garden, white picket fence, and sidewalk on which to walk the children.

The Carrolls had moved to a city transformed by the war. New government agencies had been created and existing ones expanded dramatically, leading to the construction of temporary office buildings along the Mall and around the Washington Monument that housed tens of thousands of new, mostly female office workers. A severe housing shortage led to the proliferation of overcrowded boarding houses, home to fresh-faced newcomers from remote farms and small towns across the country. They had changed Washington from a sleepy Southern town to what seemed then to many Americans the center of the universe. It would soon become the center of the defense industry. The largest office building ever constructed in the world, the Pentagon, had been completed in January 1943 just 16 months after construction had begun.

Washingtonians professed to be worried about the threat of bombing attacks—military personnel manned anti-aircraft guns around the city, and a bomb shelter was built underneath the White House—and they planted victory gardens to subsidize the severe food shortage and held drives to collect scrap metal. But for the Carrolls, used to the death and destruction they had lived through in London, the city seemed a peaceful and safe haven indeed. They could finally settle in with their own family, in their own house, and live for the first time a more undisturbed day-to-day existence.

■ ■ ■

The Carrolls' more comfortable home life, however, didn't lessen their intense commitment to the war effort. Carroll as usual plunged into work. He settled into OWI's Washington office, where he was put in charge of devising plans and policies for American propaganda directed at the European Continent, including radio broadcasts, news services, films, leaflets, booklets, exhibits, and other means of influencing public opinion. These plans had to be in harmony with American foreign policy, which was somewhat vaguely defined by the White House and State Department. His principal activity was to produce weekly directives governing the United States propaganda strategy. To do so, at the beginning of each week he would gather his staff of about twelve regional specialists to get their intelligence estimates and ideas. His team included some of the most knowledgeable experts at the time—the historian Leo Gershoy for France and the Austrian social psychologist Hans Speier for Germany, for example. Together with one or two of them he would draft the European part of the directive. Carroll would then take the train to New York to explain the principal features to the broadcasters and the editors of the OWI news service that went out daily to OWI outposts and embassies. He would then meet with OWI staff to discuss longer-term projects, such as pamphlets, books, films, and exhibits.

Carroll, with others who had taken over from Sherwood and his colleagues, was mostly concerned with supporting military objectives aimed at winning the war. He also recognized that most of Europe was hungry for hard news that would somewhat balance the propaganda campaigns coming out of Germany. Dedicated internationalists, his staff also knew at this point in the war that once liberation of Europe had been achieved, they would need to make information about the United States and its peacetime aims more available.

A sample of their work in early 1943 shows the rationale they used in imploring the French people to understand why the Allies were bombing their country, and to take up arms against the Germans in the effort:

> *THE USAAF sends the following message to the French people:*
>
> *We attack the enemy wherever he is; in Germany, first; in the Balkans together with the Soviet Army, in France and Belgium. Wherever railways serve to transport German troops, German munitions, German supply, we strike.*
>
> *We know that you are undergoing German occupation. You are undergoing the Vichy policy. You are undergoing Darnand's militia. We know that for four years the enemy has inflicted upon you physical and moral oppression, lies, constraint, hunger.*
>
> *As in 1914–18 shells had to be fired on the invaded departments, so today Allied bombs fall on the soil of France.*

"They know all that," you say, "and yet they bomb us?"

We know that these bombardments add to the sufferings of some of you. We do not pretend not to know it. It would ill become us to pretend to alleviate these sufferings by expressing the sympathy we feel for you.

We therefore say to you:

We trust in your comprehension to do all you can to get away, insofar as is possible, from railway centers, marshalling yards, sidings, locomotive dumps, repair shops.

THE DESTRUCTION OF ENEMY COMMUNICATIONS IS A MILITARY NECESSITY. IT IS A TOKEN OF YOUR LIBERATION.

A later directive took the mandate of communicating with the occupied peoples further and emphasized the role it would play in winning a final victory. Such propaganda was aimed at encouraging resistance, and at encouraging those under occupation to proceed as if victory was around the corner. It was also aimed at infiltrating German thinking by persuading them that their defeat was imminent.

Carroll was crucial in implementing this change. He was seen by Elmer Davis as "intelligent, moderate and conciliatory in his opinions," and colleagues in both the military and the State Department recognized it. Now unhinged from having to report to Sherwood and armed with better access to military intelligence and strategy, he began to think through a series of propaganda campaigns aimed both at enhancing PWD/SHAEF's military objectives and, when feasible, presenting to the world the Allies' democratic objectives.

▪ ▪ ▪

Carroll's first idea came shortly after he had rejoined OWI in March 1944. The Allies, in a deliberate and deadly advance up the boot of Italy, had been moving north since January 1944, and in late May were rapidly approaching Rome. Although Italy had formally surrendered to the Allies five months earlier, the Germans had held the Italian capital for over a year, claiming to use it as a communications center and billing it as an "open city." In truth, the Wehrmacht was using the ancient city as a staging and transport center for its armies. Day and night their convoys drove through the capital on their way to the southern front. Rome lay open to attack, and American forces, reeling from their controversial bombing of the historic monastery of Monte Cassino one month earlier, were worried that the city would become a similar battleground. Carroll felt that the destruction of ancient Rome would be sure to draw moral outrage from around the world. Rome had been the capital of Italy for almost 70 years, but large parts of the city were more than 2,500 years old. The neutral Vatican City sat at its center, and the Vatican also owned many churches and other buildings throughout the city. But both Eisenhower and Winston Churchill were adamant that Rome be captured.

After reviewing the reports of German occupation from the international press, Carroll and his team decided to launch a propaganda campaign with a twofold objective. The first was to fix the onus for any upcoming destruction of Rome firmly on the Germans. The second, much more ambitious, was to combine the force of world opinion with Allied military pressure to bring about a German withdrawal from Rome. Carroll's office began by convincing President Roosevelt to issue a worldwide statement criticizing the Nazi record on religion. Carroll drafted the communication, which Roosevelt read during a press conference on March 14, 1944. In the statement Roosevelt warned the world that "Hitler and his followers have waged a ruthless war against the churches of all faiths...." and that the Germans had "now transformed the Eternal City into a military center, a logical move in the Nazi policy of total war." The Allies did

In addition to worldwide appeals to stop the destruction of Rome, Carroll ordered leaflets to be dropped to the citizens of Rome imploring them to "do the impossible to prevent the destruction of the city…" including preventing the setting of mines under bridges and government buildings.

not want to make a battleground of Rome, he said, but this did not depend on them alone.

Roosevelt's press conference was the first time OWI had enlisted the president in a propaganda campaign. Simultaneously, Carroll instructed OWI's staff in London and in other neutral European capitals to send in any fresh material on Nazi contempt for religion and asked for Nelson Rockefeller's Agency for Inter-American Affairs to stimulate cries of concern and outrage from the Catholic hierarchy in Latin America. Day after day, pleas, denunciations, and other relevant news, including that of a German massacre of Italian partisans in Rome, were pumped through the international press into Germany and the occupied and neutral countries of Europe. The cross-fertilization of messages stimulated more pleas for Rome to be saved and cries of outrage against the Nazis.

Gradually, newspapers in Spain and other European countries began to run stories describing the German threat to Rome. Italian radio stations under Nazi control began to react, broadcasting that the Germans would begin to transfer out of Rome anything that might be regarded as a military target. Although this was not believed by the Allies, the campaign had started to turn the tide of worldwide opinion against the Germans. In a few weeks, the Germans did withdraw from Rome and the city was spared. Hitler reported that he had ordered the withdrawal of the German troops to the northwest of Rome in order to prevent its destruction.

Carroll never considered that OWI's propaganda effort could be fully credited with the Nazi withdrawal. But he did believe that at least some of the onus of protecting Rome from destruction had fallen on the Germans, and that this very well might have made a difference. If public outrage had made the Germans uncomfortable in Rome, then—combined with military objectives—it had certainly influenced their decision to withdraw from the city. When Lieutenant General Mark Clark, commanding the U.S. Fifth Army, veered off the plan to surround German soldiers retreating from the south and instead struck directly at Rome on June 4, 1944, there were no Germans to be found. The ancient capital had been spared.

On the evening of June 5, 1944, President Franklin Roosevelt welcomed the fall of Rome with a few words, "One up; two to go." The city was the first of the Axis powers' capitals to be taken, and it had emerged remarkably unscathed. Pope Pius XII, who had received criticism for refusing to condemn German atrocities during the Nazis occupation, acknowledged to a happy and boisterous crowd gathered in St. Peter's Square that summer evening that perhaps the most important aspect of the Allied victory was that Rome would escape relatively unscathed.

▪ ▪ ▪

Even as events were unfolding in Italy, by far the most attention being given by Carroll's European division as well as PWD/SHAEF in London throughout the spring of 1944 was the planned invasion of Normandy, scheduled for early June.

The London office of PWD/SHAEF had grown to more than 1,600 staff and had become a major center of activity. Work ranged from developing leaflets to drop during the invasion to preparing flyers to be carried by the Allied troops ensuring safe passage for German soldiers who agreed to give themselves up. The leaflet campaign alone was becoming a monstrous effort. In advance of and during the Normandy invasion alone, the Allies dropped nine million leaflets, and even more millions in the three months that followed.

From Washington, Carroll continued to issue directives and to give policy advice to PWD/SHAEF. It was clear that the majority of Germans were now aware that they could not escape defeat, yet despite this there was little evidence that German resistance would come to an end. Carroll began to formulate another idea related to preparations for the invasion. A major challenge facing Supreme Allied Command was the desperate need to overcome Germany's mastery of the air before the planned invasion. Eisenhower's planners believed that unless the Luftwaffe could be rendered largely impotent, the Allies would not be able to establish and hold beachheads on the French coast. This observation got Carroll thinking.

▪ ▪ ▪

Throughout 1943, the Allied air forces had engaged in Operation Pointblank, aimed at subjugating the German air force by 1944. Their tactics had been to target German cities in addition to its factories and other installations vital to the German aviation industry. The damage to German cities was considerable, but Hitler continued for the most part to commit his fighters to air battle over enemy territory, not to protect the homeland. In addition, despite heavy losses on both sides, the Reich could not keep pace with Allied production, nor in replacing pilots killed. Hitler and Goring refused to admit this to the German public, even going so far as to argue that the destruction of German cities "actually works in our favor, because it is creating a body of people with nothing to lose—people who will therefore fight on with utter fanaticism."

Carroll had the idea of baiting Goering and the Luftwaffe. His strategy was to undermine the Luftwaffe's prestige with the German people, who would put pressure on their leaders to make the air force come out to protect them. After he won an ironclad approval from the Joint Chiefs of Staff, Carroll drew up a directive aimed at taunting the German high command by issuing radio broadcasts about the American daylight raids on Germany. Through OWI's German broadcasts, American generals and spokesmen began to make taunting statements such as "Where is the Luftwaffe?" The same message was printed on hundreds of thousands of leaflets and dropped over Germany. The leaflets asked why Field Marshal Herman Goering was letting Allied planes bomb civilian populations without resistance. Broadcasts emphasized the impotence of the Luftwaffe, and questioned why its planes were just sitting on the ground amidst the attacks.

Soon after the campaign began, the U.S. War Department's intelligence service began to receive reports that the campaign was "definitely embarrassing" the Germans. And although there could be no definitive proof, the Luftwaffe in April and May began to respond more actively, sending up more and more fighters to engage with bombers attacking German cities.

"Where is the Luftwaffe?" Leaflet dropped over Germany in the lead-up to D-Day, March–May 1944.

During the month of March 1944, the Germans had made approximately 1,800 "interception sorties" against American bombers. In April, the number rose to 2,500 and in May to almost 3,200. The Allies, including the daylight raids by the U.S. Eighth and Fifteenth air forces, claimed destruction of 1,315 enemy aircraft in aerial battles compared with 920 in the peak bombing month of February and 951 in March. The May figure represented more than a quarter of the German front-line strength. This was what the Allied air forces wanted, and it was the result that Carroll's propaganda campaign had hoped for. The prioritization of fighter deployment to defend the Reich was crucial. It stripped fighter cover away from the battlefields, leaving German troops without any force capable of holding air superiority over their lines.

Proof of the campaign's effectiveness was demonstrated by Josef Goebbels himself, who began to give personal attention to the bombing attacks in his propaganda. In statements he repeatedly gave to the German press and over the radio in April and May 1944, he insisted that the enemy had not eliminated the Nazi fighter capacity, but that the Luftwaffe had only been grounded constantly by "climatic conditions." In addition, he magnified to the German public the effect of the few dozen German bombers that had flown over England in the same time period, until the force seemed equal to that of the Allied bombings. Despite these efforts, Allied intelligence still reported that Germans were asking, "Where is the Luftwaffe?"

Later reports from defectors said that the leaflets criticizing the Luftwaffe had also broken the morale of German soldiers in the field, who had become concerned for the safety of their families at home and angry at Goering. They had communicated this frustration back to their families, who also began to put pressure on the Luftwaffe.

The Allied air bombing campaign and associated propaganda strategy, however, was not accomplished without cost. As a result of the strategy, many more Allied planes were also shot down in April and May than ever before. Allied airmen paid the price. The military and propaganda campaign had hardly begun, for example, when the British lost 94 heavy bombers in a night attack on Nuremberg, Germany. It was the heaviest loss of the war in a single raid.

The British complained vehemently to the United States, calling for an end to the night raids they had been undertaking. But the Supreme Headquarters Allied Expeditionary Force (SHAEF) under Eisenhower, which had gained control of all Allied air forces in March 1944, continued to support the effort, directing bombers over routes in Europe that had been deliberately selected to bring out the maximum opposition from the Germans. Carroll called it "a cruel expedient," but acknowledged that its purpose was to save lives in the long run.

The sacrifices of the Allied air forces during this period had their crucial strategic effect: when the Allies landed on Normandy's beaches on June 6, 1944, the Luftwaffe was nowhere to be seen. Carroll always recognized that this was primarily thanks to the American and British airmen who for more than a year and a half had ground down the strength of the German air force. But he also credited those in the Allied air command who had not been afraid to use unorthodox methods—such as propaganda—to achieve their aim. Carroll later recalled that he'd felt that the many thousands of lives saved on the beaches of Normandy had in some significant measure justified the steep losses of Allied aircraft crews over Germany during the Pointblank campaign.

▪ ▪ ▪

As the propaganda campaign unfolded after the Normandy landings and the Allies advanced toward Germany, OWI became more engaged in military efforts than ever before. "From now on," noted a central directive issued by Carroll in July, "our propaganda offensive will run boldly in advance of our military offensive. We shall proceed on the implicit assumption that the German will to resist can be broken and will be broken by next December."

Carroll had been working since 1942 to understand the best way to do this. Much of it, he strongly felt, depended on the Allies' understanding of the German character, and the hold Goebbels had on the German people. Goebbels followed Hitler's example by using the credible lie, which by continuous repetition in time took on the force of fact. The truth, for Goebbels, was not important, for propaganda, he declared "had nothing to do with the truth." The "credible" lie he had repeatedly told the German people at the start of the war was that the use of military violence by the Wehrmacht had been morally defensible and necessary to prevent the country from becoming a victim of foreign aggressors. In 1943, after the Nazi defeat at Stalingrad and the heightened bombing of German cities, it became increasingly difficult to reconcile official news stories from reality. Goebbels knew he had to counteract this—even though at the time he had complete control over the national news media—because foreign news broadcasts were making their way into German homes.

His tactic was to scale up his rhetoric by increasing Germans' fears about the Allies, saying to the German people that total war was necessary to prevent Germany's enemies from destroying the country. As the Allied forces fought their way across France and entered Germany in 1944, Goebbels ramped up his strategy of terror to the German people even more. He ranted over and over again, that defeat meant the end of the existence of the German people. In a July 8, 1944, speech in Eastern Germany, he proclaimed that the Allies "pursue a plan of exterminating us root and branch, as a nation and as a people...." On July 13, he wrote, "One has only to think of the program of hatred and destruction proclaimed by the Anglo-Saxon governments—not to mention the Bolsheviks, who would turn the whole of Europe into a veritable hell." On October 27, Goebbels broadcast over the German network:

> *We will not let them make a potato field of our Reich, and we will not let them change our country into a hell. Neither will our women and children be exterminated, nor will our workers and soldiers be sent to Siberia ... there is only one answer for a people which loves honor and freedom, and that answer is: To fight at all costs until victory is won.*

Such messages were also making their way into the psyche of soldiers in the front lines. One transcript from a Goebbels lecture, found in the diary of a German soldier captured in France in October 1944, outlined what would happen if the German army met with defeat. The Allies intended to "sterilize the men and drag them off to Siberia. Our girls and women are to be exterminated and our youth to be raised along Bolshevik lines...." Another fear among the soldiers was that 12 million foreign workers from captive nations who were then toiling under Nazi rule would "rape German women and murder German children if the German army collapses."

▪ ▪ ▪

Carroll almost daily listened to information he received about how well Goebbels was managing the news for German listeners, which was carefully monitored by OWI's Overseas Branch. He began to think breaking Goebbels' hold over the German people was an almost impossible task. It was made even more difficult, he felt, by Roosevelt's policy of "unconditional surrender." The policy, which had been agreed to at the Casablanca Conference in January 1943, was put in place to ensure that the Germans would be offered no other inducement to surrender that might enable them to claim, as they had in 1918, that they had been tricked into submission. Roosevelt was adamant in its implementation. But for Carroll it fed right into Goebbels' message of fear and was a propaganda nightmare. What "unconditional surrender" meant was so vague that it enabled Goebbels to conjure up in the German mind all kinds of horrors that would descend once the fighting stopped, and gave him more ammunition to encourage the Germans to continue the fight.

Carroll had argued as early as September 1943 in a memo to the State Department that a directive be drawn up that would spell out to the German people that surrender would not mean annihilation but an end to the horrors of war and an orderly occupation. But both the military and State Department refused to approve the request. It was not until General Eisenhower—who knew well the power of psychological warfare—issued a terse statement in December 1944 outlining what "unconditional surrender" meant, that Carroll and his team were able to further counter Goebbels' messages. The statement assured the German people that while National Socialism would be rooted out and destroyed, basic functions of government would be allowed to continue and the rights of German citizens upheld. Carroll saw the statement as a godsend. While stern in tone, it provided an antidote to Goebbels' "Strength through Fear" propaganda. Carroll and his staff moved forward on a major campaign to broadcast these terms to the German people.

Carroll also worked to develop a directive that emphasized that a German defeat would be due to "overwhelming force," and thus enable the German military and the German people a way out with honor. The theme recognized the bravery of the German soldier; it also emphasized the fair treatment of captured German soldiers and the failure of German leadership.

TRANSLATION OF WG 50

THE FUTURE OF GERMANY

The following statements are from the report made by President Roosevelt to the American Congress on March 1, 1945. In that report he discussed the decisions reached jointly by the United States, Great Britain and the Soviet Union at the Yalta Conference.

WE will not desist for one moment until unconditional surrender. The German people, as well as the German soldiers, must realize that the sooner they give up and surrender, by groups or as individuals, the sooner their present agony will be over. They must realize that only with complete surrender can they begin to reestablish themselves as people whom the world might accept as decent neighbours. We made it clear again at Yalta, and I now repeat:

Unconditional surrender does not mean the destruction or enslavement of the German people.

„We did, however, make it clear at the Yalta Conference just what unconditional surrender does mean for Germany. It means the temporary control of Germany by Great Britain, Russia, France and the United States. Each of these nations will occupy and control a separate zone of Germany—and the administration of the four zones will be co-ordinated in Berlin by a control council composed of representatives of the four nations."

"Moreover, unconditional surrender means the end of National Socialism and the Nazi Party with all its barbaric laws and institutions. Unconditional surrender means the end of all militaristic influence in the public, private and cultural life of Germany."

"For the Nazi war criminals, unconditional surrender means quick, just and severe punishment. Capitulation means also the complete disarmament of Germany, the final extirpation of German militarism, the destruction of all German war material, the end of German war industry, the demobilization of all German armed forces, and the absolute dissolution of the German General Staff which has so often disturbed the peace of the world. For the damage she has done, Germany will have to make reparations in kind—by surrendering plants and machinery, rolling stock and raw materials."

"We will not, as after the last war, commit the error of demanding reparations in the form of many which Germany could never pay. We do not want the German people to starve, or to become a burden on the rest of the world. Our objective in handling Germany is simple—it is to secure peace of the future world."

"The Future of Germany," which following the Yalta Conference assured the German people that unconditional surrender did not mean "the destruction or enslavement of the German people." English versions were printed for all British and American pilots and crew assigned to drop the leaflets. It was believed that if the airmen knew what the leaflets said, they would be more conscientious in carrying out their mission.

This latter element had been strengthened in July 1944 with the assassination attempt on Adolf Hitler's life. Following the attempt, Carroll and his team sent directives outlining that the failed effort signaled widespread internal dissension and strife within the Nazi hierarchy. Goebbels, recognizing that Hitler's seemingly miraculous survival could strengthen his allure to the German people, successfully launched a counter campaign to make it clear that it had only been a few unpatriotic and cowardly generals who had tried to take the Fuehrer's life. He ratcheted up his deification of Hitler; proclaiming with Heinrich Himmler that the Fuehrer was in good health, his abilities never failing. In the end this worked to Hitler's advantage. He became even more sanctified by the German people.

PWD/SHAEF, at Carroll's recommendation and knowing the mystic hold Hitler had over the German people, had avoided personal attacks on the Nazi leader up until the attempt on his life in the summer of 1944. But as the Allies advanced in the fall of 1944, Carroll felt more was needed. He submitted for approval by the Joint Chiefs a new directive that would bait Hitler to speak. The directive questioned why the German people had not heard from Hitler. Was his health failing? Had he been seriously hurt in the July 20, 1944, bombing? Had he felt he could not face the Germans because he knew that the outlook was hopeless?

Goebbels reacted by more energetically proclaiming that the Fuehrer was in good health, his abilities never failing. In a desperate last-ditch effort to persuade the German public to continue the fighting, Goebbels used the initial breakthrough during the Battle of the Bulge on Christmas Eve 1944 to elevate Hitler to immortal status. Hitler, according to Goebbels, "transcends everything ordinary and human.... he has a sixth sense and is endowed with eyes to see what remains hidden from others ... he is the miracle of Germany...."

Even during Hitler's last days, Goebbels' propaganda machine had done its work. In a famous newsreel of Hitler, taken on his fifty-fourth birthday, on April 20, 1945, he is seen pinning the Iron Cross on a 12-year-old boy brought to Berlin to defend the city. The boy years later recalled that when Hitler pinched his check and told him to "Keep it up," the boy had the feeling that "he had done something remarkable." "It never entered my mind," said another member of the Hitler Youth, a 16-year-old working as a messenger in Hitler's bunker during the last days of the war, "even then, as the bombs rained down, that we would lose." All in all, more than 30,000 troops from the Hitler Youth would die in the Allied onslaught on Berlin.

In the end, neither Carroll nor any of the Allied propagandists ever succeeded in breaking Hitler's hold over the German people. Their belief in their Fuehrer remained to the bitter end. Later, in thinking over his wartime experiences, Carroll admitted that it was difficult for the American people to understand Hitler's hold on the country. "What they overlooked," he wrote, "was that the Germans had been conditioned to receive this kind of message; that their critical faculties had been weakened by more than ten years of totalitarian propaganda." He warned that long-term exposure to such propaganda, following a severe shock such as the German people experienced during and following World War I, could cause a similar result elsewhere, a warning to the United States and other countries in the West.

"The Hitler legend," wrote Carroll, "would bear watching."

*A self-confident "Bud"
Carroll at 12 years old.*
Credit: Carroll family

*Professor J.L. O'Sullivan (left) joined the Marquette Journalism
School Faculty in 1924, the year Carroll enrolled. Freshman Wallace
Carroll (right) would soon find his way into Sullivan's classes.*
Credit: Marquette Hilltop, 1924

The squat, black teletype machine was omnipresent in every newspaper and radio station in the country.
Credit: James P. Blair/ Newseum Collection

Carroll, here outside Paris, went to London as a foreign correspondent at age 22 and stayed on the continent for the next 14 years.
Credit: Carroll family

The Stavisky riot, February 6, 1934, in which mounted police attacked rioters; Carroll carried a dying participant to the American embassy following the upheaval.
Credit: Public Domain/Wikipedia

*Ethiopian Emperor Haile Selassie warns the League of
Nations General Assembly on October 3, 1935, of atrocities
committed during the Italian invasion of his country.
Selassie was met with catcalls and jeers from the Italian
press but was later named* Time's Man of the Year.
Credit: Library of Congress

*As UP's diplomatic reporter based in Geneva, a 28-year-old
Carroll confers with delegates to the League of Nations (1935).*
Credit: Carroll family

Carroll became a life-long friend to Rosamond and Rifat Tirana, here shown having coffee in Geneva. Carroll thought Rosamond "the most beautiful woman in Europe." Her husband, a noted economist, was the Albanian delegate to the conference and later published The Spoils of Europe *in 1942, an early warning of Hitler's atrocities.*

Credit: Carroll family

A seven-year-old Peggy in sailor suit with her father and a guide at the top of the pyramids, circa 1920. Peggy grew up traveling the world as the daughter of Dr. Wilbur A. Sawyer, who headed the Rockefeller Foundation's Public Health Service.

Credit: Carroll family

Margaret "Peggy" Carroll at 18; she would go on to graduate with a degree in economics from Vassar in 1934. One year later she was recruited by Gil Winant to work with him at the International Labor Organization in Geneva.

Credit: Carroll family

Peggy and Carroll skiing in Chamonix, France, 1938.
Credit: Carroll family

Peggy and Carroll leaving their wedding ceremony at the
U.S. Consulate in Geneva on May 25, 1938.
Credit: Carroll family

The Carrolls' wedding reception at Les Clos Fleury, Chambesy, a restored castle in Geneva, was attended by the "who's who" of the pre-war international diplomatic community.
Credit: Carroll family

UP's offices were housed at the News of the World Building on Bouvarie Street, London, at the start of the war, circa 1939. Later the building would be bombed and destroyed during the Blitz.
Credit: Rex Features via *The Guardian*

Carroll interviewing British fighter pilots during the Battle of Britain in June 1940. He marveled at their willingness to risk their lives daily, while retaining a "sense of humor."
Credit: Carroll family

"Life never seemed so unreal," Peggy Carroll wrote of the Blitz. More than 43,000 civilians lost their lives, with a million homes destroyed.
Credit: George Greenwell/Mirrorpix/Getty

Marquette Journalism Alumnus Reports Russian Conflict for United Press

Between bombing attacks on his way up to the Russian front lines, Wallace Carroll (in tin hat), United Press London bureau head, halts with his Soviet army guides while a soldier camouflages their car to conceal it from Nazi pilots, whose bombs have been striking too close for comfort. Carroll for several months was on special assignment to Moscow and recently returned to New York via Siberia and the Philippine Islands. While on the Hilltop, Carroll was a member of Sigma Delta Chi and edited the Journal.

Wallace Carroll, MU Alumnus, Lives Life of World Adventure

Dialing In...
MU Radio Workshop

Vying for honors as Marquette graduate success story number one is

hotel room in which he was quarter-

speed, barely clearing trees, telephone

RADIO SPEECH: Deviating from its usual program, this week the Mar-

Carroll meeting with Russian generals during a trip to the front lines following the Nazi invasion. Carroll was among the first foreign correspondents to enter the Soviet Union in August 1941, and to report that the Russians would stand up to the Nazi invasion.

Credit: *Marquette Tribune*, January 8, 1942.

Our Present and Future Relation to Russia

Mr. Carroll Attempts to Answer Questions We Are All Asking

WE'RE IN THIS WITH RUSSIA.
By Wallace Carroll.... 264 pp....
Boston: Houghton Mifflin Company.... $2.

Reviewed by
WILLIAM L. SHIRER
Author of "Berlin Diary"

Wallace Carroll

William L. Shirer's review of Carroll's first book, We're in This With Russia, *published in October 1942. Shirer, calling Carroll "a quiet, shrewd and very intelligent young American journalist," praises his accounts of the Russian defense of Moscow. The book later proved to underestimate Stalin's future ambitions in Eastern Europe.*

Credit: *New York Herald Tribune,* October 4, 1942.

Peggy with four-month-old baby Margaret in Hastings-on-Hudson, New York, February 1940. Margaret was born after Peggy crossed the Atlantic at the height of German submarine sinkings of Allied ships in October 1939.
Credit: Carroll family

Popular radio host Elmer Davis who became director of the U.S. Office of War Information, circa 1942.
Credit: AP

Adolf Hitler and his Minister of Propaganda, Josef Goebbels.
Carroll would become the Allied counterpart to Goebbels in
"winning the hearts and minds" of occupied Europe.
Credit: Roger Viollet/Getty Images

Gordon Gray, heir to the Reynolds tobacco fortune, owned the Winston-Salem Journal *and* Sentinel *for more than 50 years. He considered the newspaper a "public service" and plowed profits back into its operations.*
Credit: *Winston-Salem Journal*

Carroll's friend James A. "Scotty" Reston in 1945 soon after winning his first Pulitzer Prize. Reston would recruit Carroll as his news editor after taking over the helm of the New York Times *Washington bureau in 1955.* Credit: Historic Images

As news editor of the Washington bureau of the New York Times, *Carroll and Reston would recruit and mentor the "gold standard" of journalists during their leadership. Three here (L-R) are Russell Baker, Tom Wicker, and Anthony Lewis.* Credits: (L-R) Jill Krementz, *Winston-Salem Journal,* AP

Winston-Salem, looking north from Fourth Street, showing the Union Bus Station and the Hotel Robert E. Lee, circa 1963. When Carroll arrived as editor and publisher of the Winston-Salem Journal *and* Sentinel *that year, R.J. Reynolds tobacco was still the city's largest employer, but the town had begun to diversify and prosper.*
Credit: Winston-Salem/Forsyth County Public Library

N.C. School of the Arts founders (L-R) Philip Hanes, John Ehle, Rosemary Harris, and Charlotte Hanes. Good friend Carroll joined the effort by writing a front-page editorial calling for the school to be located in Winston-Salem.
Credit: UNC School of the Arts

'Quo Vadis?'–to the Top

Journal Washington Bureau

WASHINGTON — The inside story of President Johnson's decision to seek peace in Vietnam and how he was influenced by an editorial from the Winston-Salem Journal and Sentinel has just come to light in Washington.

In a detailed article about the struggle over Vietnam policy within the Johnson administration, the Washington Post reported that the wavering President was "particularly impressed" by the Journal and Sentinel editorial. It was after reading the editorial, the Post said, that he made his decision to seek negotiations.

The President announced that decision in a television talk last March 31. He also announced at the same time that he would not seek re-election.

The Journal and Sentinel editorial, entitled "Vietnam — Quo Vadis?" was written by Editor and Publisher Wallace Carroll. It appeared in the Sunday paper

WALLACE
CARROLL

... wrote
editorial ...

A story published in the Winston-Salem Journal *confirmed how Carroll's editorial had influenced the pullout from the Vietnam War.*
Credit: *Winston-Salem Journal,* February 11, 1969

Carroll (top row, third from left) sat on the Pulitzer Prize Board from 1970–1974. Standing to his left (in 1973) are Ben Bradlee and James Reston. Credit: Pulitzer.org

Carroll announces the awarding of the Pulitzer Prize to Winston-Salem Journal *staff in May 1971.*
Credit: *Winston-Salem Journal* and *Sentinel*

Carroll spent ten years (1974–1984) as Samuel J. Ervin Lecturer on Constitutional Rights at Wake Forest University. Here he introduces his friend, former secretary of state Dean Acheson, during a lecture at Wait Chapel.
Credit: Carroll family

Carroll's son, John Carroll with Dean Baquet, shortly following John's resignation as editor of the Los Angeles Times *on July 20, 2005. John Carroll was, according to Baquet, "the Willie Mays of journalists," and among the most highly respected editors of his time.*
Credit: Al Seib/*Los Angeles Times* via AP

Peggy and Wallace worked in support of the preservation of the New River Valley. Here they greet guests at a fund-raising event in Winston-Salem. Due in part to their efforts, in 1976 the New River came under the protection of the Wild and Scenic Rivers System; in 2020 it was declared the nation's latest national park.

Credits: Carroll family and Public Domain, Wikapedia.

Carroll maintained his prominence as an influential political voice following his retirement from the Winston-Salem Journal *in 1974. Here he greets former president Jimmy Carter, circa 1984.*

Credit: Carroll family

CHAPTER 11

"PERSUADE OR PERISH"

*"In war there are no prizes, neither for those who won it,
nor for those who lost."*

—Unknown

With the end of the war approaching, in the spring of 1945, Wallace Carroll and his boss, Elmer Davis, were determined to see first-hand the devastation the war had brought to the European continent. In early April, they boarded a flight to London and then Paris, where Carroll noted the "tear-stained faces" of the French upon hearing of Franklin Roosevelt's death. Several days later, they crossed the zigzag defenses of the Siegfried line and flew into Germany. Landing in the pockmarked Aachen airport, they were taken by the Army several miles into the city.

Before the war, Aachen, the westernmost city in Germany, had been a town of 165,000. Now about 15,000 people were living in ruins. A drive around town gave Carroll the impression of complete devastation. No building was left intact, except for Charlemagne's ancient Aachen Cathedral. Even so, Carroll and Davis remarked on the relatively healthy look of the people and the food in the shop windows. They had come to Aachen to see what a defeated Germany looked like. What they came away with was a feeling that Aachen residents, although thoroughly beaten and docile, had little feeling that they had been co-responsible for the war and its related crimes.

In contrast, as Carroll and Davis toured Germany, they noted the many survivors of Hitler's regime, "the slave workers, the starved and beaten prisoners of war, the survivors of the torture chambers, the political prisoners with the smell of death in their hair and the look in their eyes of men who had seen more evil than the mind can bear." Recognizing the extent of the suffering, Carroll reached the conclusion that the attempts to change the hearts and minds of the Germans had largely failed; that perhaps the only way propaganda could have made a difference would have been if it had been concentrated on the German soldier, who, upon venturing forth from Germany, had come face-to-face with the truth.

Recognizing this, Carroll began to formulate a strategy for reeducating the German people that was not based on the Allies rushing in with flags flying and pamphlets extolling the virtues of America. Rather, he thought it important to win back hearts and minds, and to do this would require a willingness on the part of the Germans to accept their guilt before coming to the Americans. "Everything I saw in Germany convinced me that this was the right course," he wrote. "The Germans are only too willing to laugh off the 'spot of bother' they have been causing the rest of us these past few years. Only by an aloof and stern attitude can we hope to convince them that they did anything wrong."

▪ ▪ ▪

Carroll would never have the chance to put his theory into practice. Four months after he and Davis returned to Washington D.C., on August 31, 1945, President Harry Truman disbanded OWI. For his part, Carroll, while recognizing the organization's "outstanding contribution to victory," acknowledged that propaganda had been a "weapon of definite but limited utility." But he also saw its vital role beyond merely achieving military objectives. The power to persuade, as he called it, would be crucial in the post-war world, and especially in ensuring that Western Europe would remain free from Soviet control. He lamented the fact that the United States still failed to see the need for a strong information effort to counter the propaganda being issued by the Soviet Union, propaganda that had reduced America's hard-won standing as proponents of freedom and self-determination worldwide.

Carroll summed up his attitude toward the use of propaganda during the war, "We had made a point of frankly reporting military reverses and Allied casualties because this helped to win the confidence of our audience." For him it wasn't about telling the truth or not telling the truth. "What we did hold back was mainly news of political dissension, ... such as the Giraud, de Gaulle difficulties and the disputes between the Western powers and the Soviet Union over Poland and other European countries." He would later write that there was a "fallacy" in the widespread belief that the propagandist's choice is between truth and falsehood. If it were as simple as that, his course would be easily determined. "Our real difficulties," he would write, "came over a choice between giving the news and withholding it, between the practices of journalism and the dictates of war, between the urge to inform and the passion to save lives, between common honesty and plain humanity."

In the end, President Harry Truman as well as many historians acknowledged that the efforts of OWI, Carroll and the other propagandists had played a valuable part in helping to win the war. Carroll himself would later acknowledge that shifting from defensive messaging (i.e., in response to Goebbels' claims) to offensive messaging (i.e., themes of Allied dominance and Nazi defeat) had shifted the balance of the "information war" toward the Allies. More important was the synchronization of propaganda messaging with military intelligence and strategy. This proved to be effective. What had at first seemed a slick Nazi propaganda machine, at least before it was properly challenged, in the end faltered. Its messaging became out of sync with realities on the ground, especially after the disaster at Stalingrad. The result was predictable—when messaging is not backed up by the truth, Carroll believed, in the end it inevitably fails. For Carroll, propaganda was never about divorcing reality from the truth. Perhaps this was why as a journalist he was so willing to join the war effort.

As the war came to an end, he would continue to believe that learning to enter into the minds and emotions of former enemies would be the way to ensure lasting peace. "Despite all the emphasis on the behavioral sciences," he wrote, "we remain insensitive to the effects of our actions and words on the pride, the hopes and the nervous systems of other peoples." The way to do this, he felt, was to accompany actions with words, … "policies, actions and words must always be part of the broad effort at persuasion—persuasion that binds the nations to us by ties of confidence and faith."

Yet he had also learned a lesson about trusting the Russians. In the summer of 1945, just following the war and while still at OWI, he wrote a directive saying that the Americans had been loyal allies during the war, but the Russians had not reciprocated. The time had come, he believed, for the United States to take a harder look at the Soviet Union. Although Truman ignored the directive, it would become one of the first official documents of the Cold War.

▪ ▪ ▪

After six years of immersion in the conflict, first covering war-torn London and Russia and then in deep involvement in the Allied war effort, Carroll was exhausted. So much so that in late 1944 he had been forced to take time off and travel to Florida to recover from what most likely was exhaustion.

While he was not ready to jump back into full time work—
and was without a job regardless—he still felt compelled to
capture his experience and thoughts about the war years. Settling
into their home in Chevy Chase, he soon began working on what
would become *Persuade or Perish,* a 400-page, in-depth look at the
use of propaganda and psychological warfare during the war.

Persuade or Perish, again finished with lightning speed in early
1947, traced in detail the use of psychological warfare, from the
bungling African campaign and the Darlan affair in 1942 through
to the invasion of Germany and the "Götterdämmerung" of
Goebbels. It dealt with the initial development of propaganda
in Europe at the start of the war, when Carroll was based in
London, through to the planning of the assault on the Continent
and the Allied advance across Europe to the final defeat of
Germany. Because of the trust he had gained from members
of the Joint Chiefs of Staff and high-level officials in the State
Department, Carroll had access to—and had remembered—
detailed information about Allied propaganda efforts. And as
in all his writing, the book would point out both the effort's
successes and its failures.

Propaganda was still a new term, and Carroll's account
would become among the first to acknowledge its effects, as
well as to define what the United States needed to do post-war
to ensure that the ideals the Allies had fought for were once
again implanted throughout Europe. The new struggle, he wrote,
would go "by the name of political warfare, psychological warfare, or propaganda warfare." In essence it would create a new
"cold war" between the East and the West.

In a heartbreaking moment in late 1947, Carroll had sent
the completed manuscript to Gil Winant for review before it
was published, only to have it returned following his old friend's
suicide in November of that year. Struggling with depression
and deeply in debt, Winant had shot himself in the head at his
New Hampshire home on the day after his book, *Letter from*

Grosvenor Square, was published. He was, according to Lynne Olson in *Citizens of London,* "an exhausted, sick man." Recalling what Winant had done for them in Geneva and London, Carroll and Peggy were devastated. Distraught, Carroll locked himself away to write a deeply personal remembrance of Winant, which he never published:

> ... *this modest and self-effacing American was perhaps the best Ambassador this country ever sent to England. If you went among the miners of Wales, they would tell you, "Your man Winant, he's all right." And if you talked to the textile workers of Lancashire or the shipyard workers along the Clyde, they would say, "We know Winant—he'll never let us down." No one could ever tell you how he did it and you had to fall back on Herbert Agar's saying about "that strange process of osmosis by which the British people learn that there's a good man around."*
>
> *Gil Winant was too good an observer and too sensitive to the affections of his fellow men not to be aware of this feeling and to be warmed and cheered by it. But that was not what he was after. He wanted the people of Britain to know the American people as he knew them. He wanted them to know the shrewd, kindly farmers around Concord, New Hampshire, where he had spent three terms as Governor. He wanted them to know the open-hearted men and women of the ranches of the southwest where he had been an oil prospector. He wanted them to know the workers of the steel and textile mills, the coal mines, the railroads and shipyards, to whose welfare he had dedicated a great part of his life.*

When Carroll's *Persuade or Perish* was finally published in 1948, it met with good reviews. The book was cited as "an altogether excellent account by a scholarly, analytic journalist" who had not only led propaganda efforts during the war but had spent eleven years as a correspondent covering Europe. *Kirkus Reviews* also pointed to the book's conclusions, which stressed the pressing necessity of creating "a fourth arm to our [military] services with the shadow of Russian expansion," which would consist of a "strategy of persuasion" to meet the growing Soviet threat. "A lively and exciting book," the review continued. "A timely book for today, as well as a dramatic account of this particular branch of warfare as it operated through the war years."

Persuade or Perish also made the case that the war was not a purely military operation—something that could be "won" and that would be the end of it. Carroll believed that, like all wars, it was a political operation, a method for imposing and maintaining policy. But too often policy had been set aside until the military phase ended, with the result that faith in the United States' declared aims received a setback from which it had not recovered. With each sacrifice of policy to the immediate needs of battle the notion that the war was "about" something became more outmoded. And the deep respect which America had first inspired became outmoded also. "Public opinion," wrote Carroll, "is a reality that must be faced just as squarely as any other." It was a reality that Carroll felt the United States had chosen to neglect.

The book drew the attention of higher ups in Washington, including Secretary of State George Marshall, Assistant Secretary of State Dean Acheson, and Frank Wisner, a former OSS operative and Russia expert, who had been recruited by Acheson to join the State Department. In June 1948, Marshall had delivered his famous Marshall Plan speech at Harvard University, in which he outlined the need for an economic aid plan to help the devastated nations of Europe and their citizens to recover from the ravages of World War II. When the plan was finally approved by Congress one year later, Averell Harriman, who Carroll had known in London during the war and who had been appointed to co-direct implementation of the Marshall Plan, called on Carroll to head up its communication strategy in Europe. Carroll, citing that he wanted to "get to know the

United States better," after fourteen years in Europe, declined the offer. His decision had also been influenced by the hazardous birth of his and Peggy's third child, a girl named Rosamond, or "Posie," born December 6, 1947, and named after their old friend from Geneva days, Rosamond Tirana. The birth had been difficult for Peggy, and in fact she had almost died due to blood poisoning. At the last minute, Carroll called his secretary to get the word out to his friends to donate blood. The first to arrive was Rosamond, hence the name Posie was given to the new baby. The incident left him shaken, and perhaps less willing to be away from home or to ask Peggy to move with the now three children once again across the Atlantic.

He turned instead to writing an article for *Life* magazine that caused some stir among those working with Truman in devising a post-war strategy in dealing with the Soviet Union, when it was published in 1949. The article, based on intelligence he had gathered from former members of the German High Command, made the argument that Hitler could have won a quick victory in Russia shortly after his invasion of the country if he had been open to the help offered by millions of Soviet soldiers and civilians in what is now Ukraine, who were eager to overthrow Stalin and the Soviet system and ready to join the German forces when they first invaded in the summer of 1941. According to Carroll's reporting, German generals were eager to use these volunteers, first as service troops, then in German combat units, and, toward the end of the war, in units of their own as large as divisions. Their efforts, however, were thwarted by Hitler, who ordered Soviet civilians and soldiers to be shipped off in cattle cars to become slave laborers in Germany and prisoners of war. Many thousands were penned up to starve or die of disease. Hitler's determination to permit nothing but misery to be offered to the Soviet peoples also frustrated the German generals' promising efforts to use an authentic Soviet war hero, Lieutenant General Andrei Vlasov, as a rallying point for a liberation movement against Stalin.

"It Takes a Russian to Beat a Russian," contained the first report of this Russian rebellion against Stalin. Until then little had been written about the vast extent of anti-Stalinist dissidence in Russia. Nothing had been known of it when Carroll was a correspondent in Moscow in the fall of 1941. All that had been reported was that the Red Army was being pushed back at an appalling rate and that the fronts were collapsing in Ukraine and the Kursk region.

Carroll later admitted that, while historically accurate, the article was propagandistic in tone. The Cold War was just beginning, and the U.S. military was ready to discredit Stalin as much as possible. Many hardliners agreed with Carroll's argument that the military should use psychological warfare and propaganda to explore fissures in Soviet society, including offering support to its minority populations. The article was very well received, and continued to burnish Carroll's reputation as both a Soviet specialist and a leading thinker on psychological warfare. Beginning in 1948, he had been asked to speak on the topic at numerous institutes, including the National War College, where *Persuade or Perish* had become required reading, and the Foreign Service Institute.

By this time, however, Carroll had been out of steady employment for three years—and he needed a job. Soon after his book was published, his friend Frank Wisner, then deputy director of the CIA, told him about a prominent North Carolinian, Gordon Gray, who had just been appointed secretary of the army and who also owned two papers in North Carolina, the *Winston-Salem Journal* and its sister paper, the afternoon *Sentinel*. Gray was looking for an executive editor for the *Journal*. Wisner introduced Carroll to Gray and the two hit if off immediately. "He is witty, learned and urbane and, as far as I have seen, adjusts well to any situation," Gray said of Carroll at the time, "I think his capacity for good writing is not excelled by anyone." Gray offered Carroll the job, and he and Peggy visited Winston-Salem. Both thought it would be a good place to raise their children, so Carroll accepted the position.

The offer would propel Carroll down a new path, one that would lead him out of the bureaucracy he found so frustrating and back to his true passion—journalism.

SECTION IV

BACK TO THE NEWSROOM

CHAPTER 12

SONG OF THE SOUTH

"…newspapering is less a means to earn a living than way of life in itself, a silent brotherhood sharing a secret understanding."
                              —Paxton Davis, author

G ordon Gray, the owner of the *Winston-Salem Journal* and *Sentinel*, was an exceptional man—born into privilege but raised to believe that he had to earn his own way in the world. To Gray, public service was everything, and he would strive to ensure the community in which he had been raised—Winston-Salem, North Carolina—would prosper.

Gray was the second son of Bowman Gray Sr., who in 1949 was the president of the R.J. Reynolds Tobacco Company, and the first person outside of the Reynolds family to hold that position. At the time, Reynolds Tobacco was among the largest companies in the country, and its influence in the Winston-Salem community was profound. Bowman Gray Sr. was known for having worked his way up through the ranks, and his commitment to hard work and self-discipline was legendary. His son Gordon had been forced to learn those same lessons well. At age 10, he had been put to work in the lowliest job in the tobacco factory, pushing hogsheads of tobacco across the floor. In later summers, he would advance to machine operator, but he still was expected to arrive at 7:20 a.m. each day and, like everyone else, to work the normal 55 hours per week.

Gordon's older brother, Bowman Gray Jr., would take over the helm of R.J. Reynolds, but Gordon would go on to an impressive career outside of the tobacco company. At 18 he left Winston-Salem to study at the University of North Carolina and later at Yale Law School, where he would graduate at the top of his class. At the outbreak of World War II, when he was 36 years old, he waited in line with the other men at the local Army recruiting office to sign up as a buck private in the Army, boarding a bus with the other recruits for Fort Bragg. Within seven years, he had soared through the ranks to become Secretary of the Army, rising first as a captain serving in Europe under General Omar Bradley, and then as Assistant Secretary of the Army, appointed by President Truman. He would then quickly move up to Secretary—the first former buck private to ever do so—and to command more than 658,000 men and a budget of $1 billion.

Gray's advance was partly due to his acknowledged brilliance—his score on the IQ test given to all recruits who enter the Army was the highest anyone at Fort Bragg had ever seen. It was also due to his acknowledged hard work and excellent judgment, according to those who knew him. He was an "idea" man who knew a great deal could be accomplished if he didn't care who got the public credit.

In 1937, when he was 28 years old and working for a local law firm in Winston-Salem, Gray had purchased the *Winston-Salem Journal* and the *Sentinel*. His only previous experience at publishing had consisted of a year as editor of the *Fir Tree*, the Woodberry Forest yearbook, business manager of *Carolina Magazine* at Chapel Hill, and editor of the *Yale Law Review*. But the city's conservative elite pushed him to make the purchase, believing they could control the paper's coverage through him. Gray proved the city leaders wrong. Although he knew little about newspaper publishing, he applied his usual work ethic to the running of the paper, and was wise enough to rely on others who knew more about the business than he did. Within a year of its purchase, the paper had doubled in size, and its staff more than tripled. Gray also began, for the first time, to insist on coverage of the Black community, whose leaders saw this as a breakthrough in race relations. The small-town *Journal* and *Sentinel* had become a regional operation, with a reach like that of a major metropolitan daily. Both papers served an area that stretched northwest into Virginia.

Gray had continued to support the papers throughout his duties in the war and shortly thereafter. By 1949, both papers were still thriving, but with the explosive growth in the city, Gray believed more substantial coverage was required. Gray felt Carroll would bring stature to the *Journal* and the *Sentinel*. And for Carroll, it meant steady employment, a boss who liked and respected him, and a great deal of independence, including time off to continue his consulting in Washington. Fresh from the dark intrigues of post-war Washington, Carroll looked forward to the environment of a medium-size town newsroom, which reminded him of his UP days.

It also meant more time for his growing brood of children. Having survived the war, both he and Peggy were ready for a quieter time. As one old friend recalled, "They had been through a lot." Both, in fact, would always say they hated the fireworks on the Fourth of July since they reminded them of the bombings during the Blitz. Peggy also remembered fondly her sojourns in the South as a teenager, and realized that in Winston-Salem they might have an opportunity to make a difference in an increasingly prosperous community on the verge of social change following the war.

At the time, however, it must have seemed a huge change for such a cosmopolitan couple. Peggy recalled her first dinner party where she thought it "best to come right out and confess my Yankee antecedents." Both Carroll and Peggy would eventually grow very fond of the slower life in Winston-Salem; the friendships they would develop there would have a profound effect on them both for the rest of their lives.

■ ■ ■

Winston-Salem, North Carolina, it was often said, had "the sweet smell of tobacco" wafting throughout its tree-lined streets. By the late 1940s, it produced more tobacco products than any other city on earth and more men's knit underwear (from the Hanes Mills) than any other place in the country. Home of the world's largest tobacco industry, the R.J. Reynolds Tobacco Company, the city had been created in 1913 from two towns— Winston, founded in 1851 and named for Revolutionary War hero Major Joseph Winston, and Salem, founded by Moravian colonists as far back as 1766. Hence, it was the city that lent its name to the famous Winston and Salem cigarette brands, not the other way around.

By 1949, when the Carrolls arrived, it was among the largest cities in North Carolina, with a population of about 85,000 residents. The town had undergone a boom in the late 1800s and through the 1920s due to the explosion of the tobacco industry. But the Depression and war years had left it suffering. Buildings and roads had deteriorated, and slums festered, especially in Black neighborhoods. The city's hospital was antiquated, its school system crowded, and its library a disgrace.

The post-war years brought some renewed prosperity, and the city was beginning to remake itself. It had embarked on the construction of a major expressway that would run around the downtown area, as well as a series of parkways to relieve traffic congestion. A new medical school and modern hospitals were making it a leader in health care. The City County Planning Board in 1948 drew up a master plan that included redeveloping the inner city, left blighted as residents increasingly moved to the suburbs. That year, the city had established an Arts Council to promote and coordinate activities in the visual and performing arts, the first of its kind in the country. Two years later, it would host Wake Forest College's move from the town of Wake Forest, near Raleigh, to the western outskirts of Winston-Salem, a change facilitated by a $10.7 million gift from the Z. Smith Reynolds Foundation toward the college's endowment and a grant of 320 acres, formerly part of the Reynolds family estate, to house it.

In addition to the tobacco industry, the Hanes Knitting Company, Hanes Hosiery Mills, Western Electric, Wachovia Bank and Trust Company, Krispy Kreme Doughnuts, and Piedmont Airlines all made their home in the city. In 1940, three companies—R.J. Reynolds, Hanes Hosiery, and P.H. Hanes Knitting—had employed 60 percent of the city's workers. By 1949, the addition of new companies diversified and expanded the job pool. People from outside the region had begun to flock to Winston-Salem, shattering the town's previous provincialism. New people brought new ideas, and the city was evolving.

But it still had a way to go to pry itself from the control of the business elite, led by the heads of Reynolds Tobacco, Hanes Mills, and Wachovia Bank. It was also deeply divided, not just economically between the business elite and low-income workers, but also by race. Segregation reigned. Although African American and white employees worked together in the city's factories, Blacks went home to their own separate neighborhoods, schools, and churches. They were denied access to most restaurants, movie theatres, and museums and discouraged from shopping in the tonier department stores. By 1949, roughly 35 percent of the city's population was African American, a figure that had not changed over the past 30 years, yet African Americans had little clout in the city's institutions.

But this, too, was changing. A new progressive mayor, Marshall Kurfees, was elected in 1949 against opposition from the city's business elite, and he pledged to not only clean up the slums but to further integrate the city government. He began to appoint African Americans to the fire department and city boards, and to raise federal money and private donations to clear the city's slums. The city also boasted the first African American teacher's college—Winston-Salem Teachers College, which was the first Black institution in the nation to grant degrees for teaching in elementary schools. The new prosperity had also begun to filter through to the Black workers, who increasingly sought jobs outside of the factories, opening cafes, barbershops, and funeral homes, among other small businesses.

■ ■ ■

The Carrolls happily settled into the southern town in the summer of 1949. By this time, Margaret, the oldest, was nine; John was seven; and Posie was just under two. Three years later, on July 4, 1952, a fourth child, a daughter named Patricia was born. The children attended the public schools, which were then still segregated, and ventured out into the country to explore the tobacco farms where Margaret remembered they were given a lesson in how to cure tobacco by representatives of the Reynolds company. Carroll would regularly take Margaret and Johnny to the minor league baseball games at the newly built Bowman Gray Stadium. Peggy, who had always loved the outdoors, reveled in their nearness to the mountains and the lush greenness of their new home and garden. "It is almost too pretty to come in and write a letter," she would write to her mother. "I never saw such a long fall. The trees are all still wonderful colors. They are the leafiest trees I have ever seen." She continued to expand upon her talents as a hostess and to pull together a good meal for guests.

Highly extroverted and always willing to accept a social invitation, her job, according to her daughters, was to be the eyes and ears for Carroll in the community. She would more than accomplish that task, joining a wide array of women's organizations, from the Parent Teachers Association to the YWCA. And as they had hoped, Winston-Salem proved to be an excellent place to raise their children.

For the cosmopolitan Peggy, it was a new world. With her usual powers of observation, she found the atmosphere of a relatively small southern town intriguing, "I find living here very pleasant indeed but I have a constant feeling of having dropped back a couple of generations," she wrote her mother that summer. "In some ways this society must be like that in which Grandma Sawyer grew up. Its roots are very recently rural and so incredibly strongly rooted in the church. The people are as nice as could be, and look you in the eye with innocent friend-liness and cheerfulness. They never seem to put on a false front or jockey for position, or even cut each other down. It makes me feel that all the people I knew in other places must have been awfully sly, scheming old twerps.... They are a wonderful public to write a newspaper for."

▪ ▪ ▪

By the time Carroll assumed executive editorship, the *Winston-Salem Journal* and the *Sentinel* had reached a circulation of significantly more than 35,000 and begun to attract national attention Carroll was executive editor of the morning *Journal,* which had a sister paper the afternoon *Twin City Sentinel;* on Sundays, the two papers combined to become the *Journal* and *Sentinel.* The *Journal,* whose editorial staff was separate from the *Sentinel*'s, in particular, began to attract new hires, often drawn from all parts of the country, who had no allegiances or family ties to the monied men in Winston-Salem's power structure.

The paper's reporters and city leaders would often agree on coverage of topics, but more often than not, the two sides had clashed. As a result, several previous editors had been sent packing. Carroll knew he had to walk a rather fine line with the city's leaders but was determined to show the paper's editorial independence. His relationship with Gray often helped smooth the way when contentious issues arose.

Carroll had only been in his job for a few weeks when this independence was tested. He backed a young, upstart journalist—Paxton Davis, who was then on his first job out of Johns Hopkins University—in uncovering the misuse of funds, poorly trained staff, and downright horrible conditions at the city hospital. Nurses, after the hospital administration had ignored their complaints, had called Davis to report on a doctor who performed surgeries while drunk and carelessly prescribed drugs to patients. The county commissioners had gotten wind of the story and fired the nurses. The commissioners then dispatched Jim Hanes, the chairman of the county commissioners and scion of the Hanes Mills family, to Carroll's office in an attempt to kill the story. Carroll "explained [to Hanes] that there was no way he was going to suppress it," according to accounts.

Thus began a rather long and public fight between Carroll and the city's commissioners, with Carroll continuing to support his reporters' accounts. "These nurses (who left the hospital) supported their charges with sworn affidavits," Carroll recalled. "They sacrificed their jobs, and they put their careers in jeopardy. People do not usually do that kind of thing unless they believe strongly in the truth of what they say. Their voices needed to be heard." The commissioners, angered at the publishing of the story, didn't hold back in their criticism of Carroll and the paper. They issued a statement saying the "charges so flagrantly and recklessly published and encouraged by the local newspapers were without foundation," and claimed that Carroll and the *Journal* had abused the "freedom of the press guaranteed by both the federal and state constitutions."

Carroll not only continued to have his reporters investigate the story, he wrote a reply on the paper's editorial page in which he cited the number of calls the paper had received from people congratulating it for taking a stand. "The staff," remembered Carroll, "was just happy as hell and glad to have a manager who stood up for them." Eventually the *Journal*'s continued coverage led to the discovery that the doctor involved had been practicing medicine without a license, and that no one had bothered to check his credentials. Shortly following this discovery, the hospital was closed. Carroll and his reporters had been right all along; their coverage and the closing of the hospital were written about in papers across the state.

The young reporter Davis would never forget the backing he had received from Carroll in writing about the incident. "Most editors would have taken it away outright," he remembered. Instead, Carroll partnered Davis with a more seasoned reporter so both could follow through on the story. Davis had loved "every overwrought and possibly overblown minute" of the coverage, he recalled, displaying the attitude of many of the reporters on staff.

The hospital incident gave the staff a good idea of who their new executive editor would be. Carroll wouldn't flinch from covering tough issues. He was "calm, measured, precise," Davis wrote in his memoir, *A Boy No More*, "and his experience and good sense gave the *Journal* both perspective and depth." If they met Carroll's high standards, reporters sensed they could freely investigate their stories and would be backed up in reporting them. They also knew Carroll's experience made him in some ways overqualified for the job. "After I sized him up," wrote the *Journal*'s popular columnist Roy Thompson, "I wondered what he was doing here. I still wonder." Nonetheless, they felt lucky to have someone of his caliber at the helm.

For Carroll, it was a return to the rollicking good fun of daily reporting. Davis would later describe the sights and sounds of the newsroom:

> *The stairs creaked, the building was rank with the smell of printer's ink, and the walls shook as the presses in the basement launched the final edition of the afternoon paper....*
>
> *After supper the newsroom would come alive with a steady stream of people and the clang of typewriters and ringing telephones. The newsroom would grow busier and louder as the ten o'clock deadline for the first edition neared. Phones rang incessantly and pneumatic tubes whooshed off or thunked back down from the composing room. Chaos subsided after the first edition was safely put to bed, and the staff relaxed for the first time since supper. They bought soft drinks from a vendor who came through the newsroom each evening with zinc pails of cold sodas. Reporters and editors settled back with their Cokes and read the first edition, warm and slightly moist from the press, for typographical errors.*

The staff was a motley crew of eccentric reporters: Managing Editor J. Worth Bacon was "a big, blond man who would invariably come in with the second-highest hand in poker games and was prone to fits of anxiety over whether the paper would come out in time to make the midnight train that took it to the *Journal*'s northwest territories." Bill Woestendiek was a big bear of a man from upstate New York and former editor of the *Daily Tar Heel*, who covered the courts with his "broad, naïve face" that won the confidence of his sources. Hoke Norris, the senior reporter at 38, covered the coveted city hall beat and was the "raw-boned and tow-headed son of a Baptist minister—but fiercely agnostic and a two-fisted connoisseur of spirits." Jim Rush, a transplant from New England, "ran the copy desk with a ferocious demand for daily perfection, an eye for the subtleties of English grammar, and the skills to deliver the news clearly and effectively."

The *Journal* also hired Mary Garber, one of the first women journalists in the country to cover sports. In a career that lasted seven decades, she would receive over 40 writing awards and numerous honors. And in 1949, Gordon Gray had added an African American journalist to the staff. A. Alexander Morisey was the first Black reporter in the South to work in a formerly all-white newsroom. A former teacher at Bennett College in Greensboro, North Carolina, his primary job was to prepare the Sunday "Negro Page," but his stories about Blacks in the city started appearing with other news throughout the newspaper. Keeping with the racial conventions of the time in North Carolina, however, Gray had a separate restroom built for Morisey adjacent to the existing men's facility in the newsroom, something Morisey hated but learned to live with.

■ ■ ■

The *Journal* was also a good place to advance a journalism career. Tom Wicker, who joined the *Journal* staff in 1951, later became the paper's Washington correspondent and chief of the Washington Bureau of the *New York Times*. His well-known column, "In the Nation," would run in the *Times* for 25 years. While at the *Journal*, he would be continually working on a novel when he wasn't writing or editing stories, and his subsequent polished writing style contributed greatly to the paper's stature. The columnist Roy Thompson, who was good enough to write for any newspaper in the country, would stay at the *Journal* for 38 years. His offbeat features and one-sentence paragraph style established him early as a star. His colleague Chester Davis, a native of Bozeman, Montana, won numerous awards for his features and investigative reporting. By the mid-1950s, he had won more writing awards than any other reporter in the state, including a National Headliner Award for his coverage of conservation issues.

Two women reporters, both hired by Carroll at a time when newsrooms were dominated by men, also went on to illustrious careers. Barbara "Bonnie" Angelo (later Levy) left the *Journal* to work for the New York City area daily, *Newsday*. She became a Washington reporter for *Time* magazine and later its London bureau chief. Marjorie Hunter, who began at the *Journal* as women's editor, went to work for the Washington bureau of the *New York Times* where she covered Capitol Hill and the White House for more than 30 years.

Ronald McKie, a journalist from Australia, spent the summer of 1952 visiting the *Journal,* and he immediately noticed that the newsroom was different from others he had seen. "I have never worked in a friendlier, happier office," he wrote. "There is an atmosphere of individualism and tolerance and extremely intelligent direction and control." He went on to note that employees felt appreciated and part of an organization that was interested in them not merely as producers but as human beings. As Barbara Levy would recall, the *Journal* was "a place of rollicking fun and unmatched collegiality, of unquenched enthusiasm and fierce pride in work."

The paper was also known for its carefully edited and stylishly written copy. Carroll placed a premium on precision, in words as well as content. Reporters' worst fear was seeing a story they had written or edited displayed on the newsroom bulletin board, accompanied by one of Carroll's blue slips pointing to some grammatical error. No one "died suddenly" in the pages of the *Journal.* That would be redundant. Neither did anyone do anything at "six o'clock on Tuesday afternoon." It was "6 p.m. Tuesday." Reporters kept their personalities out of stories, and editors worked to eradicate any trace of opinion or bias. Bylines were given out sparingly, based on merit.

As Tom Wicker would later recall, "We were proud of the *Winston-Salem Journal* because of its standards, and we were proud of ourselves because we met those standards, night after night." When he worked there, he thought "... the *Journal*, was the most widely admired paper in North Carolina, at least among journalists. The basic reason was that it reflected the character of its community, even in its limitations as well as in its strengths."

Perhaps Paxton Davis summed it up best when he wrote in *A Boy No More*, "Journalism can be a serious occupation, and some of the older hands must have realized it; but for me and the *Journal* companions of my generation it was simply the best fun on earth."

■ ■ ■

And fun aside, there was also much to report in Winston-Salem. The town was wealthy, strongly oriented to business, and its leading families had put down solid cultural and economic roots there. Community spirit was very high, according to Wicker; the town had an active arts center, hosted many lectures and music events, and boasted a good symphony orchestra. Fund-raising for the United Fund was always high, and if the public did not come through, the major businesses made up the difference.

On the other hand, Winston-Salem was not a city to question itself too deeply, and the *Journal* sometimes reflected that quality, too. The names of leading citizens and companies could be left out of disagreeable stories, and there was always a tension between whether or not to turn over "local rocks to see what might be beneath," according to Wicker. One of those issues was the recognition that the city really did have slums—mostly Black neighborhoods where sewage bubbled to the surface and rental houses owned by politicians and city officials had condemnation notices tacked to the doors. In 1951, the city's Redevelopment Commission used federal money and private donations to build low-cost housing and provide space for small businesses to relocate downtown. The *Journal* covered the sometimes-negative effects of the tearing down and building of new roads that threatened Black neighborhoods and historical landmarks, but it no doubt could have done more. Similarly, as Wicker pointed out, during this time, it reported little on the cigarette-cancer connection, coverage of which had barely begun. But what it did do was provide solid coverage of most community affairs, excellent feature writing and photography, and a high degree of literacy and accuracy.

It also delivered—especially in contrast to regional newspapers of today—an amazing amount of in-depth national and international coverage. In truth, it read more like a national publication than a regional one. Carroll was largely responsible for this level and quality of international reporting, and would even write his own stories. One such story was written on October 17, 1951, the day after President Truman—in a major international event—came to Winston-Salem to officially break ground for the new campus of Wake Forest University.[1] While there, he gave a major foreign policy address urging the Soviet Union to disarm, to which Carroll gave front-page coverage in the *Journal*. Writing under the byline of "staff reporter," Carroll ran his story under the headline "President Offers Bid for Peace: Speech is Major

---

1.   Truman's trip was made at the urging of Gordon Gray, who had played a key role in the establishment of Wake Forest University. The city's leaders had recognized that the one thing the town needed was a first-rate college, so in 1946, the Z. Smith Reynolds Foundation offered Wake Forest College, located near Raleigh, North Carolina, a $10.7 million endowment if it would move to Winston-Salem. The Charles and Mary Babcock Foundation (heirs to the Reynolds fortune) contributed a 320-acre tract on the outskirts of the city. The North Carolina Baptist State Convention, which controlled operation of Wake Forest, gave its consent to the move, provided the college retain its name and remain under the control of the convention. Today the university, since separated from the Baptist Convention, has grown to be one of the top private universities in the country.

Policy Statement." It was, according to Carroll, a statement that would be studied in every capital of the world. "It is important to remember as our defense program begins to turn out more and more weapons and our alliances for defense begin to take effect, that our basic objective—our only objective—is peace," said Truman. "Peace for the world." Carroll then wrote:

> *All in all, the speech was the most forceful justification which any administration spokesman has put forward for the American and allied defense programs.*
>
> *The President seems to be speaking first of all to the many Americans who have wondered why the nation is spending so much on weapons of destruction and whether this means war with the Soviets.*
>
> *He was speaking, secondly, to the many troubled people outside the U.S.—America's allies from London to Manila, from Athens to Tokyo, who have been told by the Communists that America is trying to push them into war against Russia. To these people he said: "The rulers of the Kremlin can plunge the world into carnage if they desire to do so. But that is something this country will never do.*

As always, Carroll was presenting the news, but it also reflected his world view, one that went beyond just his consideration for the peoples in his hometown or even of the United States. That compassion extended to what at the time was a growing issue within his own country, and particularly in the South—desegregation.

■ ■ ■

African Americans had lived in the Winston-Salem area as early as the late 1700s, first as slaves and later, in the late 1800s and early 1900s, as workers in the surrounding tobacco farms and their cigarette-producing factories. By the 1930s many of them worked for the R.J. Reynolds tobacco company. In 1944, a union, Local 22, made up mostly of Black workers, was established at the company, and labor unrest over workers' hourly wages began to build. The company accused the union, as did *Journal* publisher Gordon Gray, of being infiltrated by Communists, a charge that was never proven. In 1947, the union went on strike, and about 6,000 employees—the great majority of them Black—took to the picket lines. The strike was unusually orderly, but several days after it had begun, the *Journal* ran a story, "Communist-Union Collusion is Exposed in City," on the front page, alleging that members of the union were Communists. But it failed to back the story up with any proof. Both the editor at the time, Leon Dure, and Gray were ardent anti-Communists and had pushed forward with the paper's coverage of the issue. The result was the launch of a grand jury investigation into the union, as well as the hiring of a lawyer to prosecute Communist party members in the city.

The strike, which lasted 38 days, ended when Reynolds management met some of the union's demands. Discredited and harassed—and no doubt further weakened by the newspaper's coverage—the union lost its power and was decertified in 1951. But it had served an important purpose. It had unified Blacks in the city for the first time and driven the number of Black voters on the rolls substantially higher. Those voters placed the first African American alderman, Kenneth R. Williams, on the city's board in November 1947.

This was the racial backdrop when Carroll arrived in Winston-Salem in 1949; and it also made clear that Gordon Gray, if and when he desired, might not shy away from involvement in the paper's coverage. Carroll had made few if any public statements about his stance on segregation before he arrived in Winston-Salem, but he had written about its dangers vehemently in *Persuade or Perish*, indicating the moral harm it caused not only the country itself but its international reputation as well. "By continuing to discriminate against some of our citizens on racial or religious reasons," he wrote, "we convince hundreds and millions of friends abroad that we *do not stand for equality and justice of which we make so much*."

Nonetheless, on arriving in Winston-Salem, he decided it best to maintain a somewhat neutral public profile on the issue. He launched instead a new feature for the paper, which consisted of a weekly forum on a current topic, designed to elicit the public's views. Among the first issues addressed was anti-Jim Crow legislation. The responses indicated that while Blacks felt some advances had been made in bringing about greater equality among the races, these advances were not as significant as many whites liked to believe.

Peggy noted this, in a letter to her mother, in which she outlined her experience with the issue "…Whites think the situation is generally satisfactory or nearly so, and the Negroes naturally don't. The most liberal woman I've talked to here, and who has done a great deal to break down the barriers—even *she* quotes the director of the Negro YMCA as saying that she prefers it in the South because here the white people hate Negroes as a whole but love individual Negroes, whereas in the North they profess to like the race but don't like the individual members of it. I can't tell you how many times versions of this attitude have been reported to me. I can't myself believe that any modern Negro would trade his right to go to law school, for instance, for the benevolent patronizing love of a white woman."

Many in the business community on the whole saw the issue of desegregation as a fact that couldn't be ignored and hence were supportive of the new Mayor Kurfees's progressive efforts. With backing from the paper, Kurfees would eventually succeed in "desegregating public libraries, city buses, ministers' conferences, the public golf course, remove signs indicating separate restrooms and drinking fountains in public buildings, abandon separate seating arrangements in Reynolds Auditorium, the Coliseum, the baseball park and community center; employ of some African Americans as mail carriers, police officers and members of the fire department." Not all of this would be accomplished during Carroll's tenure as executive editor of the paper, but steady progress was made.

When the Supreme Court issued its decision in *Brown v. Board of Education* in May 1954 making the segregation of schools illegal, the paper—with backing from Carroll and his editorial page editor, A. Reed Sarratt—strongly supported the decision, saying that desegregation had been long overdue. The paper urged compliance with the new law, stating that local solutions should be found to avoid further enforcement from the national government.

Carroll remembered a speech Sarratt gave to the Rotary Club following the decision, in which he argued that there was no need to fear sudden and complete integration, and how the men attending had "fidgeted in their chairs." They were against Sarratt from that moment onward, Carroll recalled. But Sarratt never wavered in his support for desegregation. "He wasn't sticking his finger in anybody's eye, but he was going to stand up for what was right," said Carroll. Carroll would leave the paper one year later, but Sarratt would continue his outspoken support through the paper's editorials. Carroll would revisit racial tensions eight years later when he returned as editor and publisher of the *Journal* and *Sentinel*.

■ ■ ■

While Carroll enjoyed the atmosphere in the newsroom and the interactions with his smart and iconoclastic group of reporters, he was never able to quite take his foot out of Washington. While serving as executive editor of the paper, he still managed—with Gordon Gray's blessing—to serve as a consultant to both the State and Defense Departments, as well as the Voice of America, on psychological warfare. He also gave numerous talks on foreign policy across the state, developing a reputation for being well-informed on issues of national security.

In July 1950, he wrote "an appeal for peace" published in the *Journal* and republished across papers in North Carolina. The appeal was in support of the Stockholm Peace Petition, which had been launched by the World Peace Council in March 1950 to promote nuclear disarmament and to prevent nuclear war. "The war in Korea is a danger to the peace of all people," the appeal read. "We believe that the war can be stopped and that peace can be saved if the North Korean forces will obey the United Nations and go back to the starting point. We invite all friends of peace to sign this document." Again, the appeal was picked up across papers in North Carolina, further establishing both Carroll and the *Journal* as leaders in reporting on international affairs, as well as in favor of limiting military action abroad. It also demonstrated that Carroll was not afraid to express opinions that might be in opposition to Gordon Gray's strong anti-Communist beliefs. This stance was strengthened when Carroll wrote several editorials questioning the United States' involvement in the Korean War.

In fact Carroll, who had continued to impress Gray, was called on by him during this time to participate in what would become for Carroll a significant indoctrination in the byzantine nature of the Washington bureaucracy. Gray was then serving as the Chancellor at the University of North Carolina, but had continued to stay involved in intelligence work in Washington, D.C. In 1951, he was asked by President Truman to head up the newly formed Psychological Strategy Board, which was tasked with forming, coordinating, and planning psychological operations with foreign entities. The Board was set up to produce propaganda that would win the opinion of people around the world and prevent the spread of Communism. It was developed just as the Cold War was beginning and Washington was struggling to define the power relationships that then existed between the United States and Russia.

Gray asked Carroll to come to Washington to consult with the new Board. Carroll had already been consulting for the U.S. High Commissioner in Germany on how to counteract growing hostility with the Soviet Union over its influence in newly freed Eastern bloc countries, and had taken several trips to see on the ground the situation between East and West Berlin. He willingly agreed to the assignment.

He was asked to join a team preparing a paper on the U.S.'s long-term objectives toward the Soviet Union and the resources the United States had at its disposal to pursue its aim. Carroll later recalled that the overarching goal was to work to create a climate in which freedom could expand and thrive and the Soviet Union's goal of expanded and repressive rule would be diminished. The paper solidified his friendship with then Secretary of State Dean Acheson, who saw it as a "useful exposition of American purposes in the world" and who went on to use parts of it in his speeches. In it, Carroll argued that the power struggle soon to be called the Cold War would require all of the United States' resources—political, economic, diplomatic, propagandistic, and military. He advocated for the use of what he called "persuasion" and what others would call "psychological warfare," in facing the growing Soviet threat. But such persuasion had to be based on a coordinated and long-term approach to foreign policy, best delivered by senior public officials—the President and Secretary of State—who could marry their "persuasion" to concrete policy goals.

In February 1952, Gordon Gray submitted the report on the organization and work of the Psychological Strategy Board to President Truman. He commended Carroll for the work he had done on the paper, and cited the need for the United States to "help lead the world through this time of turmoil in such a way that ... there shall be an expansion in the areas of freedom and knowledge...." In the end, Truman decided not to publish the report. His advisor, Charles "Chip" Bohlen, had been reluctant to take any authority for directing foreign policy away from foreign service officials working in the field, so he had encouraged Truman not to follow through on any of the recommendations. Carroll, frustrated at the bureaucratic infighting within the State Department, questioned what his role, if any, could be. In 1952, Truman disbanded the Board and Carroll's paper was never published.

Despite the frustrations, Carroll's work within the administration had broadened his contacts in the diplomatic and international community. He was perhaps better connected with the "wise men" in the Truman administration than many knew. In addition to Dean Acheson, Carroll was friendly not only with Bohlen, a key adviser to Truman, but also with Paul Nitze, who as director of Policy Planning for the State Department played a key role in the development of the United States' Cold War strategy. He had also rekindled his friendship with Richard Helms, who was then rising through the ranks of the CIA, later to become its director. His friendship with Helms developed while Helms was Deputy Director for Plans in the CIA, working with Carroll's old acquaintance Frank Wisner, who was then director. At the time, Helms was overseeing the defense of the agency against attacks from Senator Joseph McCarthy. Starting with an infamous speech in 1951, McCarthy, a fellow Wisconsinite, had begun his campaign of accusations of Communist infiltration, not only against the Defense Department but also the State Department, the administration of Harry S. Truman, the Voice of America, and the U.S. Army.

Carroll believed, as did the "wise men," in an international world order grounded in the principles of democracy. But he also, like them, tended to be practical, realistic, and non-ideological. But, unlike Carroll, they were seen by many to be rather heavy-handed in their approach to the Soviet Union, and to put less emphasis on the need to win over the hearts and minds of the people living in foreign countries and more on military might as a deterrent to further expansion.

With the election of Eisenhower to the presidency in 1952, this collection of advisers had been disbanded. Yet Carroll continued to stay in touch with them. And Eisenhower's election would give him yet another powerful acquaintance, this time one who held the highest office in the land. His understanding of international affairs, as well as his extensive contacts, would prove to be invaluable.

CHAPTER 13

A CALL TO WASHINGTON

"Journalism is in fact history on the run."
                                        —Thomas Griffith

C arroll, accepting that he perhaps could have little effect on what happened in Washington, settled back into his work at the *Winston-Salem Journal,* where he continued to enhance his reputation as a leading personage in the South. In addition to his work at the *Journal,* he spoke at the Naval War College and other venues about psychological warfare, being generously given time off by Gordon Gray, and was appointed by the Ford Foundation to chair a committee aimed at studying the University of North Carolina's curriculum on human behavior. He also took on chairmanship of the prestigious Nieman Fellow Selection Committee, which chose the most promising journalists nationwide to participate in a year-long sabbatical at Harvard University.

He was enjoying the extra time he could spend with his family, as well as his life in Winston-Salem, when he was approached in late 1954 by his old friend James Reston about an interesting job prospect. Arthur Krock, the chief of the Washington bureau of the *New York Times,* had recently decided to retire after twenty-one years in the post. Reston, a star reporter for the *Times,* had been asked to replace Krock. Reston asked Carroll to join him in Washington as his deputy.

Reston at the time was one of the most courted journalists in the country. He had won a Pulitzer Prize nine years earlier, based on a series of articles he had written about the 1944 Dumbarton Oaks Conference, at which the United Nations had been planned. A reporter with an uncanny skill at getting high-level government officials to open up to him, Reston felt that the Washington assignment would give him leeway to establish a bureau that mirrored his journalistic ideals. It would also enable him to hire the best in the business. Reston was a master at identifying and attracting talent, but he needed a second-in-command, a "field commander" who would ensure respect from his reporters amid the frenzy of producing the daily news. He knew Carroll had the steady character and sound judgment to take on the job.

Their history together went back to the war when, in 1942, Carroll had gotten Elmer Davis to recruit Reston to join, briefly, the Office of War Information in London. While there he had introduced Reston to then Ambassador Gil Winant. Winant later recommended Reston to Arthur Hays Sulzberger, then publisher of the *Times*, and not long after that the young reporter had been hired to come to New York as Sulzberger's assistant, getting him out of the war-torn British capital. Thus, Carroll had been instrumental in launching Reston's lifelong career with the *New York Times*. The two had remained steadfast friends, and there was no one Reston wanted more for the position than Wallace Carroll.

It was not easy to lure Carroll back to the capital, however. He prized his editorial independence at the *Journal,* and he and Peggy enjoyed the more laid-back lifestyle of Winston-Salem, both for themselves and for their children. Most likely, if the friendship had not been so strong—had Carroll and Reston not so much enjoyed each other's company and shared so many of the same beliefs—Carroll would not have made the move. But he still had one foot in Washington, and felt compelled, with Peggy's agreement, to take up the offer. The position also would offer him the opportunity to go back to reporting on international affairs, drawing on his well-heeled contacts in the government. Once his editing duties were under control, he had every intention of continuing to file stories.

Reston was delighted. He considered Carroll the best editor he knew, remarking in his autobiography that "[Carroll] could have edited the Gettysburg Address and improved it." As important, he knew Carroll would not only be respected but also well-liked by his reporters, which was important to Reston. Carroll, he knew, was "unfailingly kind [and] took an interest not only in their work, but also in their families and their ambitions, and wrote funny, mocking verses in his spare time." Reston also recognized that the more low-key Carroll would do the hard day-to-day work of running the newsroom.

■ ■ ■

Thus began—from 1955 to 1963—what came to be known as the golden years of Washington coverage for the *New York Times*. Reston's reputation immediately raised the profile of the bureau, first discreetly, given his smooth demeanor, but then mostly through his and Carroll's ability to attract and retain the country's most talented journalists. Before Reston and Carroll took over, the bureau had been a dumping ground for reporters unable to make their mark in New York. Both refused to take the castoffs from the home office and started to recruit the best talent they could find. Their intention was to turn the office into an alert and aggressive news organization. "The *Times* was a mediocre newspaper, then," Carroll later remarked. He and Reston recognized that the key to improving the office was to hire the best and then demand the best of them. Reston would later compare his recruiting strategy to that of the New York Yankees' Casey Stengel. Casey "was always a better manager when he had Joe DiMaggio or Mickey Mantle in the field," wrote Reston. Together he and Carroll would build what became the best collection of newspaper journalists under one roof in the capital.

Reston's "Scotty's boys" were a special breed—"usually tall, educated at better universities and brighter than they first seemed to be," according to Gay Talese in his history of the *New York Times, The Kingdom and the Power.* Most of them, like Reston and Carroll, were from the Midwest, and had the easy manner of small towns, as opposed to the fast-talking city-sharp effect of reporters working out of New York. Reston and Carroll got to know their reporters individually and let them loose to cover what they deemed important areas of government. "They made sure their reporters were appreciated, introduced them to prominent residents of the capital, lobbied management to pay them well, and asked nothing of them in return except loyalty to the paper."

▪ ▪ ▪

The bureau, made up of about 20 reporters, operated out of a nondescript office building overlooking Farragut Square, a few blocks from the White House in downtown Washington. Desks were lined up in one room, where there was a "lively din of clicking typewriters, shouts of 'copy,' and telephone conversations that could be heard by one and all." Reston, whose office was in the corner, would often walk across the newsroom chatting with reporters and offering suggestions from his contacts around town. He would sit on the corner of a desk and pick the brains of a reporter, making subtle suggestions about the stories they were covering. When he felt something was missing, he would arrange a kind of Socratic dialogue with the reporter until, miraculously, the reporter himself would realize what more needed to be dug up. "Reston cheered us on and tapped his sources when asked, but he rarely told us how to do our jobs," recalled Max Frankel, who joined the Washington Bureau in 1961. "Unlike most of the editors in New York, he dared to presume that we knew the territory."

Carroll's own "office" was a desk at the end of the long line of reporters' desks, and it was he, more than Reston, that did the nitty gritty of assignments, as well as oversaw the editing of stories. According to John Stack in his biography of Reston, Carroll was a good but tough editor, and in many ways more hard-boiled and demanding than Reston. For example, when David Halberstam joined the *Times* years later, Carroll made him rewrite his first story for the paper five times. Halberstam would go on to win a Pulitzer Prize for International Reporting for his coverage of the Vietnam War.

Carroll, according to Reston, had a way of getting his reporters to write leads that combined the personal with the professional. As an example, Reston recalled how Carroll and Allen Drury, a reporter who had come to the *Times* from the *Washington Evening Star*, had combined on a lead paragraph of a story about playwright Arthur Miller's testimony before Congress in 1956, "Arthur Miller revealed to a congressional committee today a past filled with Communist connections and a future filled with Marilyn Monroe."

Both Carroll and Reston hated breathless, "Christ how the wind blew," copy and had a rule against saying that anything that happened in Washington was "unprecedented." Both abhorred pretense and felt the best way to get ahead of the news was to look for it not at the center among the higher-ups, but at the fringes where anonymous officials usually were the ones who told the "big shots" what was coming up. Carroll, Reston later remembered, "brought from Milwaukee a studied respect for the English language, and from the UP and his wartime intelligence activities the instincts of an amateur spy. He was a student of foreign affairs … and knew many of the foreign service officers in the State Department." Most important, perhaps, was that "his sense of history was keen as his sense of humor."

Both Carroll and Reston also actively socialized with those they covered, which was the modus operandi of the day for journalists. As *Times* reporter Max Frankel wrote, reporters "golfed with senators, swam with White House aides, and called cabinet members by their first names." He recalled Reston inviting Felix Frankfurter, then Supreme Court justice, to his inaugural lunch at the paper. Frankfurter talked freely about his fellow justices and "reminisced about his daily walks to work with former Secretary of State Dean Acheson." Carroll fit right into this milieu; his reputation during the war was well-remembered in Washington circles and his contacts within the intelligence community were unparalleled. To watch Carroll work the phones "to confirm a hot tip about strife in or outside the FBI," recalled Frankel, was "a humbling experience."

The *Times'* chief competition during this time was the *Herald Tribune*, and both Carroll and Reston considered their coverage a success if they were able to scoop it. Nothing delighted them more, Reston later wrote, than "the thought of waking up the *Herald Tribune* at midnight with howls of protest from their home office about some story we had and they didn't." He and Carroll instituted daily meetings on the theory that "the sum of our brains and legs was necessary to outthink and outnumber the *Herald Tribune*."

"Wally was one of the best and nicest editors in the business," said a young staff reporter at the time, Alvin Shuster. "He had intelligence, common sense, great contacts everywhere and a wit that no one could match. It took all his skills and humor to manage a staff of immense talent and to stand between that staff and an often-demanding New York office."

Their cooperation was seamless, according to a young Donald Graham, who was hired by Reston as his assistant in the summer of 1963. Reston, according to Graham, spent most of his time writing his column, hiring for the bureau, and arguing with the people in New York. He was the famous one, while Carroll, although well-known within journalistic circles, took on a lower profile and was really running the bureau. To Graham, Carroll was the consummate newsman: "At the time I was forming my impression of who was and who wasn't a good newspaperman," he recalled. "But I had no doubt about Mr. Carroll. He was just impressive, and had the right ideas about the newspaper business."

▪ ▪ ▪

The list of Reston's and Carroll's recruits reads like a who's who among journalists of the 1950s, 1960s, and beyond. Among the most well-known was Russell Baker, whom Reston had lured from the *Baltimore Sun* in 1954. Baker would become the paper's White House, State Department, and Congressional reporter, as well as its "designated poet." He later became famous for his column "The Observer" that ran in the *Times* from 1962–1998, and was the winner of two Pulitzer prizes. He won even greater fame when he became the host of the popular PBS show *Masterpiece Theater* from 1992–2004. Baker was a frequent visitor at the Carroll household, delighting the children, who would later recall fondly his storytelling and gentle demeanor.

Tom Wicker, whom Carroll knew from his Winston-Salem days and of whom Wicker had said "gave me a high sense of the particularity of my work and the camaraderie possible within it," joined the Bureau in 1960, just in time for the early excitement of the Kennedy era and the drama that followed. Wicker happened to be riding in the vehicle directly behind President Kennedy in Dallas in November 1963 and filed the first on-site report of the tragedy. He later took over as head of the Washington bureau, where he'd filed his influential column "The Nation" from 1966–1992.

Wicker was hired as a replacement for another young reporter who would go on to national fame, Allen Drury. Drury had been the bureau's Congressional reporter and, while at the *Times* in 1960, had published his best-selling novel, *Advise and Consent*, often described as the definitive Washington tale of political intrigue. The novel won the 1960 Pulitzer Prize for nonfiction and launched Drury on a long and successful career as a novelist.

Both Reston and Carroll understood that the world was getting too complicated for the generalist journalist, so they looked for reporters with expertise in specific fields. One of these was Anthony Lewis, who joined the *Times* in 1955, the day before winning the Pulitzer Prize for his previous employer, the *Washington News*. Lewis set the standard for coverage of the Supreme Court, earning praise from "so vigilant a critic of the press as Justice Felix Frankfurter," according to Reston. He went on to win a second Pulitzer Prize in 1963 for his coverage of the Court. Carroll, recognizing his talent, encouraged him to make use of his time during a four-month newspaper strike in 1962–63 to write *Gideon's Trumpet*, which illustrated the case in which the Court held that states were required to provide counsel for indigent defendants charged with serious crimes. *Gideon's Trumpet* won numerous prizes and was later made into a motion picture starring Henry Fonda.

Others hired at the time included war correspondent Peter Braestrup, who went on to become an international correspondent for the *Times,* author of a definitive book on the Vietnam War, and founder of the scholarly journal the *Wilson Quarterly*. Max Frankel, who would win the Pulitzer Prize in 1973 for his coverage of Richard Nixon's trip to the People's Republic of China, joined the Washington bureau in 1961. Jonathan Yardley, whom Reston had hired fresh from his graduation from the University of North Carolina at Chapel Hill, began his journalism career as Reston's assistant, and was given his first reporting assignments by Carroll. Yardley remembered how Carroll would send him out despite his inexperience and vouch for him with management. Carroll later got him a job at the *Greensboro News and Record.* Yardley went on to become a well-known book critic for the *Washington Post* and to win a Pulitzer Prize for literary criticism. He never forgot Carroll's kindness to him.

Carroll also helped persuade Reston to hire women journalists, not something Reston was inclined to do, according to several reports. In 1961, Carroll brought on Marjorie Hunter, who had worked for him at the *Winston-Salem Journal.* Hunter never believed Reston understood entirely her frustrations at being a female reporter, including being banned from the main floor of the National Press Club in the early 1960s. Carroll supported her when she barged into Reston's office one day after she had been relegated to the Press Club's balcony to cover the visit of a foreign dignitary. Reston's response was to wonder, "What's wrong with Maggie?" But Carroll backed her, and Hunter later went on to a long and distinguished career with the *Times.*

■ ■ ■

By this time, Carroll had evolved deeply held beliefs in what journalism—and journalists—should be. At the top of his list was independence. Yet Carroll had learned through his war experience that with independence came responsibility. For him, certain things did not need to be exposed in the press; to both Carroll's and Reston's way of thinking, government should be reported on, but not seen as the enemy. Both had lived through the London Blitz, and Carroll, in particular, understood the dangers involved in making classified information publicly known in a precarious world. This attitude would change in the years ahead, as Carroll increasingly saw the press's role as holding government to account; Carroll had perhaps always believed this, but such reporting needed to be done with careful judgment as to its ramifications.

In 1955, he had developed a theory he called the "tyranny of objectivity," which he presented that year in a Nieman paper. The paper was most likely prompted by the rise of Joe McCarthy, in which Carroll thought the news media had been complicit. Objectivity, he believed, was a discipline that reporters, editors, and publishers impose upon themselves to keep their own feelings from affecting the presentation of news. As such it seems a fine ideal. But to Carroll, its rigid and almost doctrinaire interpretation could lead to a lack of responsibility, or what he called the "objectivity" of the half-truth. Simply presenting the facts was not enough, he argued. Good reporting needed to add a third dimension—meaning. Reporters needed to dig down through the surface facts and fill in the background, interpret, and analyze. He felt that McCarthy had been able to exploit the news media's "objectivity" in printing what he'd said without analysis of whether it was true or not. He had made newspapers his accomplices in his reign of terror.

"I am sure," Carroll wrote, "that if a scholarly study were made of the part played by American newspapers in the rise of Senator McCarthy, it would show that the Senator understood the deadly virtues of the American press much more clearly than we do ourselves. Such a study would show ... [he] was able to exploit our rigid 'objectivity,' in such a way as to make the newspapers his accomplices."

McCarthy knew, according to Reston, that "big lies produce big headlines," and McCarthy took advantage of that fact. He would make an outrageous statement one day, and embellish it a few days later, all the time keeping himself on the front pages of the newspapers. Journalists needed to see beyond this ploy, and to back up their coverage with analysis that went beyond just reporting what someone had said. Just putting quotation marks around McCarthy's false charges was not sufficient.

As illustration, Carroll referred to Reston's reporting. In 1948, Reston had covered a speech by Governor Thomas E. Dewey, the Republican candidate for president, in which Dewey had claimed he was the author of the bipartisan foreign policy of the time. Reston reported the claim but went further. He dug into the memoirs of Secretary of State Cordell Hull and wrote in a sidebar story what Hull had said about the origins of the bipartisan foreign policy—proving Dewey's claim wrong. Thus, Reston had gone beyond mere reporting to digging deeper into what was the truth.

It seems an innocent example today, but believing that journalists had to be capable of interpreting the news as well as reporting it was the bedrock upon which journalists like Reston and Carroll built their coverage, and it was still a relatively new idea in the early to mid-1950s. When a reporter had solid evidence that a statement was misleading, both felt, he had an obligation to report it. The overriding principle was that any practice that allowed newspapers to be "used" should be carefully scrutinized.

Carroll went on to describe three principles he adhered to: the first was to bring this "third dimension" of meaning to reporting on everything covered. The second was to find, train, and pay reporters who could do such three-dimensional reporting; and, finally, to be an editor and publisher who would back their reporters up with strong editing and protection from higher-ups who might be wanting to point coverage in a particular way. Overriding all of this, however, was his extraordinary attention to detail and an absolute commitment to accuracy, fairness, and finding out what was really going on. He demanded this from his reporters, and was always pushing them to do better, to be the best in the business. The aim of the reporter was to reach the highest common denominator of the mass audience, not the lowest.

Years later, when the technological revolution was taking place in the industry, he would reiterate the importance of every newspaper person to cultivate "a passionate interest in the meaning and the substance of the news, in the essential truth of what we print, in the relevance of that essential truth to the questions that the American reader will want to answer." He warned of newspapers' tendency to mirror their audience's interests and tastes rather than to dig down to report on what he felt were the essential issues; the press's responsibility was not to give their readers "a glittering mosaic of events" but rather a coherent and substantive picture.

In a speech delivered to Kappa Tau Alpha, the national society for the promotion of scholarship in journalism, in 1956, Carroll also expressed his view of the newspapers' role in society. Good newspapers were needed in every town big enough to support them, he said, and what they should do is "hold up a mirror to the community so the people can see and understand the workings of a democratic society." Papers needed to bring the outside world closer to their readers, to convey the fascination and excitement of national and world affairs, "which give the reader a sense of participation in current history." Papers should help their readers attain the "understanding they will require to become good citizens of the communities and of the nation and of the world." Newspaper careers, Carroll believed, proved the day's greatest opportunity for community leaderships. Carroll had practiced what he preached in becoming executive editor of the *Winston-Salem Journal*. In that, he believed, as did Gordon Gray, that journalism was about public service, and one that was vital to the health of the nation.

But also worth noting was the fun both Reston and Carroll saw in being a journalist. Neither could have imagined a better profession. In an article published in 1955, Carroll wrote that "the gathering, writing and editing of the news is hard, exacting work. It is done at times under severe pressure, and it may often involve the reporter, and his editor, in unpleasantness, hardship and even danger.... Let all this be granted, but acknowledge that a good newspaperman is likely to fall asleep at night feeling a bit sorry for all those millions of men and women who are condemned to earn their living in ways that are drab and dreary."

▪ ▪ ▪

The fifties were, according to Reston, "not exactly a heroic period," especially when compared with the "creative Forties and the turbulent Sixties," but they still produced a fair share of history-making news.

Carroll, in addition to his editing responsibilities, could not stay away from reporting on international affairs, his métier since the early 1930s, even before covering the League of Nations in Geneva for United Press. There was hardly a journalist more well-versed in the nuances of international diplomacy, or well-known across the country. As a foreign correspondent, his byline (often accompanied by a photo and biography) had been on the front pages of dozens of newspapers for more than two decades. Reston encouraged him to use his well-earned contacts and to return to reporting. Carroll would do so.

When he joined the *Times* in 1955, John Foster Dulles had been secretary of state for two years and was President Eisenhower's most influential foreign policy adviser. A staunch anti-Communist—to Dulles there was no grey area—nations were either part of the "free world" or part of the Soviet bloc—and the nuclear threat stood out loud and clear. He was aided in his thinking by his brother Allen, who at the time was head of an expanding Central Intelligence Agency. Both Dulles brothers believed in the policy of massive deterence and brinkmanship—often referred to as "saber rattling"—against the Soviet Union, in an effort to stem its growing influence in Eastern Europe. They advocated an aggressive stance against Communism throughout the world, and, during Dulles's State Department tenure, concentrated on building up the North Atlantic Treaty Organization (NATO) and other anti-Soviet alliances.

There was general agreement within the government, according to James Reston, that to guard against the nuclear threat required a war of "stealth," as Reston called it, since the Soviets were expanding their authority by subversion and proxy wars. But for the press this caused a dilemma. Journalists would have to decide what information about the inner workings of the government they should make available to the public.

Early in the decade, it had been the *Times* policy to trust the government on issues of national security, but this had begun to change in 1954 when the CIA covertly overthrew the government of Guatemala. The CIA had accused, without evidence, a *Times* reporter for his coverage of events surrounding the overthrow, calling it "unreliable," and the *Times* had taken the reporter off the story. Following this, the CIA expanded its efforts to interfere with the normal reporting activities of the *Times*.

In this atmosphere, Reston and Carroll had to walk a thin line between what to divulge and what to withhold. Carroll himself recalled times when they withheld information from the public about CIA agents being captured or CIA planes being shot down over East Germany and the Soviet Union. Reston became increasingly uncomfortable with this situation. In appealing to the *Times* hierarchy, he finally got publisher Arthur Sulzberger to agree to a policy where if the government wanted the paper to print something, they would do so if the government allowed it to be attributed. If not, the paper would "impose our own judgment as to whether or not it is true and only use the story if we believe it is true."

As the 1960s approached, this willingness to withhold information began to wane even more. Increasingly, newspapers were reporting events from an independent vantage, recognizing they were more accountable to their readers than to their sources. The issue came to a head in May 1960, when the Soviets shot down a U-2 reconnaissance plane flown by Francis Gary Powers. Both Carroll and Reston knew the United States was flying high-altitude spy missions over the Soviet Union in this single-engine jet, nicknamed the "Dragon Lady." The Soviets also knew and had been quietly protesting the flights to Washington. But Reston, at the request of the CIA's Allen Dulles and Sulzberger, had agreed not to report the missions. When Powers was shot down, the Eisenhower administration decided to deny that the plane had been spying, lamely arguing that Powers had been on a weather reconnaissance mission and lost his way, drifting into Soviet airspace. Powers' capture was a huge embarrassment for the United States, which Nikita Khrushchev took full advantage of. Carroll later wondered if it had been right not to disclose the spy flights to the public.

Carroll could be the soul of discretion, hence his numerous contacts continued to keep him well informed of the inner workings of both the CIA and the State Department. He, of course, also knew Eisenhower from his days in London with OWI, and had been impressed with Eisenhower's appreciation of the role psychological warfare could play in winning the war. Nonetheless, he didn't shy away from reporting stories about Eisenhower as he saw them. Although his reporting duties were somewhat sporadic, in 1956 he sharply criticized the government's response to the Suez Canal crisis in an article that was syndicated by the *Times* across the country. "The judgment of some of the most experienced diplomats here today [in Washington]," wrote Carroll, "was that the Suez dispute had brought about a dangerous shift in world power, with the West a heavy loser...."

The Suez Canal crisis had erupted in October 1956, when Israeli armed forces pushed into Egypt toward the canal, which Egyptian President Abdel Nasser, with backing from the Soviet Union, had nationalized. Ship traffic through the canal carried two-thirds of the oil used by Europe. The Israelis were soon joined by French and British forces, which nearly brought the Soviet Union into the conflict. Soviet Premier Nikita Khrushchev threatened to rain nuclear missiles on Western Europe if the Israeli-French-British forces did not withdraw. Eisenhower, Carroll felt, had sent too measured a response to the Soviets, letting down his British and French counterparts. In the end, Egypt and the Soviet Union prevailed. The Israeli-British-French troops withdrew, resulting in the resignation of British Prime Minister Anthony Eden. Carroll, at the time, had argued a hard line against the Soviets, and was chagrined by Eisenhower's lack of support for the Western powers.

After the Suez crisis, Britain and France found their influence in the world weakened, with the United States and the Soviet Union playing a dominant role in global affairs. Carroll did little reporting during this time. It's likely that he was too busy directing the overall news for the bureau. He never outwardly expressed through his reporting his opinion of Eisenhower's policies, but in general, according to his daughter, he thought the President—who suffered a major heart attack in 1958 and was in poor health—was insufficiently engaged. Carroll recognized the serious threat posed by the Soviet Union's policy of expansion and the threat of nuclear war. But he was not a hawk along the lines of John Foster Dulles. While believing the United States had to stand up to the Soviet Union, he also believed the country needed to keep its alliances with the European nations and other allies strong, and to project a united front among the Western Democracies to the world.

During this time period, in October 1957, he also found time to diverge from his reporting on international affairs to publish a piece about Eisenhower's decision to dispatch the U.S. Army's 101st Airborne Division to Little Rock, Arkansas, to protect nine Black students who were entering an all-white high school for the first time. Arkansas Governor Orval Fauber had brought in the state's National Guard in an attempt to block the integration of the school; Eisenhower countered by federalizing the Arkansas Guard and sending 1,000 of the Airborne troops in for good measure. The action had caused an uproar in the South, and Carroll, recognizing the bind this action had put other Southern governors in, wrote that the President would do well to undertake a measured approach with the governors, fearing that any gains would be wiped out by violence and set integration efforts in the South back years. Later he would defend President Kennedy's commitment to enforcing desegregation on similar grounds—that too much direct pressuring from the President might turn off support from Democratic senators and governors who would be integral to ensuring Kennedy's aims would be met.

■ ■ ■

Returning to international reporting, Carroll would be sent in 1959 to the London Bureau of the *New York Times* to cover diplomatic initiatives aimed at quelling the tension between the United States and the Soviet Union. His initial aim was to report on the British preparations for the upcoming visit of President Eisenhower to the United Kingdom and the promise of a meeting between Eisenhower and Soviet Premier Khrushchev. While there he would also cover a meeting of the Council of Foreign Ministers, comprising diplomats from the United Kingdom, the Soviet Union, China, France, and the United States. The assignment recalled his days covering the League of Nations, and he would file numerous stories from the conference, which was to last throughout the summer.

Carroll saw the meeting of foreign ministers as an attempt for the United States to "barter a meeting for Soviet Premier Nikita Khrushchev with President Eisenhower in exchange for a pull back from threats to West Berlin," which was then still permitting the free flow of people between East and West. There was much anticipation that it would lead to a thaw in the tense relations around the divided Berlin. In the end, Khrushchev did meet with Eisenhower in the United States in the fall of 1959, but the meeting of ministers accomplished little; the West would only agree to a peace treaty with a united democratic Germany, not to separate East and West Germany, and the Soviets refused to change Berlin from an occupied city to a demilitarized one.

More worthwhile, perhaps, was the opportunity the assignment gave Carroll to take the whole family to the British capital, as well as to tour his old stomping grounds in Geneva. Carroll's daughter Patricia remembers the voyage of the four children, accompanied by Peggy (Carroll had flown on ahead) on the Queen Mary, albeit in third class, across the Atlantic, and the "car and driver" that routinely came to pick Carroll up from their London apartment to take him to his office. The family would use the trip as an opportunity to tour Europe, where they could practice their French and meet many of their parents' friends still living on the continent. At the time, Margaret was twenty years old and a sophomore at Lawrence College in Wisconsin. John was a senior in high school, and Posie and Patricia 11 and 7, respectively. Carroll may have been sent to Europe somewhat as a reward for his work, and it was a welcome chance to introduce their children to places where he and Peggy had met, lived, and established their careers.

■ ■ ■

With the election of John F. Kennedy in 1960—and most likely following the family's summer in Europe—Carroll began to ramp up his coverage of the CIA and of international affairs, writing more stories himself, rather than overseeing the work of others. Carroll found Kennedy refreshing after Eisenhower, and he also felt a level of sympathy toward Kennedy's world view. Kennedy, he would write, would actually read briefing notes and otherwise do his homework on foreign policy issues, and seemed willing to cut through the endless Washington bureaucracy in seeking a relationship with the Soviets. Kennedy was looking, Carroll believed, "to erase a widely held image of this country as an insecure giant, brandishing an atomic bomb and arguing morosely to large areas of the world that anyone not with him is against him."

But he also acknowledged that Kennedy's first experiences with the Soviets had been difficult, and that his early mistakes would color his outlook further into his administration. This was well illustrated three months after Kennedy's inauguration when, on April 17, 1961, the president authorized the CIA to undertake a secret invasion of Cuba, which had been planned under the Eisenhower administration. The invasion was to be led by Cuban exiles who had fled the country following Fidel Castro's Communist takeover in 1959. The aim was to overthrow the Castro regime. The resulting invasion, called the Bay of Pigs, after the beach where the invasion forces landed, turned out to be a disaster. After three days, the forces were forced back to the beach by Castro's forces; 114 were killed and more than 1,000 captured. The failure of the mission led to major shifts in international relations between Cuba, the United States, and the Soviet Union. It was also a major embarrassment for Kennedy.

Both Reston and Carroll had received information that the Bay of Pigs invasion was scheduled to occur, but Kennedy, who had gotten wind that the story might leak, had called *Times* Executive Editor Orvil Dryfoos to insist that the paper not run the story. Reston agreed with Dryfoos, after consulting with Allen Dulles at the CIA, that it was in the national interest not to publish the timing of the invasion. When they finally did report on the invasion attempt, the paper was heavily criticized for toning down its coverage. It also further labeled Reston, who considered Kennedy a friend, as being too sympathetic to those in power. It's unclear what Carroll thought of the invasion, but in general its failure resulted in greater skepticism from the Washington press corps about the virtues of "collaborating" with the government. In perhaps an attempt to change its coverage, shortly after the criticism, the bureau produced a tough series on the CIA's potentially questionable undercover operations around the world, a project that the paper would never have undertaken earlier.

It was Carroll who, following the invasion, was able to unearth and report on the inside deliberations within the CIA which had led to the decision to go ahead with the invasion. His contacts helped. He had become friendly with Richard Helms, who was then deputy director for plans in the CIA and in charge of espionage and covert operations. Carroll also maintained good ties with others in the organization. On April 21, 1961, he wrote that "there was among high officials of the Kennedy administration a willingness to concede privately that a serious miscalculation had been made." Helms had deliberately stepped back from becoming involved in the deliberations and no doubt was a key contact for Carroll in producing the story. Carroll also was able to report on the damage to American prestige that the failed invasion had produced, as well as to give detailed background information about how it had come about. In short, Carroll seemed to know almost everything about the internal deliberations within both the agency and the administration.

Carroll also drew on his friendship with former Secretary of State Dean Acheson, who was brought in as a principal adviser to President Kennedy and the State Department on the growing crisis in Berlin several months later. Acheson was instrumental in advising Kennedy to take a hard line against East Germany, and Carroll, likely again using Acheson as a source, was able to report on the growing test of wills between the two countries, which finally resulted in the construction of the Berlin Wall in August 1961. The Soviets had been demanding for more than two and a half years that the United States, Britain, and France withdraw their troops from West Berlin, warning that unless they did so the Soviets would make a separate peace treaty with Communist East Germany. This would then permit the East Germans to cut road, rail and canal communications and seriously hamper air traffic between West Germany and West Berlin, which lay 110 miles inside Communist territory. Their argument was based on their belief that the agreements reached in 1945 partitioning the city among the Allies were no longer in effect. Khrushchev had continued to claim that the Soviet Union would go to the aid of the East Germans if the Western Allies used force to maintain their communications with West Berlin.

Carroll had reported, quoting unnamed sources, on the ongoing hostility, as well as the administration's commitment to press the issue of self-determination for areas of Europe that the Communists controlled. The erection of the wall between East and West Berlin, undertaken in the wee hours of the morning of August 18, 1961, stunned Germans on both sides, resulting in military engagements and a series of standoffs. Eventually East Germany would erect 17 miles of concrete throughout the city. Kennedy publicly announced that he would never allow the Soviet Union to drive the United States out of Berlin, but after months of tension he decided to not escalate the military situation, being quoted as saying that the wall was "a hell of a lot better than a war." He continued to support West Berliners, authorizing the delivery of tons of food and other supplies by air to the city and, most famously in 1963, when he would visit West Berlin and proclaim, "Ich bin ein Berliner."

Carroll, at the time, would continue to report on Kennedy's increasingly hardline stance against the Soviets, writing on October 14, 1961, that "recent Soviet moves in the Berlin crisis have strengthened the conviction [within the administration] that Premier Khrushchev is less interested in an adjustment of differences than in inflicting a deep humiliation on the West, and particularly on the United States." No doubt Carroll's reporting also benefitted from his relationship with "Tommy" Llewellyn Thompson, his old friend from Geneva and best man at his wedding. Thompson was by now U.S. Ambassador to the Soviet Union, a position he had held during the Eisenhower administration and in which Kennedy asked him to remain. Thompson is credited with helping to de-escalate the military tensions with Moscow following the building of the wall, conveying to the Soviets Kennedy's desire to instill a period of "relative moderation and calm."

One year later, in October 1962, Carroll was in Rome covering the Catholic Church's Ecumenical Council meetings when tensions with the Soviet reached their high point during the Cuban Missile crisis. But he was able to contribute to reports summarizing the crisis written by *Times*'s staffers, in no doubt due to his relationship with Thompson, who by then had been brought back to Washington from Moscow to serve as one of Kennedy's chief advisers during the crisis.

The crisis arose in the summer of 1962 when U.S. intelligence reports from the CIA cited an unusual amount of secret Soviet activity in Cuba. Thousands of soldiers, hundreds of Soviet trucks, and scores of military freighters were spotted on the island. The CIA soon was able to detect that the Soviet Union was installing surface-to-air missiles. Soviet assurances that their military assistance to Cuba was purely defensive didn't ring true; the missiles being installed were useless against low-flying planes. The CIA reasoned that the rockets were being installed to cover the installation of intermediate range missiles aimed at the United States. In response, Kennedy had turned to Thompson, who was then in Washington. Based largely on his advice, Kennedy decided not to retaliate militarily but to impose a blockade of the island, backed by the possibility of military action, if the missiles were not removed. After 13 tense days of standoff between the two countries, Khrushchev announced that the missiles would be removed. The incident had brought the two nations to the brink of a nuclear war.

■ ■ ■

Carroll had written rather glowingly about Kennedy in 1961, conveying that, with his election, perhaps a new age in American foreign policy would arise. He had been disturbed that America's reputation in the world during the Eisenhower years had been based on the country "talking freely of using the bomb, scolding young nations that chose to tread the path of neutrality and carrying on endless polemics with the tireless Russians."

But the Bay of Pigs incident, as well as the advice of Acheson and Kennedy's Secretary of State Dean Rusk, had led Kennedy to consolidate even further a less than conciliatory stance toward the Soviet Union. When first elected, Kennedy and his advisers had set out with high hopes of what might be accomplished through the moral force of world opinion. He subsequently found himself compelled to rely more and more on foreign policy on "the physical elements of national power." Carroll seemed to be sensitive to this change in philosophy, writing in an article in the *Times* in October 1961, that "Every American President in time of crisis has had to seek an equilibrium between the reality of opinion and the reality of power."

Carroll would go on to cite Franklin Roosevelt's experience in World War II as an example, when Roosevelt had made a deal with Jean Darlan, Hitler's puppet in France during the Nazi occupation, to ensure an almost bloodless seizure of French North Africa by the Allies. Roosevelt, wrote Carroll, felt military might was a priority over holding the moral high ground. In an article published in the *Times,* Carroll recognized the value of real-world politics, in which force was often tantamount to political dialogue. This was a lesson he had learned during the war when he had directed propaganda efforts to support a military agenda, rather than vice versa.

While he recognized the value of "Realpolitik," however, Carroll still would hold on to the belief that "moral persuasion"—i.e., winning over the hearts and minds of those who had been defeated—was essential to ensuring continued peace. In this, he was much less a hardline defender of military action as many might have believed. It was also why he greeted Kennedy's presidency with such support and hopefulness. Years later, it would also inform his writings about the Vietnam War.

■ ■ ■

Through the late 1950s, James Reston had continued to enjoy a relatively high degree of independence from his New York superiors, seemingly guaranteed by his close relationship with the *Times* President Orvil Dryfoos and the Sulzberger family. Dryfoos was married to Marian Sulzberger, the daughter of President Arthur Hays Sulzberger, who owned the *Times*, and he had run the day-to-day operations of the paper since 1957. The relationship between New York and the Washington bureau, nonetheless, had not been easy, and by the early 1960s, it had begun to become even more difficult. Reston had garnered a reputation during his time as bureau chief for encouraging his reporters to go beyond mere reporting in their stories to analysis that could not quickly be verified by a few phone calls. He was also heavily criticized for being too close to the government leaders he covered, and hence unwilling to write about them critically. In addition, he had long wanted to open up all sections of the newspaper to his more contextual style of reporting, and this had rubbed the New York management the wrong way.

For years, Carroll and Reston had fought with the editors in New York, who would change their reporters' copy without any warning. It was so bad, according to Max Frankel, who would go on to become the *Times* managing editor, that "some days, while reading your own story, it was hard to hold down your lunch." In 1962, a new national editor, Harrison Salisbury, was appointed by *Times* assistant managing editor Clifton Daniel to bolster national coverage, and he soon began paying one too many visits to Washington to oversee the work there. Salisbury had begun to scrutinize Reston's and Carroll's reporters, whom he saw as rebellious, and the reporters complained. Reston supported their stand, but to little avail with New York management.

Carroll had already run headlong into Salisbury's scrutiny. He had written an article about the Kennedy administration's confrontation with the steel industry in 1962. Carroll had said in his story that Kennedy had been enraged at the steelmen's decision to raise prices across the board and had spoken unflatteringly of them, but Carroll did not include and attribute to Kennedy a direct quotation that would later appear in his story: "My father always told me that all businessmen were sons of bitches but I never believed it until now." Salisbury had tried to get Carroll to include the quote, even though Carroll had not heard Kennedy say it.

When Salisbury persisted, Carroll snapped back, "The hell with it—you write it yourself!" The quote, nonetheless, made it into the story, and when it was published created quite a firestorm. Regional papers picked it up, running the headline, "According to the *New York Times:* Here's What the President of the United States Thinks of You If You Are a Businessman," and Barry Goldwater, speaking in Phoenix, proposed forming a new club: "SOBs of America." Kennedy later issued a statement saying he had been misquoted. To Carroll, the fact that the quote had been run despite his objections was inexcusable, and at a minimum, risked a break in his relationship with Kennedy.

The altercation foreshadowed Carroll's departure from the *Times* one year later. He began to see that pressure from New

York would only increase. It was not the first time he had put independence and personal integrity over career advancement and journalistic stardom. The *Times* was becoming a much less personal place, more coolly corporate as it had grown larger and more important. The printers' union strike in December 1962, which had shut down all the New York daily papers including the *Times,* added to pressure on the bureau.

Many newsmen, Carroll included, felt a degree of sympathy for the strikers, who were much lower on the economic totem pole than their liberal-minded reporters and owners. But the newsroom staff also grew impatient, and Reston, in particular, began to take the side of the owners as the strike continued, seeing publication of the news as "essential" to a democratic government and therefore not to be shut down. To ease the tension, Carroll and Peggy hosted gatherings for the reporters and staff, empathizing with their concerns.

In fact, the Carrolls' residence had become over the years a sort of salon for journalists, ambassadors, and basically anyone Peggy and Carroll thought were interesting. They would host numerous dinner parties where well-known government offi-cials such as Dean Acheson and Richard Helms would gather, along with journalists and other friends. The Achesons, Helms, and Restons would vacation with the Carrolls during their annual beach holidays in Rehoboth Beach, Delaware. It was another example of the closeness between the press and the government that was not unusual in those days. "It was a small environment with fluidity between government and the press," recalled Carroll's daughter, Patricia. Peggy added considerably to fostering this environment with her lively intellect, outgoing nature, and hostessing skills. At the time, she had also taken up a part-time position at the Department of Labor, a testament to her knowledge of economics, first learned at Vassar and later when working for Gil Winant.

After 114 days, the strike ended, but it had left a bitter taste in the mouths of many. When Arthur "Punch" Ochs Sulzberger took over as publisher at age 37 after the sudden death of Orvil Dryfoos in May 1963, the writing was on the wall that a reorganization was likely to follow.

Carroll was among the first to take action. He realized, with Dryfoos gone, he had nothing to look forward to but increased pressure from New York, so, in the summer of 1963, he turned in his resignation. He had decided to go back to Winston-Salem to become the editor and publisher of the *Winston-Salem Journal* and *Sentinel*. The *Times* tried to dissuade him from quitting, offering him the Rome bureau or any other bureau that was open if he would change his mind. Reston volunteered to turn over the Washington bureau to Carroll, and Reston would devote himself entirely to his column. Carroll was appreciative, but his mind was made up; he sensed what life would be like under Clifton Daniel, whom Sulzberger had appointed as managing editor, and Salisbury as Daniel's deputy, so he was going back south. And he was happy to do it.

"I only came back [to Winston Salem] from the *Times* because I knew [Gordon Gray]'d give me absolute freedom to be the *Journal*'s editor and publisher," he remarked later. "He [Gray] started off with the right idea about what a newspaper should be, and he would never push my elbow."

▪ ▪ ▪

Unknown to nearly everyone during this period was that Reston was contemplating his own resignation. He was insulted that he had not been consulted over the appointment of Punch Sulzberger as publisher; he was now definitely out of the inner circle. In the end, he decided to stay with the *Times* but concentrate on writing a column. One year after Carroll's departure, he would turn management of the Washington bureau over to Tom Wicker.

Both Reston and Carroll had held the reins of the bureau during a time when reporters, while trying to pry as much information as possible from politicians, still had a core belief that once politians were in office, more often than not, they would try to do the right thing. This was a predominant way of thinking among many journalists at the time, as reflected in their reporting. In 1960, for example, 75 percent of evaluative references to candidates John Kennedy and Richard Nixon were positive; years later, by 1992, only 40 percent of evaluative references praised Bill Clinton or George W. Bush. To read 1963 newspapers is to enter a pre-Watergate, pre-Vietnam world. "It is to roll back a gigantic cultural loss of idealism," according to Catherine Fink and Michael Schudson in "The Rise and Fall of Contextual Journalism, 1950s–1960s."

Certainly Reston, and, to a lesser extent, Carroll, believed that the news, while serving the public, was also meant to not unjustly criticize those in power. They felt a responsibility to report with care, to withhold certain information; to treat public officials with deference. And public officials, for the most part, Carroll felt were to be given the chance to try to explain, perhaps off the record, their positions and their understanding of national problems. As Meg Greenfield—an editorial writer at the *Washington Post* from 1968 until her death in 1999—wrote, pre-sixties journalism was subject to a Washington mystique that "decreed that the people in charge in Washington knew best. They could make things happen if they wanted to. Almost all of them were acting in good faith. And they were entitled to both privacy and discretion to do what they judged necessary for the nation's well-being."

Carroll would leave the *Times* more jaded, perhaps, than Reston. He had never felt the loyalty to *Times* management that Reston did. His reporting on international affairs had been meticulous and well-informed, his editing precise, and his mentoring of young staff memorable. His many years in Europe had made him sympathetic to causes outside of the United States; seldom did he fall into the trap of United States exceptionalism. But he also was wary of the threat the Soviet Union posed with their nuclear weapons, and especially the spread of Communism.

Carroll, more than Reston, was less enamored of the powerful men in Washington. He remembered fondly the rollicking journalists at the *Journal* and felt he could contribute more to the community in Winston-Salem than he could to the political machinations in Washington. Plus, he would be in full control of the paper, as Gordon Gray had offered him the position of publisher as well as editor.

"It is obvious that in an atmosphere of silence and secrecy, the freedom of the people is endangered, even though men of the highest personal integrity may be in authority. For on some tomorrow, in all probability the honest man will be succeeded by the unscrupulous; the democratic leader, by the tyrant, the big-time political boss or political racketeer," he had written years earlier before working for the *Times*. "To the extent that the press meets the obligation to inform the public fairly it strengthens not only its position but the structure of democracy. To the extent that it fails to meet this requirement it imperils its own right and the future of free society."

Carroll would take these principles with him as he moved back to Winston-Salem. He was perhaps more well-versed in international affairs than any other journalist at the time; yet his focus would be on the Winston-Salem community. In 1963, there was still much to be addressed there.

TO GO HOME AGAIN

CHAPTER 14

OUR COLLECTIVE
CONSCIENCE AT WORK

*"The American newspaper reader is the most important and powerful
individual in the world. Upon the soundness of his judgment, the
fate of the community and the nation ultimately depend."*
  —Wallace Carroll, "Goodbye to Willie Stevens"

*"I thought he was a symbol of what a really
learned newspaperman should be."*
  —Ed Wilson, former Provost, Wake Forest University

The Winston-Salem of 1963 was a different place from the
city that Carroll and Peggy had left eight years earlier. It
was larger, younger, and richer, with a median income second
only to Charlotte's in the state. Its population had topped
100,000 for the first time, and the city had a more cosmopolitan
air. Its major industries had continued to grow. R.J. Reynolds
Tobacco was still the largest employer in town, with one out
of every five of the city's workers employed there. By 1966, its
Winston brand would become the top-selling cigarette in the
country, helping to produce total company sales of more than
$1 billion. Second to Reynolds was Hanes Hosiery and Hanes
Knitting Company, which would join with Hanes Knitting and
Dye Finishing Company to become the Hanes Corporation, the

largest maker of seamless hosiery in the world. Wachovia Bank and Trust Company, opened in Winston-Salem in 1879, had become by the early 1960s the first bank in the Southeast to reach $1 billion in deposits. And Western Electric, a subsidiary of AT&T, had opened two manufacturing plants that employed thousands of people. It was a wealthy town.

The new and wide-ranging industries that had sprung up in the early 1950s had also grown and prospered, bringing more people in from outside the state and diversifying the town's civic life. And the monied families that ran the factories and mills had continued to share their wealth with the community, building on a history of high schools, auditoriums, and recreational facilities that bore their names. They chaired charities and capital campaigns to fund the community's objectives.

As editor and publisher of the *Winston-Salem Journal* and the *Sentinel*, Carroll would be responsible for all sides of the paper—the newsroom, the pressroom, circulation, and advertising. He would replace James A. Gray III, a cousin of Gordon Gray, who had become publisher of the paper in 1959. James Gray had often sided with business leaders, projecting a less independent spirit than the *Journal* staff were used to. A significant portion of the public agreed. A poll of almost 300 readers in June and July 1959 found that the majority of Blacks and blue-collar workers thought the *Journal* was unduly influenced by the city's richest and most powerful citizens.

Carroll's appointment as publisher had the potential to change that perception and buoyed the sagging spirits of the staff. His presence reassured them that their reporting would be backed up, even though Carroll would continue to have to manage what was often a testy relationship with the powerful business leaders. Bill Hoyt, who had been fired as publisher when James Gray came in, remarked on Carroll's hiring that he was "confident that the paper won't be edited from any of the tall buildings while Wally is there."

And financially the paper was thriving. Advertising linage for the *Journal* had increased in the 1950s every year except for 1954, enabling the paper to expand. The *Journal* and the *Sentinel* published 17,714 pages in 1959, a 63 percent increase over the 10,876 published when Gordon Gray bought the papers in 1937. The resulting revenue set company records each year. Piedmont Publishing Company, parent company for the papers, had reached the $1 million mark in revenue in 1945. Seven years later revenue had more than tripled, surpassing $3 million. It would rise to $4 million in 1957, $5 million in 1962, and $6 million in 1965. As a result, the papers had expanded their staff, which by 1964 numbered 400, and invested in new equipment. Five new press units had been installed that could turn out 52,000 papers an hour, including more of the color pages popular for advertising. By 1965 three more press units would be added.

It was Carroll's good fortune as publisher to be taking the helm of a paper that was thriving financially, but it was the editorial side of the business that always interested him the most. With Gray still owning the paper and ensuring Carroll's independence, the road was open to make it among the most admired in the state and beyond. Carroll compared his role as publisher to that of a referee. His reporters and editors were left alone, guided only by an occasional nudge. Editorial staff would meet at 10 a.m. each day, but Carroll rarely talked at length. "He was a very quiet man who led by example," wrote columnist Roy Thompson, "and quite often he got exactly what he wanted." Yet he never shied away from controversial subjects. One word from him could end any debate, according to Frank Tursi, who wrote a history of the paper, *The* Winston-Salem Journal: *Magnolia Trees and Pulitzer Prizes.*

These attributes were particularly important, given the timing of his arrival. By the early 1960s, trouble was in the air for the tobacco industry. Shortly after Carroll took the reins as editor and publisher, on "a cold and cloudy day in January 1964," the surgeon general of the United States issued a report that burned to the heart of tobacco country. It said: "Smoking could kill you." The report, based on more than 7,000 articles relating to smoking at the time, concluded that cigarette smoking was a cause of lung cancer and laryngeal cancer in men, a probable cause of cancer in women, and was the most important cause of chronic bronchitis. It also pointed to a correlation between smoking and emphysema, and smoking and coronary disease. The report's release, timed for a Sunday morning to minimize its effect on the stock market, was covered in newspaper headlines across the country and on evening newscasts. It would later prove to be the top news story of 1964.

Although in the 1950s it was diversifying into food brands, Reynolds was still at that time a leading producer of cigarettes in the country. For years, the tobacco industry had fought the scientific community by saying that the health effects of tobacco were uncertain. Numerous studies financed by the trade had called into question each medical and scientific finding that came out, as the industry continued to spend huge sums of money supporting its powerful lobby in Congress. North Carolina politicians immediately questioned the surgeon general's report and challenged potential restrictions on smoking being considered by Congress. The tobacco lobby argued that further studies were needed and vowed to put more money into research.

Yet despite the financial weight of the company and its importance to the Winston-Salem community, Carroll didn't hold back on covering the story. The day after the report came out, both the *Journal* and the *Sentinel* ran 12 news stories, three briefs, and one full-page excerpt from the Associated Press on the summaries and conclusions of the surgeon general's report. It included reaction from tobacco growers and a look at how the stocks of the six major tobacco companies were faring. The coverage also highlighted the finding that smokers had a mortality rate 70 percent higher than non-smokers; a nine-to-ten-fold risk of developing cancer compared to non-smokers and at least a twenty-fold risk for heavy smokers.

"That was a shocker for people on a Sunday morning," Carroll later recalled. "But I felt very strongly that this was a tobacco community and they should know what was in store for them. I felt we had to do it." Carroll proceeded to keep the story dominant in the paper for the next three months as the Federal Trade Commission worked on restrictions on cigarette ads. In fact, Roy Parker Jr., who was the *Journal*'s Washington correspondent at the time, was told by Carroll that he wanted every tobacco story the reporter could find.

Carroll immediately felt the heat from Reynolds Tobacco and his community. "Some people at Reynolds and in the community resented it—they wouldn't talk to me," he recalled, and many readers were upset the tobacco issue received so much coverage. But the top executives never put pressure on Carroll not to run the stories, he recalled. This was due in part to their respect for Carroll's editorship. But it may also have been due to the fact that the national press at the time had fully picked up the surgeon general's report. It would not have been possible for the *Journal* not to run with it. One year later, in 1965, Congress required that all cigarette packages carry warning labels, and by 1970, television and radio advertisements were banned. Attempts to regulate the industry would continue for the next 40 years.

■ ■ ■

The 1964 threat to the tobacco industry illustrated the fine line Carroll often had to walk in presenting even-handed and fair reporting. He recognized the financial hardship the report would cause, and as a result maintained good relationships with the city's business leaders, many of whom had a long history of supporting projects that benefitted the Winston-Salem community. Two of these were R. Philip Hanes, chief operating officer of the Hanes Corporation, and Smith Bagley, grandson of the founder of R.J. Reynolds. Both became close friends of the Carrolls and would figure prominently in upcoming projects that would advance the city's reputation and well-being.

Phil Hanes at the time was 37 years old, and in 1964, he would become chief executive officer (CEO) of the Hanes Corporation, a position he would hold for the next twelve years. Like Gordon Gray, he believed no one was entitled merely by their birth to run a company. He had advanced from office drone to company salesman, vice president, president, and then, finally, CEO at Hanes. Quite the character, he was also an ardent conservationist and arts advocate and a major player in the city's cultural development that had undoubtedly made returning to Winston-Salem attractive to both Wallace and Peggy. Hanes would join the board of the Winston-Salem Arts Council in 1965 and later be appointed by President Lyndon Johnson to the National Endowment for the Arts, together with the likes of John Steinbeck, Duke Ellington, and Harper Lee.

R.J. Reynolds heir Smith Bagley, just 28 years old in 1964, had already committed himself to advancing racial civil rights and other liberal causes in his city. He would go on to support numerous philanthropic and political causes at the national level, including serving as a board member of the John F. Kennedy Center for the Performing Arts and playing a leading role in the national Democratic Party. Both he and Hanes shared a love of the arts; both would be instrumental in an initiative to establish a school for the performing arts in the state.

Carroll, too, had long been a fan of the arts, and especially of classical music. As a boy he had wanted to become a concert pianist until his father had dissuaded him of the idea, and throughout his adulthood, his favored relaxation after a long day in the newsroom was to retreat to his study to listen to his classical music collection.

Winston-Salem, too, had a longstanding identification with the arts, going back to its Moravian settlers' strong musical tradition. The city's Arts Council, created in 1949, had been the first in the nation to be formally established by a municipality. The council served as a clearinghouse for the programming, scheduling, and fund-raising efforts of the community's artist community. In 1956, leading citizens had started the Winston-Salem Gallery of Fine Arts in the former home of J. Gordan Hanes, which would later become the Southeastern Center for Contemporary Arts. Over the next decade, the city would become a regional hub for the arts, home to a host of art museums and galleries, musical and theatre groups.

In 1964, soon after the Carrolls' return, the city's arts community was presented with a new opportunity. North Carolina's governor Terry Sanford had made education his number one priority, and as part of that, he had dreamed of a school to support the performing arts. He found an ally and deputy in a professor from the University of North Carolina, John Ehle, a novelist of some note regionally, who had instigated an innovative idea in an op-ed piece in the *Raleigh News and Observer*. Ehle had argued that the university was failing its students in creative writing, dramatic art, music, and languages. Sanford had taken note, and he now called on Ehle to help realize the dream of a real educational home for the arts in the state.

Ehle was that rare person who could be both an artist and a builder of institutions. Seven of his eleven novels focused on his roots in the Appalachian Mountains; his nonfiction work ranged from an account of student civil protest in 1964 at Chapel Hill and a history of the Cherokee nation to a guide to French and British wines and cheeses, along with numerous radio dramas and biographies. It would be Ehle who would develop the idea behind the state's Governors' Schools for its brightest high school students, a state-run learning institute to provide research for improving education, and a state film board. He also added a bit of glamour to the state. In 1967, he would marry the actress Rosemary Harris, who at the time had appeared in numerous London and New York theatre productions, as well as on film. She would move to Winston-Salem, and continue a career that would span more than 70 years and bring her Tony, Emmy, and Golden Globe awards, as well as an Academy Award nomination for Best Supporting Actress for the 1994 film *Tom & Viv*.

Ehle came to be regarded as Sanford's "one-man think tank," generating ideas about what a "creative" government could accomplish in education reform. Among them was a residential school for the training of young artists. The idea was unorthodox; there were no existing models. As envisioned by Ehle and, later, Sanford, the new school would provide an environment for creativity and self-development, guided by a staff of professionals from across the full range of performing arts. The school would recognize the early start needed to develop such talents, admitting students from junior and senior high school as well as college, and it would provide instruction in the liberal arts in addition to its arts-related activities.

Since his return to Winston Salem, Carroll had become fast friends with Ehle, who soon elicited his help in hatching the idea for the school. The N.C. General Assembly, after much lobbying by Ehle and others, had agreed in June 1963 to establish the school with a $325,000 appropriation. Carroll and Ehle decided to seek additional funding from the Ford Foundation. They traveled together to New York, where Carroll played a role in introducing Ehle to Harris, whom Ehle would marry shortly thereafter. Harris would move to Winston-Salem later that year.

With funding from the state guaranteed, as well as the possibility of more funding from the Ford Foundation, the state's major cities—Greensboro, Charlotte, Raleigh/Durham, and Winston-Salem—began jousting to host the proposed art school. All were invited to submit proposals. Winston-Salem's civic leaders, led by Philip Hanes and Smith Bagley, jumped into action.

They proposed that the James A. Gray High School near Old Salem, with 22 surrounding acres, be the campus for the new school. They also proposed, even before the newly appointed

John Ehle is considered one of North Carolina's greatest writers and among its most formidable promoters of the humanities. The oldest of five children, he was born in Asheville, North Carolina, where his ancestors had lived for four generations, and from which he drew inspiration for much of his work. His first fiction book, *The Land Breakers*, chronicles the life of a pioneer family as they settle in the western mountains, and is filled with the vivid and sometimes heartbreaking details of life on the frontier. The novel began a seven-book series based on the family's evolution through two centuries. Two of his books, *The Journey of August King* and *The Winter People*, were made into motion pictures.

His wife of 64 years has proved no less remarkable. Born in India and raised in England, for many years Rosemary Harris made Winston-Salem her home. In June 2019, she accepted a lifetime achievement award at the Tony Awards, celebrating a 72-year career on the stage. At the time she was 91 years old and starring in a revival of *My Fair Lady* on Broadway. On returning to Winston-Salem, in May 2020 she gave a speech to the North Carolina School of the Art's incoming class, in which she encouraged them to recognize their unique voices and to remain "open and aware of the urges that motivate you.... No artist is pleased; there is no satisfaction, only a queer, divine dissatisfaction that keeps us marching.... Just keep marching."

board of the incipient school had picked a location, that the city come up with $900,000 to renovate the high school. "We had been trying to figure out how we could raise the money," remembered Hanes, but decided "our way [would be] to find out if we've got the money before we ask." Early on the morning of April 28, 1964, Bagley and a corps of campaigners began soliciting pledges through a phone drive, Dial for Dollars. In two days, more than 5,000 residents of the city had pledged more than $850,000, and with these funds almost miraculously raised, they enlisted Carroll to help convince state legislators to locate the new school in Winston-Salem.

"Carroll always told us not to tell people what to do in an editorial," recalled Joe Goodman, a reporter on the *Journal* at the time. But this time the newspaperman went against his own advice. The day before state legislators were due to visit the city, he sat down at his typewriter and drafted an editorial titled "Give Us the School," which he ran prominently on the front page of the *Journal* the morning of the legislators' visit. Carroll didn't pull any punches, either. We "want the school so deeply," he wrote, "we shall be glad to invest something more precious than money—our time, our enthusiasm and our affection—to make it flourish."

The dancer Agnes de Mille—a member of the incipient school's advisory board of artists, which was to decide the school's location—was impressed with the community's effort. She commented on the city's spirit following a visit, in the spring of 1964: "This was a wonderful thing to see in America.... this kind of enthusiasm for something that is so important and so absolutely unprofitable except in the spiritual sense. That these rich, rich people [the Reynolds and Hanes families], who obviously dealt in making money in one way or another, were interested now in people's souls, struck me as novel." Two days later, the legislature, based on the unanimous recommendation of the advisory board of artists on which de Mille sat, voted to locate the school in Winston-Salem; Wallace Carroll was appointed vice-chair of its board of directors.

The North Carolina School of the Arts opened in Winston-Salem in 1965 as America's first public arts conservatory, later earning the city of Winston-Salem the title "City of Arts and Innovation." The dream of an arts conservancy had come to fruition. Vittorio Giannini, a leading American composer teaching composition at Juilliard, who had been instrumental in the School of the Arts' founding, wept when he heard of his appointment as its first president. "If I can in any way help," he said following his appointment, "to give these youngsters a chance to gain a professional fame, and an ideal and a vision of what the arts can really mean ... then I really feel my life will not have been spent in vain. I am poor in words. My heart is full."

Today the School of the Arts continues to provide an environment similar to that of an artists' colony, where students are encouraged to grow, experiment, and develop their abilities to the fullest. Students study with resident master teachers who have had successful careers in the arts—from the American Ballet Theatre to the New York City Opera—and who remain active in their professions. In 2008, the school was incorporated into the University of North Carolina system, and its alumni in dance, drama, design, production, and film remain among the most successful in the country. Well-known graduates include Lucas Hedges, Tom Hulce, Mary Louise-Parker, Jada Pinkett Smith, Jennifer Ehle, and Judge Reinhold, among others.

Carroll would stay fully involved in the school's development and operation for the rest of his life, attending numerous functions, particularly in their School of Music. His good friend, the concert pianist Clifton Matthews, would become a teacher at the school, and Carroll would continue his strong friendships with Phil Hanes, Smith Bagley, and John Ehle. Carroll would later remark that helping to bring the school to Winston-Salem was among his proudest achievements, and after his death, an endowment was raised to establish a chair in piano in his honor at the school of music.

The North Carolina School of the Arts would prove to be a personal boon to Carroll as well, its presence sustaining him through challenging times that lay ahead. While he and Ehle, the governor, and some of Winston-Salem's wealthiest men were engaged in a major cultural advance for the city, there were other forces rising that would call on Carroll to use his position as editor and publisher of the *Journal* to make a difference in the community.

■ ■ ■

While Winston-Salem's dramatic success in securing the School of the Arts was still unfolding, John Ehle was deeply involved in a personal project. He had already begun his nonfiction account of three young students at the University of North Carolina in Chapel Hill who had been imprisoned for civil rights demonstrations. The account, later published as *The Free Men,* would outline the students' unsuccessful efforts to desegregate Chapel Hill's restaurants and retail stores and the arrests, trials, and sentencings that followed. Ehle had been instrumental in helping to arrange their parole in North Carolina, as well as jobs and future schooling up North. He saw the need for them to complete their educations before plunging into full commitment to a struggle that was evolving rapidly with passage of a sweeping federal civil rights bill imminent.

That bill, the Civil Rights Act of 1964, was signed into law that July by President Lyndon Johnson. The law prohibited discrimination on the basis of race, color, religion, sex, or national origin across the United States and forbade such discrimination in hiring and firing practices. It also strengthened the enforcement of voting rights and the desegregation of schools. First proposed a year earlier by President John F. Kennedy, its passage had been hard wrought. A "Southern bloc" of 18 Democratic senators and one Republican senator had almost brought efforts to enact it to an end. As Carroll had foreseen, successful implementation of the act would depend on dealing strategically with this bloc, one member of which had proclaimed, "We will resist to the bitter end any measure or movement which would have a tendency to bring about social equality and intermingling and amalgamation of the races in our states."

The issue of race had dominated the in-house thinking of the *Journal* for most of the late 1950s while Carroll had been away in Washington. During this time, the *Journal* had struggled to formulate a position on school desegregation and the integration of public buildings, choosing an approach that didn't always sit well with the city's power structure.

A major break with the city's power structure came in 1957 when the paper, led by then executive editor Reed Sarratt, objected strenuously to the school board's change in policy allowing parents to choose which schools their children attended, and that they could only attend schools close to their homes. Sarratt wrote that the school board's intervention would lead to "enforced desegregation," in that it would cause the courts to intervene and "force" integration, which he considered the worst way to handle the problem. While African American families would most likely choose to send their children to school with other African Americans, Sarratt argued that they still believed they had a right to attend desegregated schools as defined by the Supreme Court. To challenge that right was to stimulate the desire to break down segregation. The monied men, outraged by the *Journal*'s opposition to the School Board's decision, had complained to Gordon Gray, causing a shake-up in the paper's management. Sarratt was taken off the editorial page, and moved to assistant general manager, a position in which he could not influence editorial output. Later Gray would force Sarratt to resign.

Taking on the role of both publisher and editor in that context, Carroll once again had to walk the line between editorial freedom and pleasing the establishment. While desegregation of schools had been ongoing ever since *Brown v. Board of Education* in 1954, there was still tension between African Americans and whites in the community. This had perhaps been aggravated by a new series of urban renewal projects in the city that had forced the resettlement of many Black communities, including an important sector of Black businesses. Carroll's approach when he arrived back at the *Journal* was measured. An editorial written shortly after passage of the Civil Rights Act called for citizens to respect the new law even if they did not agree with it. Carroll felt an obligation to reduce tension within the community by ensuring fair and accurate reporting.

Peggy helped him in this by being his "eyes and ears" in the community. On her arrival in Winston-Salem, she had become actively involved in meetings of the interracial YWCA and close friends with one of its members, Annie Brown Kennedy. Kennedy was only the second African American woman ever licensed to practice law in the state and would later become the first Black to be elected state senator, a position she would hold for 13 years. Peggy would host meetings of the YWCA at their home as well as class parties for her daughter's integrated school. The Wellington Road house would be the place, too, where Carroll or Peggy would invite Black friends or associates for dinner, since the city's restaurants, still segregated, would have refused them service.

For the most part during the late 1960s, the city remained peaceful but not immune from racial violence. The worst episode occurred between November 2 and November 5, 1967, after a Black man, James Eller, was killed in a struggle with police. In the street violence that followed, there were about 100 fires set and about $750,000 in damage. More than a thousand National Guardsmen were called in to restore order. Carroll, according to his daughter Patricia, was at the *Journal* offices throughout the riots, overseeing its coverage to ensure that the paper's reporting did not inflame the city further. On Nov. 4, as the riots were winding down, he crafted an editorial warning the citizenry to guard against a "hardening of attitudes … a blanket condemnation of either race that could create further alienation between our people long after the last bottle has been thrown and the last looter arrested." The first priority was to restore order to the city. But he also asked readers to recognize that "there are not enough jobs, not enough decent housing, not enough opportunities" for the African American community to have a stake in things, and until this changed, such disturbances would likely continue.

Several months before the violence, the *Journal* had written about the increase in poverty among Blacks in the South: "The Deep South is wrestling now with a crisis of conscience: Does it try to alleviate the plight of these dispossessed children of poverty?" The *Journal* called on the "federal government, the nation and men of conscience everywhere … to respond to the crisis with emergency relief first and rehabilitation where possible." As usual, Carroll asked readers to keep an open mind, to look at both sides of the issue; for him, reporting the news accurately and fairly should be the paper's main focus, while achieving a peaceful, integrated city the desired goal. Years earlier, in his book *Persuade or Perish*, he had articulated his abhorrence of segregation in American culture, but he also recognized the resistance he was up against in the South, and thus centered many of his comments on the need to improve the lot of African Americans, both economically and otherwise.

But Carroll's carefully worded opinions and editorial direction would not always come without cost. A particular example was his dislike of the growing strength of the gun lobby, and he frequently wrote editorials decrying the National Rifle Association's equating the Second Amendment with the right of "every Tom,

Dick, and Harry" to carry a gun. But in North Carolina, gun ownership had long been seen as sacrosanct, vital in a rural culture where hunting was a way of life, as well as a sport, and revered as an individual right for self-defense and home protection. In retaliation, after his first editorial against the gun lobby ran in the *Journal* in 1969, his dog was found shot at the bottom of the Carroll's driveway. Carroll and Peggy had bought the dog, Bo Bo, for their youngest daughter, Patricia, several years earlier as a Christmas present, thinking that it would be a good protection should there be threats following the newspaper's coverage. Both were devastated by the dog's death, but it did not stop Carroll from continuing his editorials nor from encouraging his reporters from taking on controversial topics.

For the most part, however, Carroll succeeded in walking the line between advancing topics he cared about and further escalation of contentious issues. In truth, the *Winston-Salem Journal* and the *Sentinel* thrived under his leadership, and respect for his editorship remained strong among the staff. "He didn't wander through the newsroom looking over people's shoulders," remembered Joan Dawson, who worked as a copy editor on the *Sentinel* at the time, "but we all knew he was thoroughly evaluating our writing and editing. He let reporters and editors proceed under their own steam, prodded by an occasional nudge."

"If an argument was tainted with passion regardless of its overwhelming logic, he would reject it," wrote Joe Goodman, who would later become managing editor of the paper. Just a look from Carroll could "intimidate the hell" out of reporters who took personally the challenge to measure up to his standards. But he also was not judgmental about what his reporters were or were not capable of. The author Emily Herring Wilson, who at the time was brought in to write feature articles, remembered that he knew that not all of his staff were at the level of many he had worked with in his career, but he never looked down on anyone. He would rather shepherd them based on what he saw as their individual talents.

Carroll's son, John, who by this time had begun his own career as a reporter and editor, mirroring much of his father's professional life, also well remembered the atmosphere among the *Journal* and *Sentinel* staff, which, in part, led him to pursue a career in journalism: "The people [my father] worked with seemed more vital and engaged than your normal run of adults. They talked animatedly about things they were learning—things that were important, things that were absurd.... I felt I'd like to hang around with such people when I grew up."

Carroll was also more fun-loving than many imagined. Although quiet, he reveled in the high jinks of his staff, and he and Peggy continued to regularly host social events at their Wellington Road house. The most renowned was their annual Groundhog Eve party, during which participants had to present an "ode" to the often-maligned animal. Such odes reflected Carroll's love of rhyme and poetry. As his friend James Reston would write, "There was a touch of Lewis Carroll in Wally Carroll." His witty verses, a combination of rhyme and meter, were even by then well-known, demonstrating not only his keen sense of humor but his thorough knowledge of the English language. He would later become famous for his annual Christmas poems, which would rhythmically reflect the year's events and would be published on the front pages of both the *New York Times* and *Washington Post* for many years.

Carroll reached out, as well, to the city that was now his family's home. Although he stayed close to his Washington friends—James Reston, for one, was a regular visitor—he became first and foremost a citizen of Winston-Salem, an established Rotarian, and a vibrant member of the city's culture lobby. Within those circles, he became known for his encyclopedic knowledge of nineteenth century music and his taste for fine food, including his famous salad dressing of oil, vinegar, and mustard, and good

wine. Yet he was, according to Joe Goodman, "about as ostenta-
tious as a glass of water. The suit is dark pinstripe off the rack.
The lapels and tie are medium width. The shoes polished but
not shined…. But," Goodman continued, "perhaps his greatest
strength was his reserve, his absolute refusal to impose himself
on others or to intrude on their views. That, combined with his
great wit, made him an uncommon newsman."

A young Donald Graham, who would go on to become
publisher of the *Washington Post,* again remembered Carroll
fondly. In the summer of 1964 he was suffering the effects of
his father's suicide and looking for something to get him away
from Washington. He received a note from Carroll inviting him
to Winston-Salem to work as an intern at the *Journal.* Graham
thought it would be the "greatest thing in the world" to work
with Carroll, whom he had watched work with James Reston at
the *New York Times.* "I thought how lucky the people of Winston-
Salem were to to have him for a publisher," Graham continued.
"He seemed to reflect enormous concern about accuracy, fairness; about finding out what was really going on," Graham
remembered. "Carroll was part of a tradition that prided itself
at being the best around; he was very concerned about making
the paper better."

Carroll himself would articulate what he thought a good
editor should be: "There is only one difference between a good
editor and a babysitter," Carroll would write in an address given
to his alma mater Marquette University. "The good editor never
lets the children fall asleep. On one side, he is a mentor to his
reporters, encouraging them, restraining them when necessary,
helping them to perceive the way the wheels are going round.
On the other he is a friendly counsellor to the reader, trying to
bring the world to his doorstep and nudging him when he begins
to doze over the factors and views turned up by reporters."

Like James Reston, Carroll realized that the days of fly-by-
night reporting were gone, and that the world was becoming so

complicated that newspaper men and women had to cultivate a "passionate interest in the meaning and the substance of news, in the essential truth of what we print" rather than be swayed by what may be the interests and tastes of their audience. A good reporter "establishes the difference between the news and the truth. He or she gets the additional facts, to piece together the essential background, and thus to protect the reader from the half-truth." It is a job, he believed, as important as that of a politician in ensuring the healthy working of a democratic society. And his or her primary allegiance, Carroll believed, should be not to the owner of a newspaper, or to his government, or to the sources of his information, but to the people for whom he is writing, "to get the truth for the American people," he would write, "and to get it speedily, colorfully and accurately."

He would continue to put that belief to good use in the years ahead.

CHAPTER 15

A WORLD OF INFLUENCE

"I still believe that if your aim is to change the world,
journalism is a more immediate short-term weapon."
—Tom Stoppard, playwright

Carroll's knowledge of international affairs, along with his
many contacts in Washington, led to an exceedingly rich and
sophisticated coverage of both domestic and foreign affairs in
the *Journal* and the *Sentinel* while he was editor and publisher. A
review of the papers' international coverage during his tenure
shows a remarkable breadth and depth for a regional newspaper.
As long-term friends he could count Dean Acheson, an archi-
tect of the Cold War, who by 1964 was an adviser to President
Johnson; and Richard Helms, then Director of the Central
Intelligence Agency; as well as others, and he did not shy away
from using them as contacts in directing the paper's coverage.
It seemed people in power listened to what he had to say. And
what he wanted was to create not only the most admired newspaper in North Carolina, but also a paper of national influence.

A giant step in that direction came in early 1968 in response
to the Vietnam War. The war had been escalating for seven
years, with U.S. military involvement growing each year. By 1967,
more than 500,000 active U.S. troops were stationed in South
Vietnam, and opposition to America's involvement was rising.
In January 1968, the domestic tempest gained fervor when the

North Vietnamese launched the Tet Offensive, a massive attack against Saigon and more than 100 cities in South Vietnam. The attacks were aimed at fomenting rebellion among the South Vietnamese population and encouraging the U.S. to scale back its involvement. While the offensive failed to inspire widespread rebellion, it proved to be a strategic success for the North Vietnamese. The American public, watching the ferocious attacks nightly on TV, was shocked at the war's escalation. Outrage was heightened when it was revealed that the administration knew of the strength of the North Vietnamese and the likelihood of their success but had released a different story to the press. At the same time, Lyndon Johnson was facing a tough reelection campaign and was increasingly concerned about the popularity of the war.

Carroll had followed the war closely. The Carrolls' son, John, by now 25, was a correspondent for the *Baltimore Sun* in Vietnam and had lost his combat correspondent's accreditation for exposing the United States' secret withdrawal from Khe Sanh, a Marine outpost that had been strongly defended just prior to the Tet Offensive at huge cost of lives. Both Johnson and General William Westmoreland—then commander of the U.S. Military Assistance Command in Vietnam (MACV)—saw it as a strategically essential base. For 77 days, Marines and their South Vietnamese allies had fought off an intense siege, one of the longest and bloodiest battles of the war, with hundreds of lives lost. The administration refused to acknowledge the carnage, or that the Marines had actually retreated, claiming victory. To cover for the embarrassment of losing Khe Sanh and of the subsequent Tet Offensive, Westmoreland requested an additional 200,000 U.S. troops to mount a counter-offensive, an escalation that many Americans saw as an act of desperation.

John, showing an independence he was to repeat often in his career and unaware of an embargo on the news, reported the troop withdrawal. As a result, the Pentagon suspended his correspondent's accreditation, making him a cause célèbre among his fellow correspondents who strongly defended his actions. Many later claimed it was one of the most important stories of the war.

■ ■ ■

Carroll almost certainly had access to contacts in Washington who knew that the United States was indeed not winning the war. In addition, Peggy had posted a map on the wall of their home in Winston-Salem indicating John's location, as well as troop movements in other areas; they were likely also teasing out information from John's correspondence.

But Carroll had until that point conformed to what he thought Gordon Gray might be thinking about the war and had held back on publishing editorials strongly against it. "I knew without talking to Gordon Gray that he would feel that we ought to support the president of the United States when the country is at war," Carroll remembered. "I generally agreed with that as a matter of principle and went along until 1968."

But early in that year his views changed. He was now convinced that the war was against America's best interests. He wrote Gray a long memo in which he laid out the reasons why he thought the war was a mistake. "To my surprise, Gordon came back and said, 'Let's publish it,'" Carroll recalled. "We did, and I signed it because I knew it would be controversial and I would take the heat on it." The editorial was published in the *Winston-Salem Journal* on March 17, 1968. Several newspapers both within and outside North Carolina immediately reprinted it, to much positive response.

Carroll also sent copies to Acheson, a hawk and former secretary of state under Truman and one of Johnson's most trusted advisers, who had been brought in to give respectability and credibility to Johnson's foreign policy. Reporters thought highly of Acheson because "he could think clearly and even more surprising, he could stick to the main point." Much to Carroll's surprise, Acheson liked the editorial and had it disseminated throughout the State and Defense departments. He also stood in the Oval Office while Johnson read it on March 26, 1968, and remembered that Johnson was "most impressed" by it. Johnson at the time was under pressure from both hawks and doves, and Carroll's words seemed to provide a tipping point. The editorial, according to later reports, was unique in bringing together the country's national and international interests and involvement on a level of understanding accessible to the general public. Four days later, Johnson announced on a nationwide television broadcast that he would talk peace with the North Vietnamese and would not seek reelection.

"Dean certainly gave me the impression that it had an effect on the president," Carroll later said. "The important thing is that here was a small, provincial newspaper which had an effect on a major position. Of course, we didn't get out of the war, but we had an effect on the president which started him to move in that direction."

McGeorge Bundy, another of the president's men, was as impressed as his boss. "I do think I can say, looking back, that this editorial stands as an eloquent summary of the kind of thinking which came to the president from a lot of people he consulted that month," he wrote to a reporter who was doing a profile of Carroll in 1973. "All-out critics of the war might say that the editorial came late, and its all-out defenders might say that it should not have come at all. But I am one of those who think that it came at the right time, said most of the right things and said them in the right way. In that sense it was a remarkable editorial—but only par for Wallace Carroll."

The editorial, "Vietnam—Quo Vadis? We Must Open Our Minds to the Hard Choices," begins by asking the question, "What is in the best national interests of the United States?" In a carefully laid out fifteen points, Carroll argued that continuing the war would only aid the U.S.'s enemies—then the Soviet Union and Communist China. There was no long-term plan for engagement in the war, the "dominoes" of Communism in Southeast Asia and the Middle East were falling to the Chinese as a result, and Soviet power was creeping into the Mideast and countries surrounding the Indian Ocean, filling the vacuum left by the British. NATO, a crucial block against Communism, was also suffering from lack of public support.

Added to this were carefully laid out economic and social arguments—that the strength of the dollar was weakening due to the war and that America's cultural life was being poisoned by generational and political strife. Another casualty was what Carroll called "the truth." The war had "played havoc with our credibility—our credibility to ourselves and to the world." The options, then, were fairly clear: "We can rebuild our cities and raise up our people—or we can squander our young manhood and our treasure in the jungles. We can recover our role of leadership among the free peoples—or we can let them slip into the Communist embrace." And finally, "we must now see that we cannot allow Vietnam to become the be-all and the end-all of our national policies. Starting with that realization we can work our way back to our true role in the world—not as destroyers but as builders, not as sowers of fear but as bringers of hope."

The editorial showed Carroll's remarkable understanding of geopolitics as well as the national temperament. His plea to "open our minds to hard choices" reflects his long-held belief that rational argument should win out over impassioned action. Carroll's stance, as always, illustrated his faith in the power of words to persuade. "In a day when some of our national foundations are being shaken through abuse," wrote one commentator in North Carolina, "[Carroll] showed that to disagree, to argue, to reason and to have free expression to those who can respond with authority is not a restrictive opportunity. Worthy thought can still come from the smaller home fronts of the nation, and it can find its place."

For Carroll, the editorial showed that he was more than just a newsman. His understanding of the issue put him head and shoulders above most policy analysts of the time. And it was the single strongest example in his long career of the ability of words to bring about change. He would continue to publish articles against the war over the next several years, concluding in 1970 that "We Were Losing the Soul of America" in Indochina, and that it was "Time to Come Home."

VIETNAM—QUO VADIS

By Wallace Carroll
March 17, 1968

What will best serve the national interest of the United States?—that is the guts of the problem in Vietnam. Will we advance our national interest by prolonging and enlarging the war? Or will we simply advance the interests of the Soviet Union and Communist China? If we now make a cool appraisal and find that the war is actually making the world safe for Communism, we will have to open our minds to hard, new decisions.

■ ■ ■

How did we get bogged down like this in Vietnam? Did we go in as part of a considered strategic plan? Did the National Security Council or the Joint Chiefs of Staff determine that this was the place to crack the ribs of International Communism?

No, there was no long-range plan. No responsible American ever suggested in advance that we should tie down our first team in an unending war against the Communist fourth team in their kind of fighting ... in a place where we can do no real harm to the main forces of Communism. We slipped into a war that grew bigger than we ever expected. And we floundered deeper and deeper into the jungle as we talked emotionally about the containment of Communism, the aggressive designs of Red China and the "falling domino theory."

The dominos are falling all right while we remain hypnotized by Vietnam. Look first at the Middle East. Iraq, with its precious oil fields ... has come under Soviet influence. So have Syria and Egypt ... Algeria ... Cyprus.... The Soviet navy has broken into the Mediterranean in strength never dreamed of by the Tsars.... While we keep our minds and energies concentrated on Vietnam, Soviet power is flowing silently, relentlessly into the Middle East and the Mediterranean.

Soviet power is also flowing into the Red Sea and all the way down to the Indian Ocean—into the vacuum left by the withdrawing British.... Make no mistake about it: these moves are aimed at us. They are designed to deny the whole Red Sea area to our sea and air power and to force us out of the oil fields....

Now look at Europe. The Grand Alliance of NATO is falling apart.... West Germany, the key to the Continent, and the one decisive area in the entire Cold War, is growing restive because of our indifference and our clumsy handling of ... sensitive issues.... The Soviet and West German governments are beginning to feel each other out. If they ever make a deal ... the whole game of dominoes will be over. If that happens, we Americans can come home and play solitaire.

Next, consider the agony of the dollar under the pressure of the Vietnam War. Remember the dollar is more than money—it is a powerful weapon in the arsenal of the free world against the forces of disorder. It was a stable dollar that made possible the tremendous expansion of world trade in the past twenty years.... If the dollar should collapse, trade would contract, factories slow down, jobs disappear, people go hungry around the world. Riots and even wars might follow. In short, the strain on the dollar threatens the stability of the free world.

At home, the war poisons our national life and our personal lives and keeps us from dealing boldly with the crying needs of our society. The racial revolution ... is gathering pace in the inexorable way of all revolutions.... It has moved from the courts and the legislatures to the streets, from the paths of legality and persuasion to the ways of violence. This nation still has the wealth and wisdom, the compassion and the character to hold this revolution within bounds. But will it do so? The answer is doubtful so long as we pour $30 billion a year and so much of our national energy into the bottomless pit of Vietnam.

... Most of our young people are deeply, honestly troubled. They do not understand this war.... Can we afford to have their idealism turn to scorn, their faith in American democracy turn to cynicism?

The revulsion against the war among these young people and other decent Americans, is opening another danger. For the first time since Stalin's heyday, the Communists are using their old infiltration tactics with some success. Playing on the honest emotions of Americans, they are slipping into peace groups, student organizations and other legitimate associations....

The war has also divided the President and the Congress....

Truth, we are told, is the first casualty in any war. This war has played havoc with our credibility—our credibility to ourselves and to the world.... Who believes our generals after all their rosy predictions? We have even debunked our own airpower—the more we bomb, the stronger the enemy seems to grow. Seldom has there been such a crisis of confidence at home. Seldom have we inspired less confidence abroad.

By this time it must be clear that the Vietnam war is not our kind of war. True, our men have never fought with greater valor. True, no nation has ever performed such prodigies of logistics across such vast distances. But our military leaders have been unable to convert all this valor, all this ingenuity, all this outpouring of blood and treasure into security for even a single province....

Of course, we can continue to "escalate." We can throw in more men, step up the bombing.... But we have been putting in more men for 10 years, and we cannot even protect the capital and our military headquarters from mortar attack....

Well, then, we can spread the war. We can strike at the enemy forces in Laos and Cambodia. But how many hundreds of thousands of men would that take? ...

Of course, there are always nuclear weapons, and we might reach a point of desperation where we would have to use them.... Virtually every government in the world, under pressure of its public opinion, would have to condemn us.... A great gulf of fear and hate would open between Americans and much of humanity. What a fate for a people who began their national life on July 4, 1776, with a declaration of a "decent respect to the opinions of mankind!"

So what useful purpose do we serve by prolonging and enlarging the war? We are told we must show the Communists that their "wars of liberation" do not pay; well, after what this war had brought to North and South Vietnam, no one is going to be in a hurry to get the same treatment.... We are told that our national honor is a stake; but what nation has ever been a more honorable ally than the United States has been to South Vietnam? ...

The war has made us—all of us—lose sight of our national purposes. We need to stand back and get our priorities right....

We come back, then to the question: What will best advance the national interest of the United States? The evidence is overwhelming that this open-ended war in Vietnam is harmful to our national interest. The evidence is equally overwhelming that this war serves the interest of the Soviet Union and world Communism.

▪ ▪ ▪

A WORLD OF INFLUENCE ▪ 263

The options, then, are fairly clear. We can have a domestic policy and a foreign policy—or we can go deeper into Vietnam. We can regroup our forces and redirect our energies against the main forces of Communism—or we can continue to pit the best we have against the Reds' fourth team. We can rebuild our cities and raise up our people—or we can squander our young manhood and our treasure in the jungles. We can recover our role of leadership among the free peoples—or we can let them slip into the Communist embrace. The choices are as clear as that.

So let us take counsel of each other in all humility, for we have hard decisions to reach. There is no short and easy road out of Vietnam—we cannot simply scuttle and run. But we must now see that we cannot allow Vietnam to become the be-all and the end-all of our national policies. Starting with that realization we can work our way back to our true role in the world—not as destroyers but as builders, not as sowers of fear but as bringers of hope.

▪ ▪ ▪

While national recognition of the paper was advancing, it didn't come at the expense of more local and regional coverage. This was especially true during perhaps the paper's finest hour.

One of Carroll's protégées was Arlene Edwards, who at that time was a reporter on the state desk. Edwards—a tall, young woman, outspoken and flavorful—was a familiar sight in her native northwestern North Carolina. Readers of the paper could find her in a field in Yadkin County priming tobacco or in a sewing circle in Wilkes County helping with a quilt. She was also a gifted writer. In December 1969, she was working on a story about quilts being produced in the small mountain community of Deep Gap, North Carolina, one day when a mysterious man showed up in the newsroom, asking to see reporter Chester Davis. After being shuffled to his corner office, the man, who said he ran a furniture store in Surry County but did not want to be identified, told Davis that the Gibbsite Corporation, a mining company, was trying to buy mineral rights throughout the Northwest mountains of North Carolina, just to the west of the city, for strip mining. Davis passed the information to managing editor Pat Kelly, who was meeting with Carroll at the time. They decided to let Edwards check it out.

"I was a feature writer at heart and was, in short, the least likely reporter on staff to write the first story," Edwards later remembered, "UNTIL the Gibbsite officials lied to me; that made me work all the harder." Edwards, provoked, went on the hunt, and after numerous phone calls discovered that Gibbsite had obtained mineral rights to at least 13,000 acres in six area counties. There were no public records of the transactions, no leases or options were filed in any of the courthouses in the six counties, and the Gibbsite officials refused to reveal either the names of the landowners or the location of the land involved. The acreage touched the Blue Ridge Parkway, Stone Mountain State Park, a mountaintop development called Mahogany Rock, the Reynolds family's 8,000 acre-plus retreat— known as Devotion—and some of the finest trout streams in the mountains. The land was to be mined for gibbsite, which until that time had not been used for producing aluminum because of the difficulty and expense of separating it from the soil. A 20-mile-wide strip of the mineral runs from the Wilkesboro, North Carolina, area to Christiansburg, Virginia. A new method for mining it had made the Gibbsite Corporation look at this strip of land with hungry eyes.

On Christmas Eve 1969, Edwards wrote up the story, which put the threat of strip mining in the backyards of people all over the *Journal*'s circulation area. The story armed citizen groups and legislative committees that were organizing to fight the threat.

Soon after her story ran, the paper's editorial board met. John Eslinger, who was the editorial page editor, remembered the meeting. "Editorial writer Fred Hobson said he wanted to do a piece against the Gibbsite Corp. Carroll said, 'Let's don't just write an editorial; let's run them out of the northwest.'" The headline on the resulting editorial, the first of many on the subject, read: "A Sahara in Our Midst?" It was followed by story after story telling of the company's plans, the potential scarring of the land, and the destruction of an environmentally important area, also much valued for hunting, fishing, and other recreation. "The rolling hills and valleys in Northwest Carolina are among the most beautiful anywhere. But the land in Ashe, Alleghany, Wilkes, and Surry counties won't be beautiful much longer if strip mining gets a foothold in the area," stated the editorial.

Edwards spent that winter writing almost a story a day about Gibbsite's plan and the opposition forming against it. The paper also sent Joe Goodman, one of its prize reporters, to Spruce Pine in Mitchell County to describe what strip mining had done to the water, countryside, and wildlife in that area. Jack Trawick, state editor, wrote a series on strip mining in Kentucky. "It was probably the most depressing thing I've ever done in my life," recalled Trawick, "to see the land totally torn up and what it had done to people. I tried to get some of that in what I wrote. It would have been a tragedy for that to have happened in North Carolina."

Meanwhile, Joe Doster, the newspaper's correspondent in Raleigh, reported on the fears of legislators and the lack of laws to regulate strip mining. The *Journal*'s editorial pages hammered away. "If the people of the Northwest should allow strip mining to get a substantial foothold and if large parts of that scenic countryside become a virtual wasteland in a decade or so, they will have no one to blame but themselves," an editorial in late March 1970 warned.

Galvanized by the newspaper's coverage, residents in the northwestern mountains formed groups to oppose the mining and wrote to state and local officials. Almost every reporter on the staff would eventually contribute to the environmental pieces. Some described air pollution in Forsyth and Guilford Counties, while others detailed the development of Bald Head Island on the coast or explained how land use affected the state's water. When fish started dying in the Yadkin River, *Journal* stories pointed to Winston-Salem's waste treatment plant as the main culprit. Only an experienced and committed staff could have pulled it off. As Joe Goodman said, "By virtue of having covered city hall for years and covering water and sewer issues, we knew what the problem was before the city did. The day the fish started dying in the Yadkin River, we were taking pictures at the sewage treatment plant because we knew what the problem was."

On April 25, 1970, Edwards reported that the Gibbsite Corporation had announced that it was taking its mining plans elsewhere. Faced with mounting opposition and a hostile press, the company announced two months later that it was letting its options on the land expire.

"We won!" the editors of the *Journal* and the *Sentinel* wrote later. Since the *Journal*'s coverage, more than 50 years ago, no attempts at strip mining have ever been made in North Carolina's northwest mountains.

Carroll at that time was a member of the Pulitzer Prize Advisory Board, along with his old friend James Reston and the most prominent journalists of the time, including Ben Bradlee of the *Washington Post*, Robert J. Donovan of the *Los Angeles Times*, Vermont Royster of the *Wall Street Journal*, and Joseph Pulitzer III, editor and publisher of the *St. Louis Post-Dispatch*.

Carroll decided that the mining stories would be the centerpiece of the *Journal* and *Sentinel*'s 1971 submission for the Pulitzer Prize—the most coveted award in all of journalism, presented each year by the Pulitzer Prize Board, seated at Columbia University in New York City. The submission would also include numerous stories the *Journal* and the *Sentinel* had written on a host of environmental issues, including both the Yadkin River fish-kill and the Bald Head Island stories, among a whole suite of investigative environmental pieces.

When the Pulitzer board met in April 1971 to choose that year's Public Service prizewinner, Carroll had to leave the room while its members voted on the 78 entries for public service. When he returned, board members moved on to the next category without a word to Carroll. Reston, however, passed Carroll a note that read, simply, "OK." Carroll later learned that the vote had been unanimous.

Carroll, however, had to keep the news of the award a secret—even from his top executives—until Monday, May 10, when the trustees of Columbia University ratified the board's choices. On that day, Carroll broke the news at boisterous meetings with all the departments in the paper back in Winston-Salem. The *Journal* had won the Pulitzer Gold Medal, only one of which is awarded each year and which over time has come to symbolize the entire Pulitzer program.

The text of the board's recommendation was simple and to the point: "The *Winston-Salem Journal* and *Sentinel* waged an extensive campaign, including on-the-spot reportage, against environmental destruction by a proposed strip-mining operation. This campaign blocked the ecologically ruinous project."

In telling the 384 full-time employees of the paper, Carroll wrote: "We send our thanks and congratulations to every employee, for everyone had a part in putting out the newspapers that won this national recognition. And we are happy and proud that all of you, working together, were able to bring this honor to Winston-Salem and Northwest North Carolina." Letters and telegrams of congratulations flooded in from around the world. Officials with Southern Bell arrived in the newsroom with a huge cake bearing a replica of the iconic medal. The Chamber of Commerce and city aldermen passed resolutions commending the newspaper.

That the *Journal* won journalism's greatest prize for its environmental stories was only fitting—the newspaper had worked hard to establish a reputation for conservation reporting. "In general, our environmental coverage had arisen from specific reporters who had their own sources, their own range of interest, that kind of thing," remembered Goodman. And it also reflected Carroll's philosophy toward his editors and reporters. They were "guided only by an occasional nudge from the helm. Civic leaders regarded him as a powerful man. Rather it was his subordinates, each in their own sphere, who were influential in shaping opinions and dispensing facts. But he carefully monitor[ed] this influence, setting restraint as the ideal."

For many years the Pulitzer gold medal hung in a frame in the publisher's office of the *Winston-Salem Journal.* On one side of the medal is a picture of a man at a printing press and the inscription, "For Distinguished and Meritorious Public Service Rendered by A United States Newspaper During the Year 1971." On the other side is Ben Franklin's familiar profile and the words "Honoris Causa (For the sake of honor), Awarded by Columbia University to the *Winston-Salem Journal* and the *Sentinel.*"

To those who worked at the *Journal* at that time, the award was the crowning achievement of almost 25 years of journalistic excellence for the *Journal* and the *Sentinel.* Though no one knew it amid the jubilation of popping balloons and bubbling champagne, that era was ending. Two years earlier, Gordon Gray had decided to sell the paper to Media General, a communications conglomerate that was heavily invested in television news.

After the Pulitzer Prize, reporters also began to look for jobs outside of North Carolina. Less than three years later, Carroll, now 67 years old, decided to retire. Symbolically, this marked the end of the paper's "golden era." During his 11 years as publisher, Carroll, the precise newsman, had come to personify the *Journal* and the *Sentinel*. He had won the respect of the community, the admiration of his coworkers, and the trust of his corporate bosses, as well as the admiration of readers worldwide.

With Carroll out of the way, Media General began to exert its control by promoting its own people to key jobs. Charles W. Crowder, the former business manager of the Richmond newspapers, was given Carroll's job. "He was the complete antithesis to Wally. He had nobody's respect," recalled Goodman, then managing editor. Carroll, who had been on friendly terms with corporate headquarters in Richmond, "thought the appointment was a mistake, but no one at Media General asked for his advice," wrote Goodman. Carroll decided to go peacefully.

Since Media General's takeover, the *Winston-Salem Journal* has been sold to a succession of corporate conglomerates who have cut staff to ensure profits. At the time of this writing, the Pulitzer prize medal the *Journal* was so proud of stands framed in the *Journal*'s offices, a reminder of its earlier journalistic excellence.

▪ ▪ ▪

Carroll's retirement would presage the death of the kind of journalism he had reveled in throughout five decades. In the good old days, wrote Frank Tursi in his history of the *Journal* and the *Sentinel*, "newspaper people thought they were engaged in a holy calling. They were making a difference, commanding attention. Mattering. It was worth the low pay, lousy hours, grinding pace. People were attracted to the newspaper work because it was different from any other kind of job. Sure, it was a business. But in the news business, news came first and business second."

That business would change dramatically in the years ahead. In truth, it had been changing throughout the century. Radio had threatened newspapers in the 1930s and 1940s; in the 1950s television became their main competitor; by the late 1970s and 1980s as the costs of producing newspapers had skyrocketed, corporate mergers and acquisitions of local and regional news-papers were becoming commonplace. Except for a few of the most successful, newspapers would no longer be owned by individuals or families who often saw them as quasi-public insti-tutions meant to serve the public, but as money-making entities whose priority was the bottom line. The rise of the internet and cable networks as primary news sources, beginning in the 1990s and expanding in the twenty-first century, hastened the demise of traditional print news companies.

The result has lent a crushing blow to local newspapers. American newspapers cut 45 percent of newsroom staff between 2008 and 2017, with many of the deepest cutbacks coming in the years after that, according to Margaret Sullivan, media columnist for the *Washington Post*. While new—and profitable—business models are emerging, this lack of resources devoted to newspa-pers at the local level has inhibited their ability to monitor the abuse of power. This loss comes with at a heavy price. "When local news fails, the foundations of democracy weaken," wrote Sullivan in her 2020 book, *Ghosting the News*. "The public, which depends on accurate, factual information in order to make good decisions, suffers. The consequences may not always be obvious, but they are insidious."

These views were echoed more than twenty years ago by Carroll's son, John, who would articulate many of his father's values during his own career as a journalist. In an address on receiving the Editor of the Year Award in 1998 from the National Press Foundation, he spoke of how journalists were constantly being reminded that they were "functionaries of business," when in fact they should really see themselves as working for the reader—not the editor, publisher, or corporate conglomerate that might own the paper. Until his death in 2015 he would emulate many of his father's beliefs about journalism—the need for analysis of all sides of a story to understand how it should be presented; the essential role of investigative journalism in holding powerholders to account; attention to editorial detail; a low-key manner in the newsroom; and fierce support for his staff and fellow journalists. And finally—and perhaps most importantly—that despite the challenges, journalism was still a "wonderfully satisfying and entertaining way to engage the world, and that in a free society there is no mightier sword than the written word."

CHAPTER 16

TO LEAVE SOMETHING BEHIND

"A river is more than an amenity; it is a treasure."
                    —Oliver Wendell Holmes

Winding its way northward from the foot of the North Carolina piedmont into Virginia and through the Appalachian Mountains on into West Virginia runs the New River, the second oldest river in the world—next to the Nile—and one of the most spectacular natural wonders of the United States. The New River Gorge and Valley, carved by the unrelenting waters of the river's flow, is home to more than 1,400 unique species of both plants and animals. Rock climbers on its sandstone cliffs are witness to its stunning beauty, untrampled wilderness, and surrounding farmlands, shrouded in an early morning mist that seems unearthly.

The banks of the New River also claim a rich cultural history. The first European explorers arrived in the mid-seventeenth century, followed a hundred years later by a large wave of German and Scots-Irish settlers, lured by land grants awarded by King George III and then the new American government. They found a wilderness that had long been inhabited and sometimes fought over for centuries by the Cherokees, Shawnees, and Iroquois, with whom they established an uneasy peace. Through more than 200 years of history, the European settlers became a hardy lot, with a unity and tradition behind their way of life. They raised corn, burley tobacco, and cabbage in the bottomlands; grazed their cattle on the grassy upland slopes; hunted deer; ran their coon dogs; and danced to the whine of the fiddle.

Economically, the area had struggled as the twentieth century began, due in part to its isolated geography. Roads into the valley had only been paved in the 1920s, and electricity was nonexistent before Franklin Roosevelt's Rural Electrification Program had brought power to farms and homes in the 1930s. As a result, several small manufacturing industries arose, and by the 1970s, the valley was seeing more economic stability. Economic activity, however, still centered on family farms, where beef and dairy cattle were raised and cash crops included tobacco, beans, and Christmas trees.

Nowadays, many would recognize the river gorge as the land of Daniel Boone. Remnants of the region's past—native tribal artifacts including weapons, stone tools, fragments of clay pottery, and evidence of stone hearths—are hidden in the forest and tell the stories of earliest life in the Appalachian Mountains. Alongside these are vestiges of the European settlers and their descendants—historic coal structures and coke ovens, along with other surviving examples of subsistence farming. Former community sites, homesteads, and other places where the people of the New River Valley worked and lived for two centuries also dot the river's shoreline.

▪ ▪ ▪

In 1968, while Carroll was still editor and publisher of the *Journal* and the *Sentinel,* he and Peggy had purchased with resources inherited from her family 350 acres of land—literally an entire mountaintop—near Sparta, North Carolina, just 70 miles west of Winston-Salem and the county seat of Alleghany County. The land was high up on Cheek Mountain Road—the highest point in the county—and came with endless idyllic views, including of five states and farmland in Virginia. Much of the land was cleared and rented to a nearby farmer who grazed his cattle. Its fields were surrounded by woods where giant golden flame azaleas bloomed in the spring and wild cranberries were ripe for the picking in the fall. Peggy especially loved the mountaintop, the sweeping views, and the almost mystical beauty of the valley below.

Even before his retirement and before the property had a house on it, Carroll and Peggy had begun to invite friends to the farm for picnics. Among those who attended were old friends and staff from the *Journal*—John Ehle and Rosemary Harris; Wake Forest Provost Edwin Wilson and his poet wife, Emily; and philanthropist Phil Hanes and his wife, Charlotte. Their picnics promised good food and wine, good conversation, and always Peggy's deep and juicy pies—strawberry rhubarb being a favorite.

But the Carrolls were hardly people who would ever fully retire. A year after leaving the *Journal* and the *Sentinel,* Carroll had been offered a position at Wake Forest University as the Samuel J. Ervin Lecturer on Constitutional Rights. He took the assignment seriously, spending upwards of a year in the university library preparing his lectures. When he finally began to teach, he did not talk about his past experiences. His students had little idea of his standing in the journalistic community or his adventures before or during World War II. Most only had a vague notion that he had been involved in editing the local paper.

In class, he would stand in the corner of the classroom, arms folded, and ask questions about the assigned reading, which would often include Supreme Court decisions. Never loquacious, his demeanor would signal that he was someone who required their respect. "Mr. Carroll," as he was always referred to, somehow made students want to be more thoughtful and less glib. In other words, to do their best. A word of praise meant everything but was not often given. Yet he was not unkind or unapproachable. He and Peggy would often invite students to their mountain home for picnics and to small cocktail parties at their house on Wellington Road where—somehow—very distinguished people, former Secretary of State Dean Acheson and columnist George Will, for example, always seemed to show up. Years later his students would remember his class above others in the university. "He was an exceptional thinker and writer and so progressive for a fairly conservative, Winston-Salem," remembered one student who would go on to a noted legal career. "He was always a gentleman; gracious in his criticisms of weak thinking and mediocre writing," remembered another who would go on to win two Pulitzer Prizes in her journalism career.

Carroll would teach at Wake Forest University for ten years, preparing and delivering a course, *Rights and Citizens*, which covered a wide range of issues, from First Amendment freedoms to the right to a fair trial. He would also be called on to deliver campus-wide lectures on topics such as the origins of the Cold War, critiques of Supreme Court decisions, or revelations about Watergate. His memory for detail was remarkable and his addresses always carefully thought out and logical. He had the journalist's gift for storytelling, and he didn't let his audiences down. Tapes of his talks on his escapades as a foreign correspondent before and during the war would delight the numerous local clubs he was asked to speak before. Finally recognized for his achievements, he would be awarded honorary degrees from both Wake Forest University and Duke University, as well as his alma mater, Marquette University.

He would also continue to write, including book reviews for the *New York Times* and *Wall Street Journal*, and occasional editorials—one of which, entitled, "To End the Gun Terror, End the Second Amendment Hoax," published by the *Baltimore Sun* on July 4, 1993, continued his long fight against the National Rifle Association (NRA) for its interpretation of the Second Amendment. "This mighty country stands paralyzed in the face of an ever-spreading plague of guns," he wrote. Pointing to the Founding Fathers, he wrote that the Second Amendment was never meant to give "everyone an absolute constitutional right to carry a firearm." The NRA had ignored the initial phrase in the amendment, which was to ensure arms would be available when and if "a well-regulated militia was necessary to the security of a free state." The founders had never seen the amendment as enabling the federal government to have the power to ensure "the right of the people" to bear arms, but only to ensure state militias could do so if faced with an Indian uprising, foreign incursions on the frontier, or a domestic insurrection. He was able to back his argument up with a series of court decisions. Sadly, he once again predicted the danger of a proliferation of guns, especially automatic weapons, in people's hands.

All in all, the Wake Forest years were a rich time for Carroll, and even more so for the students lucky enough to have taken a class from him. Always a mentor, he would guide many into future careers and instill in them a desire to participate in the affairs of their community, to think critically and to cherish the written word. "He encouraged us to be engaged fully," remembered one student, "to argue well—in class and in writing. I left his class a more engaged and thoughtful participant in American democracy, and Mr. Carroll's lessons have stayed with me ever since."

■ ■ ■

By this time, the Carroll children had moved on to their own careers and were long out of Winston-Salem. The oldest, Margaret, a graduate of Lawrence College in Wisconsin, had worked as a writer and editor at *Congressional Quarterly* in Washington, D.C., and went on to be one of the founders of the *National Journal*. She later helped establish and served as executive director of the Investor Research Center in Washington, where she was to remain for many years.

John, following in his father's footsteps, had launched what was to become one of the most respected careers in American journalism. After graduating from Haverford College, he worked for the *Providence Journal* and as a foreign correspondent for the *Baltimore Sun*, where he covered Vietnam, the Middle East, and then the White House. He rose to editorship at the *Philadelphia Inquirer* and the *Lexington Herald-Leader*, where his staff won a Pulitzer Prize. He returned to the *Baltimore Sun* as editor and vice president, and then went on to become the editor of the *Los Angeles Times*. During his tenure, the *Times* won a record-breaking 13 Pulitzer Prizes. John would receive many awards, including being named Editor of the Year in 1998 by the National Press Foundation.

Tall and good-looking, John mirrored his father's reserve and self-effacing, gentlemanly demeanor. And like his father, his calm exterior masked a competitive spirit and fierce independence. He was known for inspiring his reporters and for giving them the time and resources necessary for them to develop their stories. He was also beloved for having mentored many journalists who would go on to fame, and who looked to him as a spokesperson for journalistic excellence. At his memorial service in 2015, *New York Times* Executive Editor Dean Baquet, his former deputy at the *Los Angeles Times*, remarked that watching John Carroll edit was "like watching Willie Mays play baseball." He was, according to Norman Pearlstine, chief content officer at *Time Inc.*, "our generation's best, most respected, best-loved newspaper editor." His life, this author has frequently thought, calls for its own biography.

Peggy and Carroll's third child, Posie, graduated from Harvard University and worked as a producer for KCBS on the West Coast, before going on to a 32-year career at IBM, first as a systems engineer then as a project and program manager.

The youngest, Pat, graduated from Duke University and would go on to work in and around government for more than 40 years, beginning with a stint as a staffer on the Hill and then in the Carter transition team and White House. She would eventually join the Department of Transportation and then work with the Arlington county government in Virginia, covering the state legislature.

■ ■ ■

Both Carroll and Peggy were determined to remain active in civic affairs—his teaching and speaking duties notwithstanding—and, if anything, to become more involved now that he was no longer hampered by his obligations as publisher. "They were optimists," remembered their daughter Posie about their dedication to civic undertakings, "and just felt they could accomplish things."

Peggy, in particular, took on a new cause that finally enabled her to showcase her vast abilities. She had begun taking friends and family—or whomever she could corral—on tubing trips down the New River. Throughout her time in North Carolina, she had been an avid outdoorswoman, organizing hiking clubs and serving as the first president of Winston-Salem's "environment committee." She now learned, to her consternation, that the American Electric Power Company (AEP), the nation's largest private utility, and its subsidiary, the Appalachian Power Company, since 1963 had been planning two dams on the river, not far from the Carrolls' farm—a project that would generate 3.9 billion kilowatt-hours of electricity annually but flood 42,000 acres of the New River Valley, inundating farms and even whole towns. The building of the dams now appeared imminent. Recognizing the disruption this would cause both to the environment and to the communities along the river, both Carrolls decided to join with residents and landowners to fight the project.

Thus began a decade-long fight that would be the Carrolls' final legacy. Peggy saw it as not just a fight to save the environment, but to save the mountain people's homes and heritage. The dispute pitted a symbiotic environmental coalition—consisting of the State of North Carolina, conservation groups nationwide, and innumerable individuals—against AEP. In the years in which they battled, the governments of three states would be drawn into the conflict, as would the federal courts. Twice, the conflict would enter both houses of Congress. President Gerald Ford would be drawn into it, as well as his challengers in the 1976 election. Senator Sam Ervin of Watergate fame would come out of retirement to fight in support of the mountain people, while George Meany of the AFL-CIO moved to battle on the other side. And caught between the two sides, belabored by one of the most sustained and ingenious lobbying campaigns in years, were sixteen crusty members of the U.S. House Rules Committee, who were to become instrumental to the river's protection. Any legislation to protect the river had to pass first through their committee, where lawmakers were divided.

The need to gain legislative approval for various facets of the dam project had caused delays in its implementation for several years. Such delays, beginning in 1965 and ongoing into the early 1970s, had enabled its opponents to organize and to garner support for their cause. Amassing a constituency that included the Washington-based Izaak Walton League, the Conservation Council of Virginia, the Allegheny Farm Bureau, and other opponents of the project, the State of North Carolina in 1974 launched a four-pronged assault on the dam project, attacking it on legislative, legal, administrative, and public fronts.

Their first move was to designate a segment of the New as a North Carolina scenic river under the Wild and Scenic Rivers Act of 1968. With this accomplished, bills were simultaneously introduced in the United States Senate and House of Representatives to study the waterway for possible inclusion in the National Wild and Scenic Rivers (NWSR) system. As a "study river," the New would be protected until a decision was made on its eligibility for the federal system. After the Senate passed the bill to designate the river as a "study river," a ferocious debate broke out in the House led by opponents of the bill. Ultimately the House Rules Committee, under fierce resistance from AEP and the AFL-CIO, refused to allow the bill to come to the House floor. As a result, assaults on the legislative front were temporarily thwarted.

Despite this setback, proposed legislation to place the New into the NWSR was again launched in 1975. By this time, members of Congress were under intense pressure to declare the river part of the protected national system. Meanwhile, public support for the river had been marshaled through an interstate organization that would become the National Committee for the New River (NCNR), which was supported by a massive public relations effort. Wallace Carroll was named a director of the NCNR, which published a newsletter and made slide presentations of the New available on request. Among other lobbying activities, bumper stickers proclaiming "The New River Like It Is" were distributed by the thousands to counter the opposition slogan, "Dam The New." A number of luminaries gave their support to the campaign: Earl Hammer Jr., creator of the television series *The Waltons,* wrote a moving piece about the New River, and former Senator Ervin was an invaluable asset when river legislation came before Congress. Preservation of the New had become a national rather than a local issue.

Simultaneously, individual Congressional members were lobbied heavily, particularly those on the House Rules Committee. The Carrolls were on the front lines of this effort. Peggy launched an intense lobbying campaign with members of the Committee that included making phone calls, drafting letters, arranging personal visits, and calling upon old friends in Washington to lobby as needed. Efforts were also made to generate letters from members' constituencies nationally to support the legislation going forward. Later she would invite journalists and members of Congress to visit the Carrolls' mountain home, to see the river, and the farms and towns that would be flooded by the dams, up close. At one point, she invited then Representative (later senator) Paul Simon of Illinois on an expedition on the New River, then served up a last-minute meal for twenty of his friends. As a result, Simon became a lifelong friend of the New River, working hard to get the legislation passed to save it.

Meanwhile, Carroll was leading the NCNR in a nationwide media effort. His strategy was to convince citizens across the country to lobby their representatives in the House and Senate to designate the river in the Wild and Scenic Rivers system and to use the power of the written word to do so. During the summer and fall of 1975, he wrote to hundreds of reporters and editors with whom he'd worked over his long career—journalists now sprinkled across the country at countless publications. He sent them information packets, outlined the reason the river was in dire need of their aid, and urged them to write editorials in support of its preservation. Most of them had never seen the river, and to some it seemed far away and irrelevant to their readers. But they respected Carroll and saw the power in the story of a bunch of mountaineer farmers struggling against a big power company.

Carroll also urged his contacts in Washington and at the *New York Times* to cover the story. Bob Poole, the Washington correspondent for the *Winston-Salem Journal*, discovered that archaeological studies, withheld by both AEP and the Federal Power Commission, indicated that the New River Valley had been continuously occupied by humans since at least 8,000 BC and that the New River, as the only river bisecting the Appalachian

Mountains, had been an important passageway for early peoples in North America. Both Poole and Ned Kenworthy of the *New York Times*—a close friend of Carroll's—wrote pieces on the findings, arguing that not disclosing this information had undervalued the river as a national resource.

By January 1976, more than 150 newspapers from every section of the country had written editorials in favor of the scenic river plan. It was acknowledged that Carroll was the primary reason such support occurred. One editorial from the *Daily Hampshire Gazette* of Northampton, Massachusetts, published in December 1975, read:

> *An editor for whom we once worked and whom we respect has alerted us to what is without question one of the most reckless and devastating acts in the nation's headlong quest for energy at any cost.*
>
> *A huge power company plans to dam up the New River in North Carolina, flood 40,000 acres of rich bottomland, pasture and forest, displace 3,000 rural folks living on the land—all to generate power to meet peak energy demands in far-off communities....*
>
> *Our editor friend believes that if the New River ... is taken into the national scenic river system, the power project will be killed. He says this will not happen, however, unless [Interior Secretary Thomas S.] Kleppe and President Ford are aware of the strong sentiment in all parts of the nation for protecting the New River.*

Press support for the New River appeared in other media as well. Dan Rather, Walter Cronkite, Harry Reasoner, and David Brinkley all featured the river in their television news programs; syndicated columnist George Will devoted articles to saving the river. *Newsweek* ran an article entitled "Of Time and the River" that favored the preservation of the New. Meanwhile, the NCNR hosted a variety of activities to mobilize support. One was a "Festival of the New" in northwest North Carolina attended by

3,000 supporters. The committee also mobilized chapters across the country to send letters and petitions to government agencies and to Congress in support of the scenic river application. By the summer of 1975, the New River Bill was becoming one of the most heavily lobbied measures of the 94th Congress.

■ ■ ■

The Carrolls' and the committee's strategy to bring pressure on key House committee members worked. Public opinion in key districts had pressured them to move the legislation forward. Peggy, in writing to her children that summer admitted "We are waiting for the other shoe to drop but, perhaps wrongly, believe the House will pass the bill." In August, when the vote came before the full House, it passed 311 to 73. Later that month, the Senate approved the bill 69 to 16. By federal law neither Appalachian Power nor any other intruder could damage the protected stretches of the river. The Appalachian Power Company had been powerless in matching the National Committee's media and lobbying blitz. "No one will ever know," wrote Peggy to her children, "how many people everywhere put in their little touches, or even which little touches were the ones that turned the tide."

Sam Ervin, on being told of the vote, acknowledged that it was "still possible in this country for the people to win over a big corporation and big labor," and *Time* magazine wrote on September 27, 1976, that "the measure does more than preserve the river and deal a precedent-setting setback to the power industry: it also safeguards a centuries-old way of life."

Later, Peggy would sum it up: "This is a story of a little man's victory, about some extraordinarily determined mountain people, of a change in the way Americans felt about what big business and government should do, about how much Americans were masters of their own fate, of some dramatic political activities, and of a nationwide rising to the defense of an unknown river."

On the sunny morning of September 11, 1976, in the Rose Garden at the White House, President Gerald Ford signed legislation placing large stretches of the New River into the Wild and Scenic Rivers System. The designation brought an end to proposals for energy development projects on the river upstream of West Virginia. The Carrolls were present at the signing. Their long arduous battle was over. Two years later, President Jimmy Carter would sign legislation putting the rest of the river under National Park Service Protection. And on December 27, 2020, the New River Gorge would be designated as the country's 63rd National Park, protecting for perpetuity the gorge's 53 scenic miles.

▪ ▪ ▪

Twenty-five years after the Rose Garden signing, at an anniversary celebration of the river's preservation, former North Carolina Congressman Steve Neal, who had played a key role in ensuring the scenic river designation, reminded those gathered for the occasion that the dam fight had shown that democracy does work. The fight, he said, was "a story of how all the special interests were lined up on one side and most of the citizens on the other side—and the citizens won." James Holshouer, who had been governor of North Carolina when the legislation finally passed, remembered the river's preservation as "the toughest fight he was in," but also one of North Carolina's "finest hours."

At the same celebration, a 94-year-old Wallace Carroll recalled the fight with great emotion, and especially the role that his wife, who had died less than a year earlier, had played in it. He had spread her ashes in the river at her request, and less than a year later his own would be tossed into the flowing waters.

Just before she died, he had written Peggy that he recalled fondly her hard work in preserving the river, and especially her support of the small farmers who had sought to preserve their way of life in the face of "a mis-directed vision of profit and power."

"I have been very happy ever since we met," he recalled. And she should know that "in him she had found a friend that would never fail her."

Together, the Carrolls had succeeded. They would leave something magnificent behind.

EPILOGUE

"The quiet words of the wise are more to be heeded
than the shouting of a ruler among fools."
—Ecclesiastes, 9th Chapter, verses 17 and 18

What constitutes a remarkable life?
When Wallace Carroll died in 2002 at the age of 95, the sanctuary at Highland Church in Winston-Salem, North Carolina, was filled to capacity with people who had come for his memorial service. There to pay their final respects were many journalists who had either worked with him or knew of his career; artists and musicians who had benefitted from their years at the North Carolina School of the Arts; conservationists who recognized the role he had played in saving the New River Valley; and last but not least, staff from the retirement home in which he lived, who had come to appreciate his kindness and attentiveness toward them. The church overflowed with the many friends and family who had enjoyed his and Peggy's company, and those who through small acquaintances had benefitted from his example over the years.

Carroll was a humble man, and his story is perhaps not well known because, unlike many of his contemporaries, he did not seek the limelight. Shunning radio and television journalism, he remained dedicated to the written word, and to a form of journalism that was grounded in the idea of public service. A journalists' journalist, he was widely respected by those who knew the business and who benefitted from his kind but demanding mentoring. For the most part, he was content to stay in the background; to encourage others and, when needed, to bring his substantial intellectual capacity to bear in writing editorials that influenced local, national, and international affairs.

Words were important to Carroll because he believed they held both power and nobility. "Let us not forget that the English language has stood us in good stead," he would recall from his World War II days, "and never doubt that we should need them again in our darkest moments." Words were a great natural resource to Carroll, "as much as the air we breathe and the water we drink." They held the power to persuade, and thus had to be precise and uncluttered, crisp and declarative. He built his life around their use.

It is perhaps difficult to understand today—when news is instantaneous and ever present—how important the written journalists of Carroll's day were in informing the public of what was going on in the world. Their judgment in deciding what and how to report on events was in many cases the only information available to the average citizen, and was often channeled through the mediums of radio and television to reach broader audiences. As difficult as it is to prove cause and effect, journalists like Carroll no doubt played a role in forming history. We would do well to remember their contribution.

Carroll also believed that journalism had a higher calling, and that was to give citizens the information they need and deserve to know in order to preserve democracy. The press is not perfect; it makes mistakes, he would acknowledge. But among the founding principles of democracy is the need for the powerful to be called to account by ordinary citizens; that the truth as presented to citizens matters; and that reasoned reporting of the truth is not only possible in our society but essential. In calling for an end to the Vietnam War in his editorial "Quo Vadis," he demonstrated the power of that approach. It did not need to come from the halls of the Defense Department, but from a trusted journalist at a regional newspaper who understood the danger the country was in. He believed it was up to citizens to decide what kind of country they wanted to live in; his job was to give them the facts and a rationale for reaching such a decision. In the end, he felt they would do the right thing.

Carroll's precision in the use of the English language also signaled something much larger about his character, remembered his son John, and that was a total truthfulness and integrity. He was a modest man who didn't wear it on his sleeve, but this integrity was evident anyway, and it had an effect on others who tried to emulate him, and in some way made them better. Together with Peggy, he brought that quality into his efforts to improve their community. Both believed they could make a difference in the lives of others. And they did.

It was this combination of achievement and modesty, intelligence and compassion that made this author want to write Carroll's story. And what an adventure his life was—the near-sighted schoolboy who rode in a horse and buggy in Milwaukee, carried a dying and bloody demonstrator as a young man in Europe, held lookout on the rooftops of London during the Blitz, dined with Josef Stalin, witnessed the destruction at Pearl Harbor, chronicled the mysteries and foibles of the Eisenhower and Kennedy administrations, and played a role in ending the Vietnam War. And finally, with Peggy, saving a precious natural resource for generations to follow.

He is probably even now looking for a typewriter to punch out a new story to send over the wire, or a piece to publish on the editorial page.

If only we could read it.

TIMELINE

WALLACE CARROLL, 1906–2002

1906: December 15, born, Milwaukee, Wisconsin.

1928: Graduated, Marquette University, Milwaukee, Wisconsin.

1929–1938: Foreign Correspondent, United Press, stationed in London, Paris, and Geneva.

1938: Covered Spanish Civil War; married Margaret (Peggy) Sawyer.

1939–1941: Manager, United Press London Bureau.

1941: Reported from the Soviet Union for United Press.

1942: Published *We're in This With Russia;* received Headliners Award for reporting on Soviet Union.

1942–1944: Director, United States Office of War Information, London.

1944–1945: Deputy Director for European Operations, Overseas Branch, Office of War Information, Washington D.C.

1947–1952: Consultant, United States State Department and United States Army.

1948: Published *Persuade or Perish*.

1949–1955: Executive News Editor, *Winston-Salem Journal*.

1951–1952: Consultant, Office of Plans and Policy, Psychological Strategy Board.

1955–1963: News Editor, Washington Bureau, *New York Times*.

1963–1973: Editor and Publisher, *Winston-Salem Journal* and *Sentinel*.

1974–1984: Samuel J. Ervin Lecturer on Constitutional Rights, Wake Forest University.

2002: July 28, died, Winston-Salem, North Carolina.

ACKNOWLEDGMENTS

When I began the adventure of writing this book, one of the things that I most appreciated about Wallace and Peggy Carroll was that in addition to their professional successes, they seemed to have raised remarkable offspring. This was proven true time and time again during the many years I worked on the book. The Carroll daughters—Margaret, Posie, and Pat—and John Carroll's wife, Lee, from the inception of the project never questioned the work, nor placed any limitations on me, and in fact demonstrated a rather remarkable faith in a first-time author. Without their collaboration and inputs—and especially Margaret's careful collection of her father's writings and her mother's marvelous letters—this book could not have been written. My only regrets are that the book was not finished before Margaret passed away, and that I never had the opportunity to meet John Carroll. But their legacy lives on through the many friends and colleagues who encouraged the book to come to light, and who supported it when it did. I hope that they would have been pleased with the outcome.

Wallace and Peggy were part of an extraordinary generation of enlightened citizens in Winston-Salem, N.C., who also made this work possible and offered early-on encouragement: Paula Duggan, for her wonderful conversation and home-cooked meals; Ed and Emily Wilson; Rosemary Harris and John Ehle; and Doug and Bingle Lewis. Thanks as well to Arlene Edwards and Joe Goodman, former staffers of the *Winston-Salem Journal*, who gave both their time and materials for use in the book. Maria Henson, a colleague of John Carroll's, was among the first to offer her support; Carol Hanner provided invaluable help early on in shaping and editing the manuscript. In D.C., Jonathan Yardley was kind enough to meet with me, and provided perhaps the best quote available about Wallace Carroll. And Mark Nelson brought his usual kindness, intelligence, and skill to reviewing it.

Roger Williams first gave life to the idea of the book. Andy Wolfe agreed to publish it, with the help of Wes Cannon and Jenny Young at Whaler Books. Karen Bowen, professional editor and designer, exercised extreme patience and care in producing the final product. Brad Coleman provided fact-checking when it was needed most; and Lisa Tracy, superb editor and chief cheerleader, made everything possible. Her skill and enthusiasm coming down the homestretch are absolutely why the book is seeing the light of day.

As all authors will attest, libraries are a writers' sanctuary. Such was true in my case. My thanks to the staffs of the Special Collections and University Archives Branch of the Raynor Memorial Libraries at Marquette University; the Belk Library at Appalachian State University; the Franklin D. Roosevelt Presidential Library at Hyde Park; and the Manuscript Division of the Library of Congress. Special thanks as well to the D.C. Public Library's Chevy Chase neighborhood branch, where I spent many pleasant days writing and gazing out through a full-length window at a tree that changed colors as the seasons progressed. A similarly pleasant venue was the North Carolina Room at the Forsyth County Central Library in Winston-Salem, N.C., where I could view the glistening skyline of a town for which I have always felt a special affection.

And finally, thanks to my three daughters—Emmie, Annie, and Georgia—who never fail to support their mother's some-times crazy schemes and resulting doggedness; my sisters, Helen

Whisman and Ann Fox; and my husband, Michael Woscoboinik—chief reviewer, fact-checker, and proofreader par excellence—and, of course, to me much more.

Mary Llewellyn McNeil
Washington, D.C.

ENDNOTES

Direct quotes from Wallace Carroll, unless otherwise referenced, are from audiotapes of presentations he made to the Winston-Salem community between 1982 to 1990. In Sections I and II, remarks by Carroll, unless otherwise referenced, are from an interview with H.L. Stephenson, former UPI Vice President, in Winston-Salem, North Carolina, in 1992. Newspaper quotations referenced through newspapers.com.

AUTHOR'S NOTE

xvi **"It wasn't a matter"**—Jonathan Yardley, "A Newspaper Man Who Stood Above the Fold," *Washington Post*, August 5, 2002.

PROLOGUE

xx **"flames swept"**—Stanley Cloud and Lynne Olson, *The Murrow Boys*, 90.

xxi **"Being a war correspondent"**—Douglas Brinkley, *Cronkite*, 76.

xxii **"The Blitz affected"**—BBC History archives (printout).

xxii **"I wasn't scared"**—James Reston, *Deadline*, 92.

xxiii **"It had immediacy"**—Cloud and Olson, *Murrow Boys*, 89.

xxiii **"Five months later"**—"How Did Public Opinion About Entering World War II Change between 1939 and 1941," United States Holocaust Museum exhibit, exhibitions.ushmm.org.

xxiii **"dined with the Churchills"**—Cloud and Olson, *Murrow Boys*, 92.

xxiii **"accepted the dangers"**—John G. Winant, *A Letter from Grosvenor Square*, 117.

CHAPTER 1

7 **"Hours too long"**—Marquette University, *Hilltop 1961*, 11.

7 **"The university's president"**—Thomas J. Jablonsky, *Milwaukee's Jesuit University, Marquette 1991–1981*, 259.

8   **"If we don't have a good press"**—Marquette University, *Hilltop 1961*, 11.

8   **"it would certainly take"**—Wallace Carroll, *Marquette Tribune*, November 27, 1924, 1.

8   **"Barber of Seville"**—Carroll, *Marquette Tribune*, April 7, 1925.

CHAPTER 2

11   **"News stories on a press"**—Robert Hanley, "Earl Johnson, 71, Led United Press," *New York Times*, January 4, 1974.

12   **"In bureau after bureau"**—Gregory Gordon and Ronald E. Cohen, *Down To The Wire UPI's Fight for Survival*, 10.

12   **"But while many considered AP"**—Ibid., 6.

13   **"men propped against the"**—"Hail of Lead Tests 'Nerve' of Gangland," *Vidette-Messenger* of Porter County (Valpariso, Indiana), February 15, 1929.

13   **"I never saw him [Johnson] rattled"**—Douglas Brinkley, *Cronkite*, 42.

14   **"great at keeping the books"**—Stephenson interview, 1992.

14   **"The lead elephant"**—Carroll, "Scores Hurt in Mad Rush from Street," *The San Bernadino County Sun*, November 11, 1930.

16   **"I fear the Americans might"**—Carroll, "Gandhi Will Shun America," *The Times* (Munster, Indiana), September 12, 1931.

20   **"A dying French youth"**—Carroll, "Horrors of Paris Riots Told by Correspondent," *Los Angeles Times*, February 7, 1934.

CHAPTER 3

25   **"scattering fear and death"**—Carroll, "Boos, Cat-calls Fail to Prevent Monarch's Plea," *The Atlanta Constitution*, July 1, 1936.

26   **"Carroll had warned"**—*Mt. Carmel Daily Republican-Register*, June 29, 1936, 1.

26   **"was the climax"**—Carroll, *Columbus Daily Telegraph*, June 30, 1936, 1.

26   **"I sat in the press galleries"**—Carroll, *We're in This With Russia*, 42.

26   **"non-recognition of Italy's conquest"**—*Columbus Daily Telegraph*, June, 30, 1936, 1.

26   **"British foreign secretary Anthony Eden"**—*Cushing Daily Citizen*, July 6, 1936, 6.

26   **"He used every device"**—Carroll, *We're in This With Russia*, 4–5.

27   **"Nothing in the annals"**—Frances Paul Walters, *A History of the League of Nations,* 712.

27   **"failed ultimately because of the reluctances"**—*Events Leading Up to World War II,* Library of Congress. 1944, 97.

27   **"I saw the magic"**—Carroll, *We're in This With Russia,* 6.

28   **"His replacement as Commissar"**—"The Fall of Litvinov: Harbinger of the German-Soviet Non-aggression Pact," *Europe-Asia Studies,* Vol. 52 (January 2000), 35–56.

28   **"Fear of war broods over Europe"**—Carroll, "Europe Rearming Madly as Fear of War Grows," *Los Angeles Times,* July 27, 1936.

28   **"The League has been so badly shaken"**—*Los Angeles Times,* July 26, 1936.

28   **"largely because it was abandoned"**—Kenneth Thompson, *Winston Churchill's World View: Statesmanship and Power* (Baton Rouge: Louisiana State University Press, 1983), 298.

28   **"You are lucky to be an American"**—Carroll, "Europe Rearming Madly As Fear of War Grows," *Los Angeles Times,* July 27, 1936.

30   **"he is not very good"**—Peggy Sawyer letter to her mother, February 3, 1938.

31   **"so painful I couldn't speak"**—Carroll letter to Peggy, August 5, 1938.

32   **"During his three-year stint"**—Jenny Thompson and Sherry Thompson, *The Kreminologist,* 18.

32   **"with grace"**—Carroll, "Career Diplomat Was 'The Playboy Who Made Good,'" *Winston-Salem Journal,* February 8, 1972.

34   **"Don't tell them what you think"**—In "Letter: A tradition reporting not what you feel, but what you know," Telecom.com, Worchester, M.A., February 18, 2018, https://www.telegram.com/news/20180218/letter-tradtion-reporting-noto-what-you-feel-but-what-you-know.

34   **"Roosevelt, who had dubbed"**—Lynne Olson, *Citizens of London,* 22.

35   **"he understands the social"**—Ibid., 22.

37   **"According to Carroll"**—Carroll, "Double City Underground Protects Barcelona resident from Raiders," *The Berkshire Eagle,* August 5, 1938.

38   **"MADRID-U.P. (August 23)"**—Carroll, "Planes Still Carry Passengers Over Franco's Blockage," *Wisconsin State Journal,* August 23, 1938.

40   **"I shouldn't have recognized him"**—Peggy letter to mother, February 16, 1939.

41   **"Food is strictly rationed"**—Carroll, "Madrid: Here's How it Looks Now," *Wisconsin State Journal,* August 24, 1938.

CHAPTER 4

45   **"Writing for a news agency"**—Peggy letter to mother, January 18, 1939.

46   **"The news agencies"**—Richard Sambrook, "Protecting Journalists: An Evolving Responsibility," *Reporting Dangerously,* summary, https://link.springer.com/chapter/10.1007%2F978-1-137-40670-5_8.

47   **"absolutely honest and fearless"**—Cloud and Olson, *Murrow Boys,* 92.

48   **"style or authority"**—Brinkley, *Cronkite,* 30.

49   **"like hearing an old friend"**—Cloud and Olson, *Murrow Boys,* 92.

51   **"a businessman's fear"**—Carroll, *We're in This With Russia,* 32.

51   **"Carroll reported that"**—*Eau Claire Sunday Leader,* April 30, 1939, 1.

51   **"who knew something about war"**—Wallace Carroll Lecture at Wake Forest University, November 1, 1973.

52   **"could not convince myself"**—Carroll, *We're in This With Russia,* 29.

52   **"Churchill, in a speech"**—Winston Churchill, broadcast on October 1, 1939, https://winstonchurchill.org/publications/finest-hour/finest-hour-150/churchill-on-russia/.

52   **"The Soviet-German pact was"**—Carroll, *We're in This With Russia,* 46.

52   **"To convince doubtful embassy officials"**—Clare Hollingworth, "The foreign correspondent who broke news of the Second World War, turns 104," *The Telegraph,* October 9, 2015.

53   **"Chamberlain, in a radio"**—Reston, *Deadline,* 80.

54   **"I cannot believe"**—Neville Chamberlain, radio address on September 3, 1939, https://avalon.law.yale.edu/wwii/gb3.asp.

54   **"the peoples of the world"**—King George VI, radio address on September 4, 1939, https://www.americanrhetoric.com/speeches/kinggeorgevifirstradioaddress.htm.

55   **"The tension"**—Peggy letter to mother, September 28, 1939.

56   **"I am so very proud of you"**—Carroll letter to Peggy November 3, 1939.

CHAPTER 5

57   **"London looked"**—Storm Jameson, "City without Children," *The Atlantic,* April 13, 2012.

57   **"The London Zoo"**—E.S. Turner, *The Phony War on the Home Front.*

57   **"The phony war gave everybody"**—Reston, *Deadline*, 87.

58   **"Perhaps most disturbing"**—Ellis, Major L.F (2004) *The War in France and Flanders 1939–1940*. History of the Second World War, United Kingdom Military Series, Naval and Military Press, retrieved October 2016.

58   **"We are told nothing"**—Lynne Olson, *Troublesome Young Men*, 257.

58   **"transformed conditions of life"**—Ibid., 248.

58   **"During the first month"**—"Life During the Blackout," *The Guardian*, November 1, 2009.

58   **"Everybody carried gas masks"**—Hugh Baillie, *High Tension, The Recollections of Hugh Baillie*, 137.

59   **"walking with destiny"**—Winston Churchill, https://www.goodreads.com/quotes/59680-i-felt-as-if-i-were-walking-with-destiny.

60   **"I have never imagined"**—Carroll, "Flanders Survivors Describe Nightmare of Blood and Hell," *Tampa Bay Times*, May 30, 1940.

60   **"We may have"**—Reston, *Deadline*, 81.

62   **"We were plainly drifting"**—Ibid., 81.

64   **"According to his count"**—"The Secret to Winning the Battle of Britain," bbc.co.uk.

65   **"What worried British Air Chief"**—"Air Pilots Biggest Need of Britain," *The Capital Journal*, Salem, Oregon, October 15, 1940.

65   **"The Greatest Day"**—Williamson Murray and Allan R. Millett, *A War to be Won*, 88.

65   **"On August 18,"**—Ibid., 88.

66   **"People in towns,"**—James Holland, *Battle of Britain*, 514.

66   **"Along the southeast"**—Carroll, "2,000 Planes in Vast Drive Over England," *The Dayton Herald*, August 16, 1940.

CHAPTER 6

69   **"I realize I would"**—Peggy letter to mother, July 15, 1940.

70   **"Often during the night"**—Peggy letter to mother, May 22, 1940.

70   **"Among the most frequently asked"**—Gil Winant papers, Roosevelt Library, "Questions About America Asked at the 'America Marches' Exhibition," paper prepared by Margaret S. Carroll.

72   **"Peggy wrote frequently"**—Peggy Carroll letter to mother, July 16, 1940.

72   **"You cannot imagine"**—Peggy Carroll letter to mother, August 27, 1940.

75   **"LONDON: Dec. 30"**—Carroll, "Churchill Sees Ruins, Rebukes Peace Pleader," *The Atlanta Constitution*, December 31, 1940.

76   **"London was in flames"**—Quentin Reynolds, *Collier's Weekly*, August 30, 1941.

77   **"The big question"**—Carroll, "Hess Believed Nazis Could Not Be Beaten, Hoped Foe Could Agree and End Fight," *The Coos Bay Times*, May 15, 1941.

77   **"Life never seemed so unreal"**—Gavin Mortimer, *The Longest Night*, 9.

77   **"As he walked around"**—Quentin Reynolds, *Collier's Weekly*, August 30, 1941.

77   **"Their strength lies"**—Peggy letter to mother, May 6, 1940.

78   **"We came home by underground"**—Peggy letter to mother, October 20, 1941.

79   **"Polls indicated"**—Statements based on percentages disclosed by Gallup surveys. Memo, Maj. Gen. Edwin M. Watson for President, 16 May 1941, *FDR Personal Letters*, II, 1158.

79   **"The reporting of the Blitz"**—Olson, *Citizens of London*, 31.

CHAPTER 7

83   **"The British"**—Carroll, *We're in This With Russia*, 49.

91   **"In another car were"**—Henry C. Cassidy, *Moscow Dateline: 1941–1943*, 109.

92   **"Henry Cassidy would later write"**—Ibid., 111.

92   **"According to Cassidy's estimate"**—Ibid., 103.

92   **"It is no heel-clicking army"**—Carroll, *Berkshire Evening Eagle*, September 27, 1941, 2.

92   **"Carroll had another observation"**—Carroll letter to Peggy, October 13, 1941.

94   **"Sokolovsky went on to"**—Henry C. Cassidy, *Moscow Dateline*, 115.

110   **"On the day of the attack"**—Carroll, "Friends Were Spies," *Minneapolis Morning Tribune*, December 31, 1941.

111   **"And since his stories"**—Gary Y. Okihiro and Julie Sly, "The Press, Japanese Americans, and the Concentration Camps," *Phylon*, Vol. 44, No. 1, 1983.

CHAPTER 8

115   **"like going back"**—Peggy Carroll, letter to Gil Winant, December 21, 1941, Gil Winant Papers, Roosevelt Library.

116 **"You doubtless know"**—Ibid.

117 **"It is the story"**—Carroll, *The Vidette-Messenger,* November 17, 1941.

118 **"As a result"**—Frank S. Adams, review of *We're in This With Russia, New York Times,* October 4, 1942.

118 **"must have a long period"**—Carroll, *We're in This With Russia,* 242.

118 **"[The Soviets'] primary aim"**—Ibid.

119 **"A country barred"**—Ibid., 245.

119 **"The refusal of the British"**—"Biennial Report of the Chief of Staff," U.S. Army, September 1, 1945.

119 ***"We're in This With Russia* consolidated"**—Adams, review of *We're in This With Russia, New York Times,* October 4, 1942.

120 **"For twelve years"**—William L. Shirer, "Our Present and Future Relation to Russia," *New York Herald Tribune,* October 4, 1942, Section viii, 1.

121 **"If the waiters hadn't removed my plate"**—Carroll, Presentation to Winston-Salem Chamber of Commerce, 1982.

121 **"Davis soon had the public's full attention"**—Alan M. Winkler, *The Politics of Propaganda, The Office of War Information 1942–1945,* 31.

121 **"At the time"**—Olson, *Those Angry Days,* Introduction.

122 **"After the war"**—Winkler, *The Politics of Propaganda,* 3.

123 **"In a further effort"**—Ibid., 26–27.

124 **"Recognizing the challenge"**—Ibid., 35.

124 **"As the war dragged on"**—Ibid., 68.

126 **"He would report to Robert Sherwood"**—Ibid., 74.

126 **"When Carroll told him"**—Carroll, *Persuade or Perish,* 6.

127 **"This straining between two continents"**—Peggy letter to Carroll, November 13, 1942.

CHAPTER 9

129 **"Huge swaths of the capital"**—Michael Korda, *Ike, An American Hero,* 268.

130 **"There have been"**—Peggy Carroll letter to mother, January 4, 1943.

130 **"Carroll later recalled"**—Carroll Papers, Library of Congress, Box 3, Folder 1, narrative history.

130 **"Interestingly, many questioned"**—Peggy Carroll, "Questions Americans Asked at 'America Marches' Exhibition," John G. Winant Papers, Roosevelt Library, Hyde Park, N.Y.

131 **"the most moving thing"**—Peggy letter to mother, September 29, 1943.

131 **"hundreds of thousands"**—Carroll Papers, Library of Congress, Box 3, narrative history.

131 **"the Ministry saw American soldiers"**—Winant Papers, Letter from Peggy Carroll, October 22, 1943, Roosevelt Library.

132 **"Eisenhower would spend"**—David Reynolds, *Rich Relations, The American Occupation of Britain, 1942–1945*, 2000.

133 **"This "flamboyant term"**—Carroll Papers, Library of Congress, Box 1, Folder 1, narrative history.

135 **"One of their first tasks"**—Reston, *Deadline*, 117.

137 **"Carroll remembers Eisenhower"**—Carroll Papers, Library of Congress, Box 3, Folder 1, narrative history.

139 **"Our great influence"**—Ibid.

139 **"It seemed to confirm"**—Winkler, *The Politics of Propaganda*, 86.

139 **"To Carroll, the President's"**—Carroll, *Persuade or Perish*, 55.

140 **"cast principle aside"**—Ibid., 51.

141 **"A month later"**—Winkler, *The Politics of Propaganda*, 89.

142 **"to create a base"**—Carroll, *Persuade or Perish*, 113.

143 **"equivalent of the Good Housekeeping"**—Carroll Summary, Carroll Papers, Library of Congress, Box 3, Folder 7, 8.

143 **"vague, unpunctual and protective"**—Reston, *Deadline*, 116.

143 **"His secretary later recalled"**—Winkler, *The Politics of Propaganda*, 77.

144 **"as bitter a man"**—Holly Cowan Shulman, *The Voice of America, Propaganda and Democracy, 1941–1945*, 106.

145 **"increased the frustration"**—Shulman, *Voice of America*, 107.

CHAPTER 10

148 **"wished he had"**—Winkler, *The Politics of Propaganda*, 108.

148 **"In effect, Barrett"**—Ibid., 109.

149 **"The Overseas Branch"**—Ibid., 125.

149 **"OWI became devoted"**—Ibid., 112.

150 **"I had practically"**—Wallace Carroll letter to Gil Winant, Carroll Papers, Library of Congress, Box 3, Folder 1.

150 **"being a mother"**—Ibid.

152 **"Dedicated internationalists"**—Shulman, *The Voice of America*, 162.

152 **"THE USAAF sends"**—Carroll papers, Library of Congress, Box 3, Folder 10.

153 **"He was seen by"**—Ibid., 164.

157 **"The leaflet campaign"**—Winkler, *The Politics of Propaganda*, 126.

158 **"actually works in our favor"**—David Irving, *Hitler's War* (New York, 1977), 574–575 in Williamson Murray and Allan R. Millett, *A War to be Won* (Cambridge: Harvard University Press, 2000), 317.

159 **"During the month of March 1944"**—Carroll, *Persuade or Perish*, 224.

159 **"This was what"**—Philips Payson O'Brien, *How the War was Won*, 291.

159 **"Later reports from defectors"**—"Former Publishers' Role in Psychological Warfare Is Focus of Film," *Winston-Salem Journal*, November 23, 1989.

160 **"From now on"**—Winkler, *The Politics of Propaganda*, 132.

161 **"The truth, for Goebbels"**—Ibid., 19.

161 **"He ranted over and over again"**—Carroll, *Persuade or Perish*, 324.

161 **"On July 13"**—Ibid.

162 **"We will not let them"**—Ibid., 325.

162 **"sterilize the men"**—Carroll, memo to Robert Sherwood, March 10, 1944, Carroll Papers, Library of Congress, Box 3, Folder 1.

165 **"transcends everything"**—Ibid., 347.

166 **"Keep it up"**—Carroll, *Persuade or Perish*, 324–325.

166 **"What they overlooked"**—Ibid., 350.

166 **"The Hitler legend"**—Ibid., 351.

CHAPTER 11

168 **"the slave workers"**—Carroll, *Persuade or Perish*, 358.

168 **"Everything I saw in Germany"**—Wallace Carroll papers, Letter to Edward Barrett, April 17, 1945, Library of Congress, Box 3.

168 **"outstanding contribution"**—Carroll, *Persuade or Perish*, 362.

169 **"We had made a point"**—Ibid., 237.

170 **"Despite all the emphasis"**—Wallace Carroll papers, Library of Congress, Box 3, narrative history, pg. 28.

170 **"The way to do this"**—Carroll, *Persuade or Perish*, 391.

170 **"he wrote a directive saying"**—Joe Goodman, "Wallace Carroll: An Eye on History," *Winston-Salem Journal*, December 16, 1973, C5.

172 **"He was"**—Lynne Olson, *Citizens of London*, 496; as told on National Public Radio, *All Things Considered*, February 3, 2010.

172 **"this modest and self-effacing American"**—Wallace Carroll papers, Note on Gil Winant, Library of Congress, Box 3, File 9.

172 **"The book was cited"**—Oxford Academic, book reviews, 511.

173 **"A lively and exciting book"**—Herbert Agar, review of *Persuade or Perish*, *Kirkus Reviews*, August 14, 1948, 10.

173 **"Public opinion"**—Agar, review of *Persuade or Perish*, *The Saturday Review*, August 14, 1948, 19.

173 **"The book drew the attention"**—Gordon Gray, cover letter of report to President Truman on establishment of Psychological Strategy Board, Wallace Carroll Papers, Library of Congress, Box 5.

174 **"He turned instead to"**—Carroll, "It Takes a Russian to Beat a Russian," *Life,* December 19, 1949.

175 **"He is witty"**— Frank Tursi, *The* Winston-Salem Journal: *Magnolia Trees and Pulitzer Prizes,* 141.

CHAPTER 12

180 **"He was an "idea" man"**—Tursi, *Magnolia Trees and Pulitzer Prizes,* 106.

181 **"The small-town *Journal* and *Sentinel"***—Ibid., 131.

181 **"best to come right out"**—Peggy Carroll letter to mother, September 2, 1949.

182 **"The city's hospital was antiquated"**—Tursi, *Magnolia Trees and Pulitzer Prizes,* 225.

183 **"By 1949, roughly"**—See "Winston-Salem's African American Neighborhoods, 1970–1950" Architectural and Planning Report, 1994, 14.

184 **"It is almost too pretty"**—Peggy Carroll letter to mother, November 14, 1949.

185 **"I find living here very pleasant indeed"**—Peggy Carroll letter to mother, August 25, 1949.

186 **"explained [to Hanes]"**—*Winston-Salem Journal, Centennial Edition,* April 3, 1997, D8.

186 **"These nurses (who left the hospital)"**—"Forsyth Board Clears Dr. Fleming of Charges," *Charlotte Observer,* August, 11, 1949, 5A.

186 **"charges so flagrantly and recklessly"**—Editorial, *Charlotte Observer,* August 9, 1949.

187 **"The staff," remembered Carroll"**—Ibid.

187 **"Most editors would have taken it away outright"**—Paxton Davis, *A Boy No More,* 199.

187 **"He was "calm, measured, precise"**—Ibid., 196.

187 **"After I sized him up"**—Roy Thompson, in Tursi, *Magnolia Trees and Pulitzer Prizes,* 140.

188 **"The stairs creaked"**—Ibid., 169.

188 **"After supper the newsroom"**—Paxton Davis in Tursi, *Magnolias and Pulitzer Prizes,* 137.

188 **"The staff was a motley crew"**—Descriptions and quotes from Davis, *A Boy No More*, 203–212 and Tursi, *Winston-Salem Journal, Centennial Edition*, April 3, 1997, D4.

189 **"Keeping with the racial"**—*Winston-Salem Journal, Centennial Edition*, April 3, 1997, D4.

190 **"I have never worked in a friendlier, happier office"**—Tursi, *Magnolia Trees and Pulitzer Prizes*, 144.

190 **"As Barbara Levy would recall"**—Bonnie Angelo, *Winston-Salem Journal, Centennial Edition*, April 3, 1997, D11.

190 **"The paper was also known"**—Ibid., 138.

191 **"We were proud of the"**—Tom Wicker, *On Press*, 38.

191 **"Journalism can be a serious occupation"**—Davis, *A Boy No More*, 203, 233.

191 **"Community spirit was very high"**—Wicker, *On Press*, 38.

191 **"local rocks to see what might be beneath"**—Ibid.

192 **"Similarly, as Wicker pointed out"**—Ibid.

193 **"It is important to remember"**—Wallace Carroll, "President Offers Bid for Peace: Speech is Major Policy Statement," *Winston-Salem Journal*, October 17, 1951.

194 **"The strike, which lasted"**—Tursi, *Magnolia Trees and Pulitzer Prizes*, 163.

195 **"By continuing to discriminate against"**—Carroll, *Persuade or Perish*, 1948.

195 **"Peggy noted this"**—Peggy letter to mother, March 6, 1950.

195 **"desegregating public libraries"**—Clarence H. Patrick, "Lunch-Counter Desegregation in Winston-Salem, N.C.," July 25, 1960.

196 **"He wasn't sticking"**—Tursi, *Magnolia Trees and Pulitzer Prizes*, 163.

197 **"The war in Korea"**—Quoted in "Slick Communist Agents Put on World Peace-Petition Campaign," *Asheville-Citizen Times*, July 19, 1929.

198 **"useful exposition of American"**—Wallace Carroll papers, Library of Congress, Box 5, File 4.

198 **"help lead the world"**—Wallace Carroll papers, Library of Congress, Box 5, File 4.

CHAPTER 13

202 **"Reston was a master"**—James Reston, *Deadline*, 210.

203 **"[Carroll] could have edited"**—Ibid., 211.

203 **"The *Times* was"**—As quoted in John F. Stacks, *Scotty, James B. Reston and the Rise and Fall of American Journalism*, 162.

204 **"usually tall, educated"**—Gay Talese, *The Kingdom and the Power*, 19.

204 **"They made sure"**—Ibid., 22.

204 **"lively din of clicking"**—Reston, *Deadline*, 210.

204 **"He would sit on the corner"**—John F. Stacks, *Scotty, James B. Reston and the Rise and Fall of American Journalism*, 163.

205 **"Unlike most of the editors"**—Max Frankel, *The Times of My Life and My Life with* The Times, 221.

205 **"According to John Stack"**—Stacks, *Scotty*, 162.

205 **"Arthur Miller revealed"**—Reston, *Deadline*, 204.

205 **"Christ how the wind blew,"**—Ibid., 205.

205 **"Both abhorred pretense"**—Ibid., 214.

205 **"brought from Milwaukee"**—Ibid., 213.

206 **"golfed with senators"**—Frankel, *The Times of My Life*, 219.

206 **"reminisced about his daily walks"**—Ibid.

206 **"to confirm a hot tip"**—Ibid.

206 **"the thought of waking up"**—Ibid., 213.

206 **"the sum of our brains"**—Ibid., 210.

206 **"Wally was one of the best"**—John Thurber, "Wallace Carroll, 95; Persuasive Editor, Among Best of His Era," *Los Angeles Times*, July 30, 2002, B10.

207 **"At the time I was forming"**—Interview with Donald Graham, April 19, 2010.

207 **"Baker would become"**—Reston, *Deadline*, 212.

208 **"so vigilant a critic of the press"**—Ibid., 218.

209 **"Carroll also helped persuade"**—Stacks, *Scotty*, 171.

209 **"Carroll supported her"**—Ibid.

210 **"In 1955, he had developed"**—Wallace Carroll, "The Seven Deadly Virtues," *Nieman Reports*, July 1955.

210 **"I am sure"**—Ibid.

210 **"McCarthy knew"**—Reston, *Deadline*, 223.

210 **"Journalists needed to see beyond this ploy"**—Ibid., 224.

211 **"Carroll went on to describe"**—Carroll, "The Seven Deadly Virtues," *Nieman Reports*, July 1955.

211 **"Years later, when the technological revolution"**—Wallace Carroll, "New Horizons—or Else," lecture delivered to annual Kappa Tau Alpha meeting, August, 3, 1956.

212 **"hold up a mirror"**—Ibid.

212 **"In an article published"**—Carroll, "Goodbye to Willie Stevens," 1955.

213 **"not exactly a heroic period"**—Reston, *Deadline*, 214.

214 **"The CIA had accused"**—Richard H. Immerman, *The CIA in Guatemala, The Foreign Policy of Intervention,* Note 47, 235–236.

214 **"Reston became"**—Ibid., 217.

214 **"impose our own judgment"**—Ibid.

214 **"Increasingly, newspapers were reporting"**—Frankel, *The Times of My Life,* 227.

215 **"The judgment of some of the most"**—*The Decatur Review,* September 28, 1956.

217 **"The action had caused an uproar"**—Wallace Carroll, "Kennedy Role on Rights," *New York Times,* May 24, 1961.

217 **"barter a meeting for"**—Wallace Carroll, "Division on West's Bid," *New York Times,* June 19, 1959.

219 **"to erase a widely held image"**—Wallace Carroll, "The Kennedy Record," *New York Times,* March 31, 1961.

220 **"there was among high officials"**—Wallace Carroll, "Cuba Setbacks Called Bad Blow to U.S. Prestige," *New York Times,* April 21, 1961.

221 **"a hell of a lot better"**—Bernard Schaefer, *Kennedy and the Berlin Wall: A Hell of a Lot Better than a War.*

221 **"recent Soviet moves in the Berlin"**—Wallace Carroll, "Soviets Aim Seen to Humiliate U.S. Over Berlin Issue," *New York Times,* October 15, 1961.

223 **"talking freely of using the bomb"**—Wallace Carroll, "Eisenhower's Four Years," *New York Times,* July 31, 1956.

223 **"Every American President in time of crisis"**—Wallace Carroll, "Soviets Aim Seen to Humiliate U.S. Over Berlin Issue," *New York Times,* October 15, 1961.

224 **"In addition, he had long wanted to open up"**—Frankel, *The Times of My Life,* 216.

225 **"some days, while reading"**—Ibid., 227.

225 **"The hell with it"**—Talese, *The Kingdom and the Power,* 301.

227 **"I only came back"**—Tursi, *Magnolia Trees and Pulitzer Prizes,* 113.

228 **"It is to roll back a gigantic"**—See Catherine Fink and Michael Shudson, "The Rise and Fall of Contextual Journalism, 1950s–1960s," *Journalism,* Vol. 15, Columbia University, 2014.

228 **"decreed that the people"**—Ibid.

229 **"It is obvious that in an atmosphere"**—"The People's Right to Know," *Winston-Salem Journal,* September 8, 1949.

CHAPTER 14

234 **"A poll of almost 300 readers"**—Tursi, *Magnolias Trees and Pulitzers,* 156.

234 **"confident that the"**—Ibid., 158.

235 **"Advertising linage for"**—Ibid., 150.

235 **"He was a very quiet"**—Ibid., 141.

236 **"It said: "Smoking could"**—Centers for Disease Control and Prevention, "History of Surgeon General's Reports on Smoking and Health," https://www.cdc.gov/tobacco/data_statistics/sgr/history/index.htm.

236 **"The coverage also highlighted"**—Steve McQuilkin, *Winston-Salem Journal, Centennial Edition,* April 3, 1997, D13.

237 **"That was a shocker for people"**—Ibid.

242 **"We had been trying to figure out"**—Leslie Banner and Douglas C. Zinn, *A Passionate Preference,* 145.

242 **"Carroll always told us not to tell people"**—Interview with Joe Goodman, Fall 2016.

242 **"The day before state legislators"**—Tursi, *Magnolia Trees and Pulitzers,* 149.

242 **"This was a wonderful"**—Banner and Zinn, *A Passionate Preference,* 152.

243 **"If I can in any way help"**—Ibid., 159.

245 **"We will resist to the bitter end"**—"The Civil Rights Act: What JFK, LBJ, Martin Luther King and Malcolm X Had to Say," *Los Angeles Times,* retrieved February 2, 2016.

245 **"A major break with the"**—Tursi, *History of Winston-Salem,* 155.

247 **"hardening of attitudes"**—*Winston-Salem Journal,* November 4, 1967.

247 **"federal government, the nation"**—*Winston-Salem Journal,* Editorial, June 27, 1967.

248 **"He didn't wander"**—Tursi, *Magnolia Trees and Pulitzer Prizes,* 141.

248 **"If an argument was tainted"**—Interview with Joe Goodman, Fall 2016.

249 **"The people"**—"The World in Reporter's Clothing: The Rise of Pseudo-Journalism in America," by John Carroll, 2004 Ruhl Lecture, University of Oregon School of Journalism and Communication, May 6, 2004.

249 **"There was a touch"**—Reston, *Deadline,* 203.

250 **"But," Goodman continued"**—Joe Goodman, "Wallace Carroll: An Eye on History," *Winston-Salem Journal,* December 16, 1973.

250 **"I thought how lucky"**—Donald Graham interview, April 19, 2019.

250 **"There is only"**—Wallace Carroll, "Goodbye to Willie Stevens," The Citizen and the News Series, address at the Marquette University Press, 1955, 121.

251 **"passionate interest in the meaning"**—Wallace Carroll, "The Substance, Not the Shadow," Seventh Annual Pulitzer Memorial Lecture, May 21, 1965.

251 **"A good reporter"**—Carroll, "The American Newspaper," pamphlet for the American Newspaper Publishers Association, 1967.

251 **"And his or her primary allegiance"**—Ibid.

CHAPTER 15

254 **"John, showing an independence"**—See "John S. Carroll dies at 73," *Los Angeles Times* (obit), June 14, 2015 and "John S. Carroll, former *Sun* editor, dies at 73," *Baltimore Sun*, June 14, 2015.

255 **"I generally agreed with"**—Tursi, *Magnolia Trees and Pulitzers*, 142.

255 **"We did, and I signed it"**—Ibid.

256 **"he could think clearly"**—Reston, *Deadline*, 154.

256 **"Dean certainly gave me the impression"**—Tursi, *Magnolias Trees and Pulitzer Prizes*, 142.

256 **"I do think I can say"**—Ibid., 142.

257 **"In a day when some of our national"**—Editorial, *Daily Times News*, Burlington, N.C., February 12, 1969, 4.

258 **"He would continue to publish"**—See editorials in *Winston-Salem Journal*, May 31, 1970, and May 17, 1970.

258 **"Vietnam-Quo Vadis"**—See Tursi, *Magnolia Trees and Pulitzer Prizes*, 142–143; also see *Winston-Salem Journal* for full editorial, March 17, 1968, 1.

264 **"I was a feature writer at heart"**—*Winston-Salem Journal, Centennial Edition*, April 3, 1997, E9.

264 **"Edwards, provoked"**—Ibid.

265 **"Editorial writer Fred Hobson"**—Sarah Abramson, "A Winning Effort," *Winston-Salem Journal, Centennial Edition*, April 3, 1997.

265 **"The headline on the resulting"**—Ibid., E9.

265 **"The rolling hills"**—Ibid.

265 **"It was probably the most depressing thing"**—Ibid.

265 **"If the people of the Northwest"**—Ibid., E8.

266 **"By virtue of having covered"**—Tursi, *Magnolias Trees and Pulitzer Prizes*, 192.

267 **"The text of the board's"**—Abramson, "A Winning Effort," *Winston-Salem Journal, Centennial Edition*, April 3, 1997, E8.

267 **"We send our thanks"**—Tursi, *Magnolias Trees and Pulitzer Prizes,* 192.

268 **"In general, our environmental"**—Abramson, "Front Lines," *Winston-Salem Journal, Centennial Edition,* April 3, 1997, E9.

268 **"guided only by an"**—Ibid.

269 **"Carroll, the precise newsman"**—Tursi, *Magnolia Trees and Pulitzer Prizes,* 195.

269 **"He was the complete antithesis to Wally"**—Ibid.

269 **"newspaper people thought"**—Ibid., 204.

270 **"American newspapers cut"**—Margaret Sullivan, *Ghosting the News: Local Journalism and the Crisis of American Democracy,* 14.

270 **"When local news fails"**—Ibid., 20.

271 **"wonderfully satisfying and entertaining"**—John Carroll, remarks adapted from acceptance speech, Editor of the Year Award, National Press Foundation, 1999.

CHAPTER 16

276 **"He was an exceptional thinker"**—Quote provided by former student, David Shouvlin.

276 **"He was always a gentleman"**—Quote provided by former student, Maria Hensen.

277 **"He encouraged us to"**—Quotes provided by former student, Jo Sager Gilley.

280 **"The need to gain legislative"**—Scott Goodell, "The New River Controversy," Boston College, *Environmental Affairs Law Review,* Vol. 8, Issue 2, December 1, 1979.

283 **"An editor for whom"**—Thomas J. Schoenbaum, *The New River Controversy,* 129.

284 **"We are waiting for the other"**—Peggy letter to children, August 9, 1976.

284 **"how many people everywhere"**—Ibid.

284 **"still possible in this"**—*New River News,* Vol. 3, Issue 1, 8.

284 **"This is a story of a little man's victory"**—See National Committee for the New River Records, circa 1912–2004, Peggy Carroll Papers, 1967–1978, Box 39.6. Appalachian State University, Boone, N.C.

285 **"a story of how all the special interests"**—*New River News,* Vol. 3, Issue 1, 8.

285 **"James Holshouer"**—Ibid.

286 **"Just before she died"**—Peggy Carroll, notes, Peggy Carroll papers, Box 38.2.

286 **"I have been very happy"**—Wallace Carroll note to Peggy, undated.

SELECTED BIBLIOGRAPHY

Main Sources:

Wallace Carroll papers, Library of Congress Manuscript Division, Washington, D.C. http://hdl.loc.gov/loc.mss/mss.home.

Letters of Peggy Sawyer Carroll, 1937–1965, unpublished.

Peggy Carroll papers 1967–1968, National Committee for the New River Records (Boone, N.C.: Appalachian State University).

H.L. Stevenson, Interview with Wallace Carroll, Winston-Salem, N.C. 1992. https://downhold.org/lowry/history1.html.

Newspapers.com. https://www.newspapers.com.

Books/Articles/Publications:

Dean Acheson, *Present at the Creation* (New York: Norton, 1987).

Michael Alpert, *New International History of the Spanish Civil War* (London: Palgrave Macmillan, 2004).

Hugh Baillie, *High Tension* (New York: Harper and Brothers, 1959).

Leslie Banner, *A Passionate Preference: The Story of the North Carolina School of the Arts* (Winston-Salem, N.C.: North Carolina School of the Arts Foundation, 1987).

Clay Blair, *Hitler's U-Boar War*, 2 Vols. (New York: Modern Library, 1998).

Douglas Brinkley, *Cronkite* (New York: Harper Perennial, 2012).

Robert A. Caro, *Working: Researching, Interviewing and Writing* (New York: Alfred A. Knopf, 2019).

Wallace Carroll, "It Takes a Russian to Beat a Russian," *Life* magazine, December 19, 1949.

Wallace Carroll, *Persuade or Perish* (Boston: Houghton Mifflin, 1948).

Wallace Carroll, *We're in this with Russia* (Boston: Houghton Mifflin Co., 1942).

Henry C. Cassidy, *Moscow Dateline*, (Middletown, D.E.: 2015).

Stanley Cloud and Lynn Olson, *The Murrow Boys* (Boston: Houghton Mifflin Co., 1996).

Virginia Cowles, *Looking for Trouble* (London: Faber & Faber, 1941).

Nicholas John Cull, Selling War, *The British Propaganda Campaign Against "Neutrality" in World War II* (Oxford: Oxford University Press, 1995).

Paxton Davis, *A Boy No More* (Winston-Salem, N.C.: John F. Blair Publisher, 1992).

John Ehle, *The Free Men* (Lewisville, N.C.: Press 53, 2007).

Max Frankel, *The Times of my Life and My Life at* The Times (New York: Dell Publishing, 1999).

David M. Glantz and Jonathan House, *When Titans Clash: How the Red Army Stopped Hitler* (Lawrence: University Press of Kansas, 1995).

Josef Goebbels, *Adolf Hitler—A Chilling Tale of Propaganda* (New York: Trident Reference, 1999).

Gregory Gordon and Ronald E. Cohen, *Down to the Wire* (New York: McGraw Hill Publishing, 1990).

John Gurda, *The Making of Milwaukee*, (Milwaukee: Milwaukee Historical Society, 1999).

Max Hastings, *Inferno, The World at War 1939–1945* (New York: Vintage Books, 2012).

Ruth Henig, *The Peace that Never Was: A History of the League of Nations* (London: Haus Publishing, Ltd., 2019).

James Holland, *The Battle of Britain* (New York: St. Martin's Griffin, 2010).

Thomas Hugh, *The Spanish Civil War* (New York: Harper & Brothers, 1961).

Richard Immerman, *The CIA in Guatemala: The Foreign Policy of Intervention* (Austin: University of Texas Press, 1982).

Thomas J. Jablonsky, *Milwaukee's Jesuit University, Marquette 1991– 1981,* (Milwaukee: Marquette University Press, 2007).

Paul F. Jankowski, *Stavisky: A Confidence Man in the Republic of Virtue* (Ithaca, N.Y.: Cornell University, 2002).

Samuel Hynes et al., *Reporting World War II* (New York: The Library of America, 1995).

Warren F. Kimball, *The Juggler: Franklin D. Roosevelt as Wartime Statesman* (Princeton: Princeton University Press, 1991).

Michael Korda, *Ike, An American Hero* (New York: Harper Perennial, 2008).

Clayton D. Laurie, *The Propaganda Warriors: America's Crusade against Nazi Germany* (Kansas: University Press of Kansas, 1996).

James Leutze, ed. *The London Journal of General Raymond E. Lee 1940–1941* (Boston: Little, Brown and Company, 1971).

Marquette University, Hilltop 1924–1928 https://cdm16280. contentdm.oclc.org/digital/collection/p4007hilltop.

Gavin Mortimer, *The Longest Night* (New York: Penguin, 2005).

Ray Moseley, *Reporting War* (New Haven: Yale University Press, 2017).

Williamson Murray and Allen R. Millett, *A War to be Won: Fighting the Second World War* (Cambridge, London: The Belknap Press of Harvard University Press, 2000).

Philips Payson O'Brien, *How the War was Won* (Cambridge: Cambridge University Press, 2015).

Lynne Olson, *Citizens of London* (New York: Random House, 2010.)

Lynne Olson, *Troublesome Young Men* (New York: Farrar, Straus and Giroux, 2007).

Hugh D. Phillips, *Between the Revolution and the West: A Political Biography of Maxim M. Litvinov* (London: Westview Press, 1993).

Curt Reiss, *Joseph Goebbels* (Stroud, U.K.: Fonthill Media, 2015).

Reporting World War II, *American Journalism 1938–1946* (The Library of America, 1995).

James Reston, *Deadline* (New York: Random House, 1991).

James Reston, *Prelude to Victory* (New York: Pocket Books, 1942).

David Reynolds, *Rich Relations: The American Occupation of Britain, 1942–1945* (New York: Random House, 1995).

David Reynolds, "The Churchill Government and the Black American Troops in Britain during World War II," *Transactions of the Royal Historical Society* 35 (1985).

Andrew Roberts, *The Storm of War* (New York: Harper Perennial, 2011).

A Reed Sarratt, *The Ordeal of Segregation* (New York: Harper and Row, 1966).

Thomas J. Schoenbaum, *The New River Controversy* (Jefferson, N.C.: McFarland and Company, 2007).

Holly Cowan Shulman, *The Voice of America, Propaganda and Democracy, 1941–1945* (Madison: University of Wisconsin Press, 1990).

John F. Stacks, *James B. Reston & the Rise and Fall of American Journalism* (Lincoln, Nebraska: University of Nebraska Press, 2003).

David Stahel, *Operation Barbarossa and Germany's Defeat in the East* (Cambridge: Cambridge University Press, 2009).

John Stevenson and Chris Cooke, *The Slum: Britain in the Great Depression* (London: Routledge, 1977).

Gay Talese, *The Kingdom and the Power, Behind the Scenes at* The New York Times: *The Institution That Influences the World* (New York: Random House, 1966).

Evan Thomas, *The Very Best Men, The Daring Early Years of the CIA* (New York: Simon and Schuster, 1995).

Jenny Thompson and Sherry Thompson, *The Kremlinologist* (Baltimore: Johns Hopkins University Press, 2018).

Nicholas Thompson, *The Hawk and the Dove*, Paul Nitze, George Kennan, and the History of the Cold War (New York: Henry Holt and Company, 2009).

Rifat Tirana, *The Spoils of Europe* (New York: W.W. Norton Co., 1941).

Frank Tursi, *Lost Empire: The Fall of R. J. Reynolds Tobacco Company* (Winston-Salem, NC: *Winston-Salem Journal*, 2000).

Frank Tursi, *The* Winston-Salem Journal, *Magnolia Trees and Pulitzers* (Winston-Salem, N.C.: *Winston-Salem Journal*, 1996).

Frank Tursi, *Winston-Salem: A History* (Winston-Salem, N.C.: Blair Publishers, 1994).

Tom Wicker, *On Press* (New York: Viking, 1978).

Paul K. Williams, Washington, D.C., *The World War II Years* (Charleston, S.C.: Arcadia Publishers, 2004).

John G. Winant, *A Letter from Grosvenor Square* (London: Hodder & Stoughton, 1947).

Winston-Salem Journal, Centennial Issue: Celebration of a Century, 1897–1997, April 3, 1997.

Allan M. Winkler, *The Politics of Propaganda, The Office of War Information 1942–1945* (New Haven: Yale University Press, 1978).

Manuscript Sources, Digitized:

Foreign Relations of the United States series, U.S. Department of State. Official documentary history of American foreign relations. Organized by presidency (but searchable by key word), digitized on State Department website. See, for example, League of Nations search results: https://history.state.gov/tags/league-of-nations. Or, search for Wallace Carroll. https://history.state.gov/search?q=Wallace+Carroll&within=documents&sort-by=relevance.

Marquette University, Special Collections and Archives, 1924–1928. https://cdm16280.contentdm.oclc.org/digital/collection/p16280coll3.

Franklin D. Roosevelt Library, Hyde Park, N.Y. President's Secretary's Files, 1933–1945. Digitized. See entries for Office of War Information, OSS, and Donovan. http://www.fdrlibrary.marist.edu/archives/collections/franklin/?p=collections/findingaid&id=502.

John Gilbert Winant papers, 1916–1947, Franklin D. Roosevelt Presidential Library and Museum http://www.fdrlibrary.marist.edu/archives/collections/franklin/index.php?p=collections/findingaid&id=173.

Manuscript Sources, Not Digitized:

National Archives and Records Administration, College Park, M.D. Record Group 208, Records of the Office of War Information. https://www.archives.gov/findingaid/stat/discovery/208.

George C. Marshall Research Library, Lexington, V.A. Papers of George C. Marshall. Records related to the June 1941 meeting on Soviet capabilities with journalists.

Selected speeches by Wallace Carroll:

"Murder, Mayhem and the Mother Tongue," delivered on receiving the By-Line Award of Marquette University, Milwaukee, Wisconsin, May 4, 1969. https://acornabbey.com/blog/?p=4547.

"The Seven Deadly Virtues," Nieman Reports, July 1955 ad, *Michigan Quarterly Review,* August 6, 1955, Vol. LXI, No. 21.

"Living up to the Constitution," delivered as contribution to the bicentennial of the United States Constitution," July 4, 1976, published by *Winston-Salem Journal.*

"The American Newspaper," published in connection with the American Newspaper Publishers Association, 1964.

"A Witness to History," talk delivered at Wake Forest University, November 1, 1971, Wallace Carroll Collection, Wake Forest University Library.

"Professionalism and the Press," delivered at the 75th Anniversary Observance of the Continuous Teaching of Journalism at the University of Michigan, May 9, 1966.

"Ralph Waldo Emerson, Thou Shouldst Be Living at this Hour," delivered to the New England Society of Newspaper Editors, Cambridge, Massachusetts, December 6, 1969.

"Good-by to Willie Stevens," delivered at Marquette University, College of Journalism, 1955.

"Professionalism and the Press," delivered at the 75th Anniversary Observance of the Continuous Teaching of Journalism at the University of Michigan, May 9, 1966.

"The Substance, Not the Shadow, A Glance at the New Journalism," Seventh Pulitzer Prize Memorial Lecture, Columbia University Graduate School of Journalism, May 21, 1965.

Permissions:

The author gratefully acknowledges the Carroll family's permission to quote from *We're in This With Russia* and *Persuade and Perish*, as well as other documents/photos of Wallace and Peggy Carroll. Permission to run images from the *Marquette Hilltop* and *Marquette Tribune* granted by the Department of Special Collections and University Archives, Raynor Memorial Libraries, Marquette University. Permission to use photos of the London Blitz and Adolf Hitler/Josef Goebbels granted by Getty Images. Permission to use the photo of Elmer Davis granted by Associated Press. Permission to use the reprint of "Quo Vadis" granted by Lee Enterprises (*Winston-Salem Journal*).

INDEX

Italicized page numbers refer to illustrations, and the insert of photographs following page 166 is indicated by "insert after 166."

Acheson, Dean, *insert after 166*, 173, 198, 206, 220, 223, 226, 253, 255–56, 276
African Americans. *See* race relations
Agar, Herbert, 133
Agency for Inter-American Affairs, 155
Algeria, 137–38, 140
Allegheny Farm Bureau, 280
American Broadcasting System in Europe, 142
American Electric Power Company (AEP) and Appalachian Power Company, 279–84
Associated Press (AP)
  competing with United Press, 12–13, 17, 45, 48, 84
  correspondents killed in WWII, 46
  as leading wire service, 11
  Reston at, 49–50
  on Surgeon General's report, 236
  in WWII Soviet Union, 91
SS *Athenia*, 55

Atlantic Charter (1941), 122–23, 125, 139
Azerbaijan, 106

Bacon, J. Worth, 188
Bagley, Smith, 238, 240–43
Baillie, Hugh, 21, 65
Baker, Ira, 142
Baker, Russell, *insert after 166*, 207
Bald Head Island (North Carolina), 266–67
Baldwin, Stanley, 27
Baltimore Sun
  Baker at, 207
  John Carroll as editor and vice president of, 278
  John Carroll as foreign correspondent for, 278
  John Carroll as reporter on Vietnam War for, 254–55, 278
  Carroll writing editorial on gun control for, 276–77
Baquet, Dean, *insert after 166*, 278
Barrett, Edward W., 148
Bartlett, Vernon, 86–88
Basra, 107

Battles of World War II. *See* Soviet Union in World War II; World War II

Bay of Pigs invasion (1961), 219–20, 223

BBC (British Broadcasting Corporation) in World War II, xviii, 86, 135

Beattie, Edward, 46–47, 76, 85

Beaverbrook, Lord, 117

Black Americans. *See* race relations

Blitz (Britain), xi, xvi–xix, 47, 120–21, *insert after 166*
British resilience during, 69–81. *See also* Britain in World War II
end of, 129
evacuation of London, 57
News of the World Building bombing, 76, *insert after 166*
St. Paul's Cathedral in bombed area of London, 74–75
start of, 63–67

Bohlen, Chip, 199

Bourke-White, Margaret, 91, 94–95

Bradlee, Ben, *insert after 166*, 266

Braestrup, Peter, 208

Brauchitsch, Walther von, 102

Brinkley, David, 283

Britain in Suez Crisis (1956), 215–16

Britain in World War II. *See also* Blitz; Churchill, Winston
American soldiers' conduct in, 131–32
appeasement attempts with Fascists, 24–27, 50–52
Atlantic Charter (1941), 122–23
blackout and ongoing bombings, 129
British Third Division visited by Carroll, 61–63
Carroll in London as UP bureau manager, x, xv, 13–17, 45–67, 69–81

Chamberlain's blunders, 50–54
declaring war on Nazi Germany, xii, 53
Dunkirk evacuation, 59–60, 62
firsthand accounts in London from Carroll, xv–xix, 54–55
Hess's arrival in Britain, 76–77
Home Guard, 61–62
incendiary bombs, resident watch for, 71–72
London destruction of May 10, 1941, 77
Marshall on British resolve, 119
Munich Agreement with Germany (1938), 27, 51
Nuremberg bomber raid, loss of planes during, 160
OWI leaflets dropped by British planes in World War II, 135, 142
Poland, pledging support to, 51
propaganda use to influence public opinion in, 133–34
respites during, 70–71, 73, 75–76
Royal Air Force (RAF), xv, 63–67, 86–87, 135, 142
Soviet relations, 51–52
War Cabinet, 132

British Expeditionary Force, 58–59

British Foreign Office, 85, 106, 132

British Ministry of Home Security, 61

British Ministry of Information, 76, 131–32, 134

British Political Warfare Executive (PWE), 135, 137, 140, 144

Brown v. Board of Education (1954), 196, 246

Bundy, McGeorge, 256

Bush, George W., 228

Caldwell, Erskine, 91

Capone, Al, 13, 71
Carroll, Emmet (brother), 5–6
Carroll, John Francis (father), 3–6
Carroll, John Sawyer (son)
  as *Baltimore Sun* reporter on
    Vietnam War, 254–55
  birth of, 116
  childhood of, 126, 150, 184
  compared to his father, 278
  echoing his father's journalistic
    values, 270–71, 289
  education and career of, 249,
    278
  on London trip (1959), 218
  National Press Foundation
    awarding Editor of the Year
    to (1998), 270, 278
  photograph of, *insert after 166*
Carroll, Josephine Meyer (mother),
  4–6
Carroll, Margaret (daughter)
  birth of, 56
  Carroll's first meeting with, 112
  childhood of, 69, 126, 150, 184
  education and career of, 218,
    277–78
  on London trip (1959), 218
  photograph of, *insert after 166*
Carroll, Marian (sister), 5
Carroll, Patricia (daughter)
  birth of, 184
  education and career of, 279
  her dog Bo Bo killed in
    retaliation for Carroll's
    editorial on gun control, 248
  on London trip (1959), 218
  on press-government relations,
    226
  on race riot in Winston-Salem
    (1967), 247
Carroll, Peggy (née Margaret
  Sawyer) (wife)
  birth of daughter Margaret, 56,
    insert after 166
  birth of daughter Patricia, 184

birth of daughter Rosamund
  ("Posey"), 174
birth of son John, 116
Black friends, hosting of, 246
on Blitz bombings, 77–79
on Carroll's appearance on
  return from Spanish Civil
  War, 41
on Carroll's assignment to
  London's UP office, 45
Daily Telegraph (London) article
  on Carrolls as "Dynamic
  Couple," 145–46
death of, 285
exhibit on America organized
  by, to educate British about
  America, 130–31
first meeting in Geneva, 29–30
greeting Carroll upon his return
  from Soviet Union, 112, 115
in London during WWII, xviii,
  49, 55, 69–76, 80, 126–27,
  130, 218
on London trip (1959), 218
marriage to Carroll, 30–31, *insert
  after 166*
New River Valley land purchase,
  274–76
New River Valley preservation
  efforts of, 279–86
personality of, 29, 31, 185, 289
photographs of, *insert after 166*
powers of observation, 185, 246
on race relations in South, 195
return from London to New
  York, 55–56, 111
social circle of Carrolls, 31–32,
  49, 80, 115–16, 185, 201, 226,
  238, 246, 249, 275, 282, 287
supporting Carroll's pursuit of
  reporting war, 37
Vietnam War, tracking son
  John's locations in, 255

Washington, D.C. move and
reuniting with children,
149–50
White House talk on WWII
conditions in Britain, 116
Winston-Salem life of, 181–82,
184–85, 202, 238, 246,
248–49
working at U.S. Department of
Labor, 226
working for Winant, 29–30, 35,
55, 70, 85, 127, 130, 145
Carroll, Rosamund "Posey"
(daughter), 174
childhood of, 184
education and career of, 278–79
on her parents' civic
undertakings, 279
on London trip (1959), 218
Carroll, Wallace (John Wallace).
See also journalism
birth of, 3
bravery of, xvii, 79
childhood of, 4–6
classical music as love of, 238
conservative appearance of, 250
as consultant to State
Department and Defense
Department, xi, 197
death of, 285, 287
education of, 5
embodying the role of
journalist, ix, xiii, 50, 209–13,
228–29, 269, 288
endowed chair at North
Carolina School of the Arts
music school named for, 244
as environmentalist. *See*
environmental issues; New
River Valley preservation
efforts
friends of. *See* Carroll, Peggy
*for their social circle generally and
names of specific friends*
gourmet interests of, 249–50

health problems of, 40–41, 144,
171
humor of, 8, 14, 50, 203, 206,
249, 250
independence and personal
integrity of, 181, 226–29, 289
intelligence of, xii, 5, 120, 206,
249
learning Russian language, 87
in London as reporter and
office manager for United
Press. *See* Britain in World
War II; United Press (UP)
at Marquette University
(undergraduate), 6–9
marriage to Peggy, 30–31, *insert
after 166*
memorial service (Highland
Church, Winston-Salem), 287
New River Valley and. *See* New
River Valley preservation
efforts
New York Times role. *See New
York Times,* London bureau;
New York Times, Washington
bureau
nicknamed "Bud," 5
Office of War Information
(OWI) roles. *See* Office of
War Information (OWI),
European Operations (based
in Washington, D.C.); Office
of War Information (OWI),
Overseas Branch (based in
London)
personality of, xii, 6, 13, 250,
275, 287–89
as persuader, xii, 257, 288, 304
photographs of, *insert after 166*
propaganda, views on. *See*
propaganda
on Psychological Strategy Board,
197–99
religious and leisure activities of
childhood, 5

in Soviet Union during WWII.
See Soviet Union in World
War II
Spanish Civil War reporting,
36–41, 93
timeline, 307–8
at United Press. See United
Press (UP)
on Wake Forest University
faculty. See Wake Forest
University
at *Winston-Salem Journal*. See
Winston-Salem Journal
WWII reporting. See Britain in
World War II; Soviet Union in
World War II
Carroll, Wallace, works of. *See also
specific newspapers for topics of
other editorials not listed here*
"Barber of Seville Has Nothing
on the Barber of Union
House" (college newspaper),
8
Christmas Day poems, 249
"Goodbye to Willie Stevens,"
233
Persuade or Perish, 6, 171–73, 175,
194–95, 247
"To End the Gun Terror, End
the Second Amendment
Hoax" (*Baltimore Sun*
editorial), 276–77
"Vietnam—Quo Vadis? We
Must Open Our Minds to the
Hard Choices" (*Winston-Salem
Journal* editorial), 255–63,
288–89
*We're in This With Russia: How
to Do Business with Stalin and
Why*, 52, 102, 117–20, *insert
after 166*
Carter, Jimmy, *insert after 166*, 285
Casey, Bob, 70–71
Cassidy, Henry C., 91–92, 94, 102
Castro, Fidel, 219

Catholicism and Catholic Church,
5, 7–8
Second Vatican Council (1962),
222
CBS, 34, 47–49, 119
censorship
German, 142
Soviet, 84, 89–90, 98
in WWII, 48, 55, 76, 79–80, 109,
126, 141
Central Intelligence Agency (CIA)
Bay of Pigs invasion (1961) and,
218–20
Carroll's relations with, 199, 215,
220
Cuban Missile Crisis (1962) and,
222
Allen Dulles as head of, 213–15
founding of, 139
Guatemalan government coup
by, 214
Chamberlain, Neville, 27, 50–54,
57–59, 62, 118
Charles and Mary Babcock
Foundation, 192n1
Chautemps, Camille, 19
Chiappe, Jean, 19–20
Chicago Daily News, 53, 70–71, 91
Chicago Sun-Times, 103
China, 24, 257
Cholerton, A.T., 91
Christie, Agatha, 17
Churchill, Winston, x
Atlantic Charter (1941) and,
122–23
becoming prime minister and
WWII leadership, 59–61, 70,
80
Carroll and, 60–61
Chamberlain and, 50–52
on Darlan Affair, 139
Hess and, 77
Ireland and, 73
League of Nations and, 28, 51
London ruins, walk through, 75

Murrow and, 48
on RAF role in WWII, 67
Rome's capture and, 154
on start of World War II, 58
CIA. *See* Central Intelligence
Agency
Civil Rights Act (1964), 244–46
civil rights movement, xii, xiii. *See
also* race relations
Clark, Mark, 156
Clinton, Bill, 228
Cold War. *See also* Communist
fears; Soviet Union; Vietnam
War
America wanting to prevent
spread of Communism, 198
Berlin negotiations in, 218–19,
220–21
Berlin Wall construction (1961),
220–21
Carroll on team preparing paper
on U.S.'s objectives toward
Soviet Union, 198–99
Carroll's views on U.S.
leadership responsibility in,
118–19, 216
Cuban Missile Crisis (1962), 32,
222–23
diplomatic initiatives to quell
tensions of, 217
Psychological Strategy Board
formed to prevent spread of
Communism, 197–98
"saber rattling" approach of
Dulles brothers, 213–14
Soviet Union, Carroll's
predictions about, 118
State Department strategy in,
199
Suez Crisis and (1956), 215–16
U.S. and Soviet Union as main
players in, 216
U.S. propaganda to discredit
Stalin, 175
U-2 incident (1960), 214–15

Collier's Weekly, 61, 76
Collingwood, Charles, 47
Colvin, Marie, 45
Committee on Public Information,
122
Communist fears
America wanting to prevent
spread of Communism, 198
John Foster Dulles and, 213
McCarthyism, 199
Vietnam War and, 257
in Winston-Salem, 194
Conservation Council of Virginia,
280
Convention of Engineers (New
York 1942), 120
Cooper, Duff, 50
Council of Foreign Ministers
(London meeting 1959),
217–18
Cousins, Norman, 121
Creel, George, 122
Cripps, Richard Stafford, 89, 103
Cronkite, Walter, xvii, 48, 283
Crowder, Charles W., 269
Cuba
Bay of Pigs invasion (1961),
219–20, 223
Cuban Missile Crisis (1962), 32,
222–23
Czechoslovakia, 50, 51

Daily Hampshire Gazette
(Northampton,
Massachusetts), 283
Daily Sketch, 87, 91
Daily Telegraph (London), 91,
145–46
Daladier, Edouard, 19–20
Daniel, Clifton, 225, 227
Darlan, Jean François, and Darlan
Affair, 138–41, 145, 171, 223
Davis, Chester, 189–90, 264
Davis, Elmer
background of, 121

initial hiring of Carroll, 125–27, 129
in Office of War Information (OWI), Overseas Branch, 124–26, 143, 148–49
photograph of, *insert after 166*
re-hiring Carroll as deputy director of OWI's European Operations, 148–50, 153
Reston hired by, 202
Roosevelt and, 147–48
Sherwood and, 143–45, 147–48
travel to see European devastation in WWII, 167–68
on WWII reporting, 115
Davis, Paxton, 179, 186–88
A Boy No More, 187, 191
Dawson, Joan, 248
Day, Clarence, 14, 18
Dayton Herald, 66
Defense Department, U.S.
Carroll as consultant to, 197
Carroll's editorial on Vietnam War disseminated to, 256
McCarthy's charges of Communist infiltration of, 199
de Gaulle, Charles, 138, 140, 169
de Mille, Agnes, 242–43
democracy
America as "arsenal of democracy," 123
Carroll's belief in, 8, 199, 277
journalism and, 229, 270, 288
MacLeish and Sherwood as pro-interventionists supporting, 123, 125
New River's preservation as demonstration of, 285
Roosevelt "Four Freedoms" speech on, 122
Spanish Civil War as fight over, 36
Voice of America and, 123–24

Democratic Women of Forsyth County, 246
de Valera, Éamon, 73–74
Dewey, Thomas E., 211
Donovan, Robert J., 266
Donovan, William "Wild Bill," 124, 126, 139–40, 143
Dos Passos, John, 36
Doster, Joe, 265–66
Dowding, Hugh, 65
Drake, Waldo, 109
Drury, Allen, 205, 208
Advise and Consent, 208
Dryfoos, Orvil, 219, 224, 227
Duke University, Carroll receiving honorary degree from, 276
Dulles, Allen, 213, 215, 219
Dulles, John Foster, 213–14, 216
Dure, Leon, 194

East Germany, 214, 218, 220–21. *See also* Cold War
Eden, Anthony, 26, 52, 216
Edwards, Arlene, 263–66
Egypt and Suez Crisis, 215–16
Ehle, John, *insert after 166,* 239–41, 243–44, 275
The Free Men, 244
Eisenhower, Dwight, x
African Torch campaign of Allied forces and, 135, 137–38, 140
on Black soldiers, 131–32
Carroll and, 215
Darlan Affair and, 138–41, 145
election of, 200
as head of Allied air forces (1944), 160
health problems of, 216
Khrushchev meeting with, 217–19
Little Rock desegregation (1957) and, 216–17
overcoming German mastery of the air, 157

propaganda campaign and, 135, 163

Psychological Warfare Branch/ Psychological Warfare Division, 137, 141, 215

Rome's capture and, 154

Suez Crisis and (1956), 215–16

Eisenhower, Milton S., 124, 124n1, 141

Eller, James, 246

Elliot, Walter, 53

environmental issues, xii, xiii. *See also* New River Valley preservation efforts

strip mining in North Carolina, 264–66

Winston-Salem Journal as Pulitzer Prize winner for coverage (1971), *insert after 166*, 267–69

Ervin, Sam, 280–81, 284

Eslinger, John, 265

Ethiopia, Mussolini's invasion of, 25–26, 28

Executive Order 9066 ordering Japanese-American internment, 111

Fascism. *See* Hitler, Adolf; Mussolini, Benito; Nazi Germany

Fauber, Orval, 216–17

Federal Power Commission, 282

Federal Trade Commission, 237

Fink, Catherine, and Michael Schudson: "The Rise and Fall of Contextual Journalism, 1950s–1960s," 228

Flory, Harry, 36

Ford, Ford Madox, 17

Ford, Gerald, 280, 283, 285

Ford Foundation, 201, 240

Foreign Information Office (FIS), 123–24

foreign policy as expertise of Carroll, 145, 151–52, 192–93, 197, 200, 205–6, 213, 229, 253

Foreign Service Institute, Carroll as speaker at, 175

Fox, Albert C., 7

France
Socialist government prior to WWII, 19

Suez Crisis and (1956), 215–16

France in World War II
Allied bombing of occupied France, 152–53

Darlan Affair and, 138–41, 145, 171, 223

declaring war on Germany, 53

Free French, 138–40

German attack on, 58–59

Vichy government, 136–38

Franco, Francisco, 36–40

Frankel, Max, 205–6, 224–25

Frankfurter, Felix, 206, 208

Gallup Poll on U.S. aid to Britain (1940), xix

Gandhi, Mahatma, 16

Garber, Mary, 189

Geneva. *See also* League of Nations

Carroll meeting wife Peggy and marrying in, 29–31

Carroll's friendships formed in, 31–35

pre-WWII life in, 23

George III (king), 273

George VI (king), 54

Germany in post-war era. *See also* Cold War *for Berlin;* East Germany

Carroll and Davis tour of, 167–68

educating Germans about the war, 168

Germany in World War II. *See* Hitler, Adolf; Nazi Germany

Gershoy, Leo, 151–52
Giannini, Vittorio, 243
Gibbsite Corporation, 264–66
Goebbels, Josef, 134–35, 142, 147, 159–66, 171
  photograph of, *insert after 166*
Goering, Hermann, xv, 64–65, 67, 157–59
Goldwater, Barry, 225
Goodman, Joe, 242, 248, 250, 265–66, 268–69
Gordon, Gregory, and Ronald Cohen: *Down to the Wire: UPI's Fight for Survival,* 12
Governors' Schools (for high school students), 239
Graham, Donald, 206–7, 250
Gray, Bowman, Sr., 179
Gray, Bowman, Jr., 180
Gray, Gordon
  anti-Communist beliefs of, 194, 197
  background of, 179–81
  compared to Phil Hanes, 238
  hiring Black journalist on *Journal* staff, 189
  hiring Carroll as executive news editor (1949), 175–76
  owner of Winston-Salem newspapers, 175–76, 180–81, 235
  Psychological Strategy Board and, 196–99
  rehiring Carroll (1963), 227, 229
  removal of Sarratt as executive editor, 245
  sale of *Winston-Salem Journal,* 268
  sharing Carroll's journalistic viewpoints, 212
  smoothing way for Carroll in Winston-Salem, 186
  Vietnam War, position on, 255
  Wake Forest University and, 192n1

Gray, James A., III, 234
Great Depression, 15–16, 18
Greeley, Horace, 11
Greenfield, Meg, 228
Greensboro News and Record, 209
Griffith, Thomas, 201
gun control, 247–48, 276–77

Halberstam, David, 205
Haldane, Charlotte, 87, 91
Hammer, Earl, Jr., 281
Handler, Charlie, 100
Hanes, Charlotte, *insert after 166,* 275
Hanes, Jim, 186
Hanes, R. Philip, *insert after 166,* 237–38, 240–43, 275
Hanes Corporation, 233–34, 238
Hanes Mills (Winston-Salem), 183
Harriman, Averell, 117, 173
Harris, Rosemary, *insert after 166,* 240–41, 275
Hart, Thomas, 108
Hastings-on-Hudson, New York (home of Peggy Sawyer Carroll's parents), 29, 55–56, 69, 111, 115–17
Heinzen, Ralph, 18–20
Helms, Richard, 199, 220, 226, 253
Hemingway, Ernest, 36, 116
Herald Tribune, insert after 166, 206
Hess, Rudolph, 76–77
Himmler, Heinrich, 165
Hitler, Adolf. *See also* Nazi Germany
  aggression and ramping up for war, 45
  air fighting strategy of, 157–58
  appeasement of, 24–27, 35–36, 50–53
  assassination attempt on, 165
  Blitz and, xvi, 67. *See also* Blitz
  credible lie used by, 161
  Czechoslovakia invaded by, 51

deification and hold over
German people, 165–66
German-Soviet Non-
Aggression Pact (1939) and,
52, 118
Hess and, 76–77
MacLeish on, 123
Munich Agreement (1938) and,
27, 51
Operation Barbarossa launched
by, 81, 83
Operation Weserübung
launched by, 58–60
photograph of, *insert after 166*
propaganda machine of, 132,
134, 152, 159–66, 167–68
radar use and, 64
refusal to admit signs of defeat,
157–58
refusal to take assistance from
Ukrainians to fight Soviets,
174–75
rise of, 18, 21, 23, 134
Rome spared from destruction
by, 156
Soviet strategy of, 80–81, 90,
97, 102
Spanish Civil War and, 36
taking personal control of
military after defeat at
Moscow, 102
Versailles Treaty repudiated by,
24–25
Hobson, Fred, 265
Hollingworth, Clare, 52–53
Holmes, Oliver Wendell, 273
Holshouer, James, 285
Hopkins, Harry, 85, 96, 117
Hottelet, Richard C., 33–34
Hoyt, Bill, 234
Hull, Cordell, 211
Hunter, Jayden, 3
Hunter, Marjorie, 190, 209

information campaigns. *See*
propaganda
international affairs. *See* foreign
policy as expertise of Carroll
International Labor Organization
(ILO), 29, 32, 34–35
Iran, 106–7
Ireland's neutrality in WWII,
73–74
Israel and Suez Crisis, 215–16
Italy in World War II
appeasement of, 25–26, 28
Monte Cassino bombing by
American forces, 154
North African campaign against,
136
Rome campaign of Allies and
propaganda to save Rome
from destruction, 154–56
Izaak Walton League, 280

Jameson, Storm, 57
Japanese Americans
Carroll reporting of fifth
columnists among, 110–11
incarceration of, 110–11, 124n1
Japan in World War II, 107–11
Japan's withdrawal from League of
Nations, 24
Jim Crow laws, 195
John F. Kennedy Center for the
Performing Arts, 238
Johnson, Earl, 11, 13, 17, 42,
45–46, 81, 84, 112
Johnson, Lyndon, xi, 238, 244,
253–56
Joint Chiefs of Staff, 132, 143,
149, 158, 165, 171
Jordan, Philip, 91
journalism
Carroll's views on, 209–13,
250–51, 287–88
community leadership role of
journalist, 212

demise of print and local
ownership of newspapers,
ix–x, 270–71
democracy and, 229, 270, 288
dramatic changes to business of,
269–71
editor's role in, 250
foreign correspondents, job
of, 14
Kappa Tau Alpha speech (1956)
on role of newspaper in
society, 212
love of the work of being a
journalist, 212–13
misleading statements and
responsibility to contradict
them, 210–11
objectivity and, 210
politicians viewed in positive
and idealistic light, 228
principles of good journalism,
211–12, 228–29
rational argument as superior to
impassioned action, 257
role in forming history, 288
trust of journalists, ix, 17, 30,
49, 80
truth, importance of, 170, 289
"tyranny of objectivity," 210

Kahn, Harold, 143
Kelly, Pat, 264
Kennedy, Annie Brown, 246
Kennedy, John F., xii, 218–25
Acheson and, 220
assassination of, 207
Bay of Pigs invasion of Cuba
(1961), 219–20
Berlin Wall construction (1961),
220–21
Carroll's opinion of and
relationship with, 223, 225
Cuban Missile Crisis (1962),
222–23
desegregation and, 217, 244

election of, 218
journalists' opinion of, 228
Soviet relations and, 219–21
steel industry and, 225
Thompson and, 32
Kenworthy, Ned, 283
Khrushchev, Nikita, 215–18,
221–23
Kimmell, Husband E., 109–10
Kirkus Reviews, 172–73
Kleppe, Thomas S., 283
Knox, Frank, 111
Korean War, 197
Krock, Arthur, 201
Kuhn, Ferdinand "Ferdie," xvi, 47,
50, 132
Kurfees, Marshall, 184, 195–96

Le Lapin Agile (Paris), 18
Laval, Pierre, 18
League of Nations
Carroll's reporting at, 23–42, 51,
118, *insert after 166*
collapse of, 26
Disarmament Conference
(1932–1933), 23–24
founding and purpose of, 24
German and Italian withdrawal
from, 24–25
ineffectuality of, 35, 51
Litvinov at, 26–28
peacekeeping force of, 24
Selassie at, 25–26, *insert after 166*
Soviet Union joining, 24
U.S. role in, 24
Leahy, William D., 136
Lee, Raymond, 63
Lend-Lease Act (U.S. 1941), 79, 96
LeSueur, Larry, 101, 119
Levy, Barbara "Bonnie" Angelo,
190
Lewis, Anthony, *insert after 166,*
208
Gideon's Trumpet, 208
Leysmith, Walter, xix

Life magazine, 91, 174
Lindbergh, Charles, 123
Litvinov, Maxim, 26–28, 118
Liverpool, 85–86
Llanstephan Castle (ship), 86–88, 96
Lloyd George, David, 51–52
Lochner, Louis, 47, 53
Lockhart, Robert Bruce, 135
London. *See also* Office of War
    Information, Overseas
    Branch; United Press (UP) *for
    its London office*
  Blitz (WWII). *See* Blitz
  culture during 1920s & 1930s
    in, 17
Los Angeles Times, 20, 98, 109
  John Carroll as editor of, 278
Louisville Courier-Journal, 133
Luce, Henry, v

MacAvoy, Dennis, 103–7
MacLeish, Archibald, 123–25
Makhachkala, 106
Manila, 107–8
Marquette Tribune, Carroll on staff
    of, 8
Marquette University
  Carroll attending, 6–9
  Carroll receiving honorary
    degree from, 276
  Carroll's address at, 250
Marshall, George C., 83–84, 119,
    173
Marshall Plan, Carroll receiving
    job offer from, 173–74
Mason-MacFarlane, Noel, 89
Matthews, Clifton, 243
Matthews, H. Freeman "Doc,"
    149
McCarthy, Joseph, 199, 210
McKie, Ronald, 190
Meany, George, 280
Media General, 268–69
Miller, Arthur, 205
Miller, Webb, xix

Milwaukee, Wisconsin, 3–4
Molotov, Vyacheslav, 28
Montgomery, Bernard, 63
Morisey, A. Alexander, 189
Morocco, 137–38
Munich Agreement (1938), 27,
    50–51
Murrow, Edward R., ix, xix, 34,
    47–49, 83
"Murrow Boys," 34, 48, 101
Mussolini, Benito, 21, 23, 25

Nasser, Abdel, 215
National Committee for the New
    River (NCNR), 281–84
National Endowment for the Arts,
    238
National Headliners Club Award,
    Carroll winning (1942), 120
National Press Club, 209
National Rifle Association (NRA),
    247–48, 276–77
National Socialist movement in
    Germany. *See* Nazi Germany
National Unemployed Workers
    Union (NUWM, Britain), 16
National War College, Carroll as
    speaker at, 175
National Wild and Scenic Rivers
    (NWSR) system, 280, 282,
    285
NATO (North Atlantic Treaty
    Organization), 214, 257
Naval War College, Carroll as
    speaker at, 201
Nazi Germany, 18, 25–26. *See also*
    Hitler, Adolf; World War II
  1941 control of Europe, North
    Africa, and North Africa, 84
  Blitz of Britain. *See* Blitz
  bombing of Barcelona in
    Spanish Civil War, 37
  Carroll's OWI campaign to bait,
    158, 158–60, 165

Goebbels's propaganda
campaign in, 160–66
Hitler Youth, 166
Hottelet in, 33–34
invasion of Western Europe,
58–59
Luftwaffe, 37, 55, 63, 65–67, 86,
129, 157–60
Operation Weserübung (April 9,
1940), 58
Poland invaded by, 49, 51–53
propaganda machine of, 132,
134, 152, 159–66, 167–68
Reich Ministry of Public
Enlightenment and
Propaganda, 134
in Rome after Italian surrender,
154
Soviet Union invaded by. *See*
Soviet Union in World War II
Tirana describing evils of, 33,
insert after 166
Neal, Steve, 285
Neruda, Pablo, 36
New Republic, 121
New River Gorge National Park,
285
New River Valley preservation
efforts, *insert after 166,* 273–75
acknowledgment of Carroll's
efforts, 287
archaeological studies and,
282–83
Carroll's media efforts for,
282–86
Carrolls' purchase of land and,
274–75
"Festival of the New," 283
history of New River, 273–74
legislation successfully passed,
284–85
National Committee for the
New River (NCNR) formed,
281–84
Peggy's role in, 279–86

twenty-five-year anniversary
celebration, 285
U.S. House Rules Committee
and, 280–81
Wild and Scenic Rivers system
and, 280, 282, 285
News Chronicle, 91
News of the World Building
(London), 46, 54, 76, *insert
after 166*
Newsweek, 148, 283
New York bureau of Office of
War Information (OWI). *See*
Office of War Information
(OWI), Overseas Branch
(based in New York)
New York Daily, 108
New York Herald Review, 119
New York Times
Carroll's Christmas Day poems
published in, 249
Carroll writing book reviews
for, 276
CIA interfering with reporting
by, 214, 219–20
Hunter at, 190
"In the Nation" column by
Wicker, 189, 207
New River Valley conservation
and, 282–83
printers' union strike (1962) and,
225–27
Reston as Washington bureau
chief. *See New York Times,*
Washington bureau
Reston as WWII reporter for,
49
Soviet Union coverage in WWII,
91
New York Times, London bureau
Carroll at (1959), 217–18
New York Times, Washington
bureau, xi, *insert after 166,*
201–29

Carroll joining as Reston's deputy, 201–4

Carroll's editorial standards at, 205

Carroll's resignation from, xii, 225–27

competing with *Herald Tribune*, 206

contentious relationship with New York management, 224–25

location and office environment of, 204–5

Reston as chief of, 201–7

Reston giving up management role, 227–28

Reston trying to keep Carroll from resigning, 227

staffing choices made by Reston and Carroll ("Scotty's boys"), 203–4, 207–9

staff regard for Carroll, 206–7

Wicker at, 189

New York Tribune, 117

New York World-Telegram, 74

Nieman Fellow Selection Committee, 201

Nieman paper on "tyranny of objectivity" (1955), 201

Nitze, Paul, 199

Nixon, Richard, 208, 228

Norris, Hoke, 188

North Africa in World War II

Allies' Torch campaign in, 136–41

Darlan Affair and, 138–41, 171, 223

Eisenhower improving press coverage of, 141

under Nazi control, 84

under Vichy control, 137–38

North Atlantic Treaty Organization (NATO), 214, 257

North Carolina Baptist State Convention, 192n1

North Carolina School of the Arts (Winston-Salem, *now* University of North Carolina School of the Arts), *insert after 166*, 238, 240–44, 287

Northern Ireland, 73–74

NRA. *See* National Rifle Association

Oechsner, Frederick, 47

Office of Facts and Figures, 123–24

Office of Strategic Services (OSS), 139, 143

Office of the Coordinator of Information, 124

Office of War Information (OWI), x

acknowledgment of efforts of, 168

creation of, 121–22, 124

in crisis, 147–48

criticisms of, 149

disbanded, 168

internal problems of, 143–46

mission of, 125–26, 129–31, 149

Roosevelt and, 121–22, 147–48, 154–56

State Department relations with, 126, 147, 171

Office of War Information (OWI), European Operations (based in Washington, D.C.), xi, 148–66

appeal to stop destruction of Rome, 154–55, *155*

baiting Nazis, *158*, 158–60, 165

Barrett as head of, 148

campaign to explain "unconditional surrender" to Germans, 162–64, *164*

Carroll and Davis travel to see
  European devastation in
  WWII, 167–68
Carroll hired as deputy director
  of, 148–50
countering Goebbels'
  propaganda in Germany,
  160–66
directing propaganda strategy,
  151–52
role of, 151–53, 160–61
State Department relations with,
  151, 163
Office of War Information (OWI),
  Overseas Branch (based in
  London), 34, 129–46
African campaign ("Torch") of
  Allied forces and, 135–37
Carroll hired by Davis, 125–27,
  129
Carroll organizing office and
  personnel, 132–33, 141, 143
Carroll's relationship with
  Lockhart, 135
Daily Telegraph (London) article
  on Carrolls as "Dynamic
  Couple," 145–46
Davis as head. See Davis, Elmer
educating British about America,
  129–30
Hottelet and, 34
leaflet bombardment by, 135,
  142, 157
medium-wave radio stations,
  142
Psychological Warfare Division
  of the Supreme Headquarters
  Allied Expeditionary Force
  (PWD/SHAEF) relations
  with, 149, 157
resignation by Carroll, 144–45
Sherwood-Carroll relations, 144
Office of War Information (OWI),
  Overseas Branch (based in
  New York), 125, 139

Davis-Sherwood relations,
  143–45, 147–48
news service, meetings with
  Carroll, 152
sample communication to
  French people, 152–53
Sherwood as head, 126, 137,
  143–45
Sherwood-Carroll relations, 144
Sherwood's departure, 148–49
Olson, Lynne, x, 172
Operations of World War II. See
  World War II
Orwell, George, 17, 36, 69
O'Sullivan, Jeremiah L., 6–9, insert
  after 166
OWI. See Office of War
  Information

Pakistan, 107
Paris, United Press office in. See
  United Press (UP)
Parker, Roy, Jr., 237
Patton, George, 46
Pearl Harbor attack, xi, 108–11,
  115–16, 124
Pearlstine, Norm, 278
Pentagon, construction of, 151
Perkins, Frances, 32
Persian Gulf, 106–7
Pétain, Philippe, 136–38, 140
Picasso, Pablo: Guernica, 36
Piedmont Publishing Company,
  235
Pius XII (pope), 156
Poole, Bob, 282–83
Powers, Francis Gary, 215
SS President Coolidge, 108–9, 111
propaganda
  British use of, 133–35
  Carroll's views on role of, 145,
    149, 153, 169–71, 224
  Nazi. See Nazi Germany
  Soviet use of, 169
  WWI, 122

WWII. *See* Office of War Information (OWI)

Psychological Strategy Board, 197–99

psychological warfare, xi, 133, 137, 142, 163, 171, 175, 197–98, 201, 215

Psychological Warfare Branch/ Psychological Warfare Division, 137, 141, 149, 157

Pulitzer, Joseph, III, 266

Pulitzer Prizes
  Baker as winner (1979 & 1983), 207
  Carroll on Board, *insert after 166,* 266
  Drury as winner (1960), 208
  Halberstam as winner (1964), 205
  Lewis as winner (1955 & 1963), 208
  Lochner as winner (1939), 47
  Los Angeles Times as winner 13 times under John Carroll's editorship, 278
  Reston as winner (1945), *insert after 166,* 202
  Reston on Board, 266–67
  Sherwood as winner (1930s and 1940s), 123
  Winston-Salem Journal as winner (1971), *insert after 166,* 267–69
  Yardley as winner (1981), 209

Pyle, Ernie, 69, 74, 80

race relations
  Carroll's position on desegregation, 194–95, 217, 245, 247
  Chapel Hill desegregation, 244
  Civil Rights Act (1964), 244–46
  Little Rock desegregation, 216–17

  Morisey as first Black reporter to join all-white newsroom, 189
  poverty among Southern Blacks as factor in, 247
  in United States, 130–31
  in Winston-Salem, 181, 183–84, 193–96, 238, 245–47
  at *Winston-Salem Journal,* 189

radio news, 12, 48–49, 108, 121, 134–35, 151, 158, 287. *See also* Murrow, Edward R.

Raleigh News and Observer, 239

Rather, Dan, 283

Reasoner, Harry, 283

Rehoboth Beach, Delaware vacations, 226

Reston, James "Scotty," 204–15
  background of, 49–50, 202
  on Carroll's wit, 249
  Cold War reporting and need for secrecy, 214
  criticisms of, 219, 224
  Dewey speech coverage (1948), 211
  friendship with Carroll, 49–50, 174, 202, 249
  giving up management of *New York Times* Washington bureau, 227–28
  hiring Carroll as Washington bureau deputy for *New York Times,* 201–4
  Kennedy and, 219
  in London during WWII, xviii, 66
  at *New York Times,* 47, 49, 133, 201–4, 224–29, 250. *See also New York Times,* Washington bureau
  at OWI, British Division, 132–33, 143, 202
  photograph of, *insert after 166*
  printers' union strike (1962) and, 225–27

on Pulitzer Prize Advisory
Board, 266–67
as Pulitzer Prize winner (1945),
insert after 166, 202
on start of World War II, 53, 57
Wells and, 62
Reuters, 46, 91
Reynolds, Quentin, 61–62, 76–77
R.J. Reynolds Tobacco Company,
179–80, 182–84, 194, 233,
236–38
Rockefeller, Nelson, 155
Rockefeller Foundation, 29, 107
Roosevelt, Eleanor, 116
Roosevelt, Franklin D., x
"arsenal of democracy" as catch
phrase of, 123
Atlantic Charter (1941) and,
122–23, 125, 139
Blacks serving in military and,
131
criticism of Nazi attacks on
religion, 154–55
Darlan Affair and, 139–41, 145,
223
death of, 167
Executive Order 9066
ordering Japanese-American
internment, 111
Foreign Information Office
(FIS) created by, 123–24
Four Freedoms speech, 122–23,
125, 139
Lend-Lease and, 79
management style of, 125n2
Nazi propaganda about, 132
Office of War Information
(OWI) and, 121–22, 147–48,
154–56
Rural Electrification Program,
274
Soviet relations and, 170
Stalin and, 108
Thompson and, 32

unconditional surrender policy
of, 162–63
Vichy France and, 138
Winant and, 34, 74
HMS *Royal Oak,* 55
Royster, Vermont, 266
Rural Electrification Program
(1936), 274
Rush, Jim, 188–89
Rusk, Dean, 223
Russia. *See* Soviet Union

St. Valentine's Day Massacre
(1929), x, 13
Salisbury, Harrison, 225, 227
Sanford, Terry, 239–40
Sarratt, A. Reid, 196, 245
Saturday Review of Literature, 121
Sawyer, Dr. Wilbur A. (father-in-
law), 29, 74, 107, 112, *insert
after 166*
Sawyer, Margaret. *See* Carroll,
Peggy
Scripps, E.W., 12
Second Amendment rights,
247–48, 276–77
Selassie, Haile, 25–26, 28, *insert
after 166*
Sevareid, Eric, xvi–xvii
Shapiro, Henry, 88–89, 99–101
Sherwood, Robert
on Darlan Affair, 139–40
as head of Foreign Information
Office (FIS), 123
as head of OWI Overseas
Branch (based in New York),
126, 137, 143–45
as pro-interventionist, 123, 125
resignation and departure from
OWI, 148–49
Roosevelt and, 147–49
There Shall Be No Night, 123
Voice of America and, 123–24
Shirer, William L., 17, 35, 80,
119–20

Shuster, Alvin, 206
Simon, Paul, 282
Singapore, 107
Smith, Howard K., 17, 47
Sokolovsky, Vasily, 93–94
Southeastern Center for
    Contemporary Arts, 239
Soviet Union. *See also* Cold War;
    Soviet Union in World War II
    Carroll's knowledge and book
        on, xi, 117–20, 169, 229
    Carroll's predictions of post-war
        policies of, 118, *insert after 166*
    Carroll's predictions of U.S.-
        Soviet relations, 170
    Kennedy and, 219
    in League of Nations, 24, 26–28
    propaganda post-war, 170,
        174–75
    Suez Crisis and (1956), 215–16
    Thompson as U.S. ambassador
        to, 32, 98, 222
    Truman urging disarmament of,
        192–93
    U-2 incident (1960), 214–15
    Vietnam War and, 257
Soviet Union in World War II,
    83–112. *See also* Stalin, Josef
    assessment of military strength
        against Germans, 83–84, 90,
        92, 94, 96, 102
    British-Soviet relations, 118
    Carroll extolling Soviet resolve
        in, 119
    Carroll's belief in Soviet defeat
        of Nazis, 119
    Carroll's dispatches from, 98,
        102, 108
    Carroll's return from (1941),
        102–10, *104–5*
    Carroll's time in Moscow, 89,
        118
    Carroll's travel to (1941), 84–88

Carroll's trip from Moscow to
    Vyazma front, 91–96, *insert
    after 166*
Chamberlain and, 51–52
change of German strategy, 90,
    97, 102
correspondents moved to
    Kuibyshev, 98, 100–101, 103
dissidence against Stalin in, 175
first victory against Germans,
    90
German-Soviet Non-
    Aggression Pact (1939), 52,
    118
morale and ability of Russian
    Air Force, 93–94, 96
Moscow, Battle of, 101–2, 108,
    117–18
Operation Barbarossa as initial
    German invasion, 80–81, 83,
    90
Operation Typhoon as German
    drive to Moscow, 97–98
partisan fighters, 95–96
political commissars' role, 98
siege of Leningrad, 91
Smolensk victory by Germany,
    90–91
Soviet Foreign Office's move to
    Kuibyshev, 98–100
Soviet strategy of war of
    attrition, 94, 102
U.S. shipments of materiel to,
    86–88
Spanish Civil War, 36–41, 93
Speier, Hans, 152
Stack, John, 205
Stalin, Josef. *See also* Soviet Union
    in World War II
    Carroll's assessment of, 117–20
    dissidence during World War II
        against, 174–75
    foreign correspondents
        admitted to Soviet Union
        by, 90

German-Soviet Non-Aggression Pact (1939) and, 52, 118
Hopkins and, 85, 96
iron will of, 108, 117
Roosevelt and, 108
Spanish Civil War and, 36
State Department, U.S.
  Acheson and, 220
  Carroll as consultant to, xi, 197
  Carroll's editorial on Vietnam War disseminated to, 256
  Carroll's relations with, 145, 149, 153, 171, 199, 205–6, 215
  OWI Overseas Branch's relations with, 126, 147, 149, 151, 163
Stavisky, Alexandre, and Stavisky Affair, 18–19, *insert after 166*
Steele, A.T., 91
Steinhardt, Laurence, 89
Stengel, Casey, 203–4
Stimson, Henry, 126
Stockholm Peace Petition (1950), 197
Stoppard, Tom, 253
strip mining in North Carolina, 264–66
Suez Canal crisis (1956), 215–16
Sullivan, Margaret: *Ghosting the News*, 270
Sulzberger, Arthur Hays, 202, 214–15, 224
Sulzberger, Arthur "Punch" Ochs, 227
Sulzberger, Cyrus, 91
Sulzberger, Marian, 224
Supreme Headquarters Allied Expeditionary Force (SHAEF), 160
  Psychological Warfare Division of (PWD/SHAEF), 149, 153, 156–57, 165
Surgeon General's report on tobacco smoking, 236

Swift, Jonathan, 129

Talese, Gay: *New York Times, The Kingdom and the Power*, 204
teletype machines, 12, *insert after 166*
Thayer, Charlie, 99
Thompson, Llewellyn "Tommy," 31–32, 89, 98, 118, 222
Thompson, Roy, 187, 189, 235
Time magazine, 26, 121, 190, 284
Tirana, Rifat, 32–33, *insert after 166*
  The Spoil of Europe (Reveille, pseud.), 33
Tirana, Rosamund, 32–33, *insert after 166*, 174
tobacco industry, xii, 235–37. *See also* R.J. Reynolds Tobacco Company
Trawick, Jack, 265
Truman, Harry
  acknowledging contribution of OWI during WWII, 169–70
  disbanding of OWI, 168
  McCarthy's charges of Communist infiltration of, 199
  post-war strategy of, 174
  Psychological Strategy Board and, 197–99
  in Winston-Salem at groundbreaking for, 192–93
Truman Committee of the Senate, 143
Tunisia, 63, 137–38, 140
Tursi, Frank, 269
  The Winston-Salem Journal: Magnolia Trees and Pulitzer Prizes, 235
Twin City Sentinel, 185

United Nations, 139
  Dumbarton Oaks Conference, 202
  Korean War and, 197

United Press (UP)
  Carroll in London as bureau
    manager, x, xv, 13–17, 45–67,
    69–81. *See also* Britain in
    World War II
  in Chicago, 9, 11
  competing with Associated
    Press, 12–13, 17, 45, 48, 84
  correspondents killed in WWII,
    46
  founding of, 12
  at League of Nations, 23–42,
    insert after 166. See also League
    of Nations
  London office team assembled
    by Carroll, 46–48, 80
  O'Sullivan at, 6–7
  in Paris, 17–21
  in Soviet Union, 83–112
  Spanish Civil War reporting,
    36–41
United States
  Carroll advocating for post-war
    leadership of, 118–19
  public opinion in, 173
United States in World War II,
    116, 121. *See also* Pearl Harbor
    attack; Roosevelt, Franklin D.;
    specific generals
  American change of mind about
    entering war, 79
  Carroll's frustration with apathy
    of Americans, 111, 120–21
  isolationist policies, 122–23
  Soviet-U.S. relations, 119–20
University of North Carolina
  Carroll as chair of committee
    to study human behavior
    curriculum, 201
  Ehle's account of students
    imprisoned for civil rights
    demonstrations, 244
  North Carolina School of the
    Arts incorporated into, 243

U.S. House Rules Committee,
    280–81
U-2 incident (1960), 214–15

Vereker, John (Viscount Gort), 59
Versailles Treaty (1919), 24–25
Vietnam War, xi, xii, xiii, 141,
    insert after 166, 205, 208, 224,
    253–63
  Carroll's editorial on (1968),
    255–63, 288–89
  John Carroll's reporting on,
    254–55
  Khe Sanh battle, 254
  Tet Offensive (1968), 253–54
Vlasov, Andrei, 175
Voice of America, 123–24, 142,
    197, 199

Wachovia Bank and Trust
    Company (Winston-Salem),
    183, 234
Wake Forest University (Winston-
    Salem), x, *insert after 166,* 183,
    192
  Carroll on faculty of, 275–77
  Carroll receiving honorary
    degree from, 276
  Carroll teaching course *Rights
    and Citizens,* 276
Wall Street Journal, Carroll writing
    book reviews for, 276
Warburg, James P., 126, 129, 136,
    139–40, 144–45, 148
Washington, D.C.
  New York Times bureau in. *See
    New York Times,* Washington
    bureau
  Office of War Information
    (OWI) bureau. *See* Office
    of War Information (OWI),
    European Operations (based
    in Washington, D.C.)
  in World War II, 150–51
Washington Post, 209, 228

Carroll's Christmas Day poems published in, 249

Wells, H.G., 17, 62

Welsh, Mary, 116

West Berlin. *See* Cold War

Western Electric (Winston-Salem), 234

Westmoreland, William, 254

Weybright, Victor, 132–33

Wicker, Tom, *insert after 166*, 189, 191–92, 207–8, 228

Wild and Scenic Rivers system, 280, 282, 285

Will, George, 276, 283

Williams, Kenneth R., 194

Wilson, Edwin, 233, 275

Wilson, Emily Herring, 248, 275

Wilson, Jeffrey, 103

Wilson, Woodrow, 122

Wilson Quarterly, 208

Winant, John "Gil"
    American soldiers in Britain and, 132
    Carroll's eulogy for, 171–72
    friendship with Carroll and Peggy, 34–35, 37, 80, 115, 129, 150
    help with Carroll's Soviet assignment, 85
    Irish assistance in WWII and, 74
    Letter from Grosvenor Square, 171–72
    Peggy working for, 29–30, 35, 55, 70, 85, 127, 130, 145, *insert after 166*
    Reston and, 202
    suicide of, 171–72
    on U.S. journalists' bravery in WWII reporting, xix

Winston, Joseph, 182

Winston-Salem (North Carolina), *insert after 166*, 237–51
    Carroll appointed to board of directors of North Carolina School of the Arts, 243–44

Carrolls considering their home, 185, 249

Carrolls' dog killed in retaliation for editorial on gun control, 248

Carrolls' first move to (1949), 176, 181–82

Carrolls' second move to (1963), 227, 229

changes as of 1963 when Carrolls moved back, 233–34

Communist charges against union in, 194

community spirit in, 191–96, 234

cultural development in, 238–44

desegregation in, 195–96

fundraising and competing for North Carolina School School of the Arts to be located in, 241–42

Gray family commitment to, 179

history and profile of, 182–84

James A. Gray High School's conversion into North Carolina School of the Arts, 241–43

leading businesses in, 179, 182–83

Moravian settlers, 182, 239

named "City of Arts and Innovation," 243

Peggy's assessment of life in, 184–85

race relations in, 181, 183–84, 193–96, 238, 245–47

race riot in (1967), 246–47

Redevelopment Commission, 191–92

slums in, 182, 184, 191–92

Truman visit to (1951), 192–93

urban renewal forcing Black resettlement in, 246

Winston-Salem Arts Council, 238–39

Winston-Salem Gallery of Contemporary Arts, 239

Winston-Salem Journal and *Sentinel*, 185–97

"appeal for peace" written by Carroll in, 197

Carroll as executive editor (1949–1955), xi, 175–76, 185, 201, 212

Carroll's management style, 235, 248–49

Carroll's retirement from, 269

Carroll's return to be editor and publisher (1963–1974), 227, 229, 234, 246

community relations with, 186–87, 192, 234, 237–38, 246, 269

congenial work atmosphere, 229, 249

desegregation position of, 245–46

editorial standards of, 190–92, 248, 250

expansion under Gray's ownership, 180–81

financial success of, 181, 235

Gray's sale to Media General, 268

Groundhog Day party held annually, 249

gun control editorials by Carroll in, 247–48

hospital exposé in, 186–87

Media General takeover and subsequent sales, 268–69

national and international coverage of, 192–93, 197, 253

North Carolina School of the Arts, supporting Winston-Salem as ideal location for, 242

on poverty among Southern Blacks, 247

public opinion of, 234

as Pulitzer Prize winner (1971), *insert after 166*, 267–69

race riot, reporting on, 246–47

staff members of, 188–90, 250

staff's regard for Carroll, 187, 190, 248–49, 269

on strip mining and environmental issues, 264–66, 282

on tobacco smoking's effects and Surgeon General's report, 236–37

Truman's call for Cold War peace initiative in, 192–93

Vietnam War, Carroll's editorial on (1968), 255–63

Winston-Salem Teachers College, 184

wire services. *See* Associated Press; United Press

Wisner, Frank, 173, 175, 199

Woestendiek, Bill, 188

women

Black women attorneys in North Carolina, 246

Annie Brown Kennedy as first Black senator from North Carolina, 246

on *New York Times,* Washington bureau staff, 209

on *Winston-Salem Journal* staff, 189–90

World War II role of, 65, 77, 92, 97, 99–100, 103

World War I, 122

World War II, xi, xii. *See also specific geographic locations*

American change of mind about entering war and, 79

Battle of Britain, xi, *insert after 166*

Battle of the Atlantic, 70

Battle of the Bulge (1944), 165

Berlin, Allied battle for, 166

bravery and death of journalists in, 46, 79

Britain in. *See* Britain in World War II

Casablanca Conference (1943), 162–63

D-Day and Normandy invasion, 63, 137, 144, 156–57, 160

Denmark invaded by Germans, 58

Dunkirk, Battle of (1940), 59–60, 62

Finland, Soviet invasion of, 58, 123

France. *See* France in World War II

Goebbels's propaganda campaign in Germany, 160–66

North African front. *See* North Africa in World War II

Norway invaded by Germany, 58

Operation Barbarossa (1941), 81, 83

Operation Pointblank (Allied targeting of German air force), 157, 160

Pearl Harbor attack. *See* Pearl Harbor

Poland and, 49, 51–53, 89

Psychological Warfare Division of (PWD/SHAEF), 149, 153, 156–57, 165

radar, importance of, 64

reporting of, 48–49. *See also specific news agencies and journalists*

Rome campaign of Allies and propaganda to save Rome from destruction, 154–56

Soviet role. *See* Soviet Union in World War II

Sudentenland ceded to Hitler prior to, 50

Supreme Headquarters Allied Expeditionary Force (SHAEF), 160

Ukraine in, 174–75

unconditional surrender policy, 162–64, *164*

United States in. *See* United States in World War II

Worth, Alexander, 91

Yadkin River (North Carolina), 266–67

Yardley, Jonathan, xii, 208–9

Z. Smith Reynolds Foundation, 183, 192n1

Zakharov, Georgy, 93

READER'S GUIDE

1. Consider Carroll's professional journey. How did he evolve? What were his guiding principles as a journalist and as an editor?

2. What do you think about the dichotomy between Carroll's roles as journalist and as World War II propagandist? How do you think he reconciled these roles?

3. What can be seen as Carroll's major reporting mistakes? What are your own views of these mistakes? Are there lessons to be drawn from them?

4. What drove Carroll's shift from international to national and then to regional journalism? How is this notable, and different, from the trajectory we see in the news profession today?

5. What is relevant today about Carroll's role with OWI and the current conflict in Ukraine? How important is propaganda to both sides in times of war?

6. How do you evaluate Carroll's role as editor and publisher of the *Winston-Salem Journal?* What effect does the demise of local newspapers have on smaller cities and towns like Winston-Salem today?

7. Why do you think the "Quo Vadis" editorial had such an important effect? Would it be possible today for it to have a similar effect? Have newspapers become less or more important in influencing public policy?

8. What do you think was Peggy's impact on Wallace's life and professional development and in her own right?

9. Outline Wallace and Peggy's personal attributes. Would they be as appreciated today?

10. What would Wallace and Peggy think of social media; the rise of Facebook, Twitter, and other platforms as "go to" places where people get their news?

11. What is your opinion of journalism today? Is it objective? Should journalists tell the differing sides of every story or stick to reporting facts as they see them? What is meant by "false objectivity"?

ABOUT THE AUTHOR

Mary Llewellyn McNeil is a former editor and writer for the *Congressional Quarterly* and the primary author of *Environment and Health*, *Reagan's First Year*, and *The Nuclear Age*. She has worked as an editor at the Smithsonian Institution and the National Academy of Sciences. During a twenty-eight-year career at the World Bank, she launched two  global publications, *The Urban Age* and *Development Outreach*, and edited *Demanding Good Governance, Lessons from Social Accountability Initiatives in Africa*. A graduate of Wake Forest University and the John F. Kennedy School of Government at Harvard University, she resides in Washington, D.C., with her husband and three daughters. This is her first full-length biography.

CPSIA information can be obtained
at www.ICGtesting.com
Printed in the USA
BVHW081451130922
646891BV00011B/603